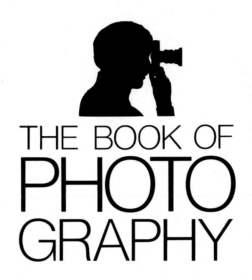

THE BOOK OF
PHOTO
GRAPHY

THE BOOK OF PHOTO GRAPHY

How to See and Take Better Pictures

JOHN HEDGECOE

ALFRED A. KNOPF
NEW YORK, 1987

Photographs by John Hedgecoe
Text by John Hedgecoe and Adrian Bailey

Published in the United States by Alfred A. Knopf, Inc., New York.
Distributed by Random House, Inc., New York.

First paperback edition published June 12, 1984
Reprinted Twice
Fourth Printing, April 1987
Library of Congress Cataloging in Publication Data

Hedgcoe, John.
  The book of photography.

  Includes index.
  1. Photography. I. Title.
TR146.H415 1984 770 83-49189
ISBN 0-394-72466-6

Printed and bound in Italy by
A. Mondadori, Verona
First edition 1976

Contents

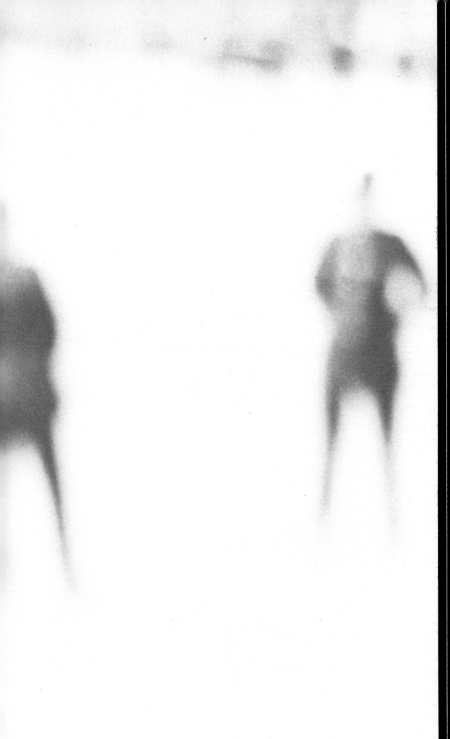

Introduction

This book is a practical approach to creative photography. It is designed to show you how to improve your technical knowledge while increasing your visual perception — to help you, in short, take better pictures. Some people are naturally more perceptive than others, but even their perception needs to be developed by conscious effort, by learning to look, to see, to anticipate and to analyze.

The text and pictures show how your skill and perception can be applied to a variety of different subjects — landscape, still life, nature, architecture, people — and by studying the photographs, you will be more able to create your own.

In this book I have tried to show most techniques and a variety of styles in common use. But as I have taken the photographs (except for the historical ones, of course) a personal style obviously prevails. By making intelligent use of this book, each individual will be able to develop his own style. By approaching photography in a creative and practical manner and learning the techniques, any photographer should be able to produce photographs as good as these.

Photographic techniques are important in helping the photographer achieve a wide variety of desired results, but technique alone cannot give a picture originality or esthetic value. Photography used in science or technology is unequalled in its factual recording abilities. But most photographers are not scientists or technologists wanting accurate records; they are people who wish to capture a given scene and in addition, to capture the emotional response they felt to the images that first attracted their attention. Photography, like any other art form, is an interpretive medium of

The quality of this picture depends entirely on photographic techniques. The subject and image was uninteresting, but by using soft focus, and over-exposing about 20 times above the given reading, most of the image has been obliterated to give an unusual result. The highlights disappeared first, then the dark shadow areas began to break up, devoured by the light. Making photographs like this becomes very much a matter of experimentation, trial and error. Take every opportunity to exploit camera, equipment and film, and to push them beyond their normal limits.

self-expression. The camera is just the tool with which the photographer expresses his creative faculties.

Modern photography allows you greater freedom to concentrate on these creative aspects because the majority of technical problems have been overcome. In the past decade the progress of photo-technology has been rapid, the new methods have made photography — once the complicated and expensive hobby of the few — available to all.

The Book of Photography seeks to emphasize the human approach and the importance of the individual eye. It shows you how to take pictures of good technical quality, but above all, *why* to take them and *when* to take them, and how to interpret and communicate through the medium of photography. The most complicated of cameras is still only a box with a lens for rendering an image — a three-dimensional one — onto a flat, two-dimensional piece of paper, to create an illusion of reality. There's little skill involved in pointing a camera at a subject and taking a picture. But to produce consistently good shots, you must be aware of the controlling factors: the time of day; the quality and direction of the light; the type of film, lens and camera; the length of exposure; the camera angle; and most important, the decisive moment of releasing the shutter.

The vital ingredient that we term "creativity" may be described as a combination of many qualities, including inventiveness, imagination, inspiration, perception. Don't be misled into thinking that creativity is entirely a heaven-sent gift to the few, for its qualities can be learned as one learns a language and, like a language, it is constantly being developed. By realizing in a composition why one shape is more important than another, and why a number of forms carefully arranged can be more acceptable than those

Photo-montage gives the photographer a freedom usually enjoyed only by painters and graphic designers. You can combine, juxtapose and vary the scale of any number of images. In this light-hearted example, six separate photographs have been placed to gether to make one picture. The method is explained on p. 208.

In these sectional pictures I used both pictorial and psychological elements to tell a story. The couple represent freedom, space, and the joys of youth. The room, on the other hand, is enclosed and restrictive, the furniture reflecting a materialistic attitude. Splitting the image emphasizes the contrast between the two subjects. Although this is my allegorical explanation, the aim is to stimulate the viewer to make his own interpretation.

In the photograph opposite my prime concern was to emphasize the feeling of movement in a static shot. I exaggerated perspective by placing the camera with a wide-angle lens at floor level, and used electronic flash to arrest the dancer in a dynamic position. The cropping of her hand, also helps to convey the feeling of space through which the dancer is leaping.

haphazardly placed, you begin to *see* better pictures and are therefore in a position to *take* better pictures. By learning to analyze the elements, observing the way in which they play their part in any given scene, and by composing them in order to show that element you wish to emphasize, your pictures will reveal a marked degree of individuality and assurance. The careless photographer taking pictures in a split second is likely to miss those necessary qualities.

People really believe the pictorial "truth" of photographs — that "the camera cannot lie." For this reason, and to free themselves of solemn representation, photographers have sometimes

tended to look for extremes: the tallest, the fattest, the most beautiful, the ugliest, the freak. They have attempted to shock us into a new awareness or perception of the world around us. The photograph can dehumanize and make trivial, it can be unsympathetic and pretentious. It can also make a comprehensive statement about people and society, and provide a factual record of a given situation. But capturing for posterity a split-second of time and recording a faithful image is no longer enough — we must add our own creative influence. This is why photography's progress in the past fifteen years has been toward a more liberated vision,

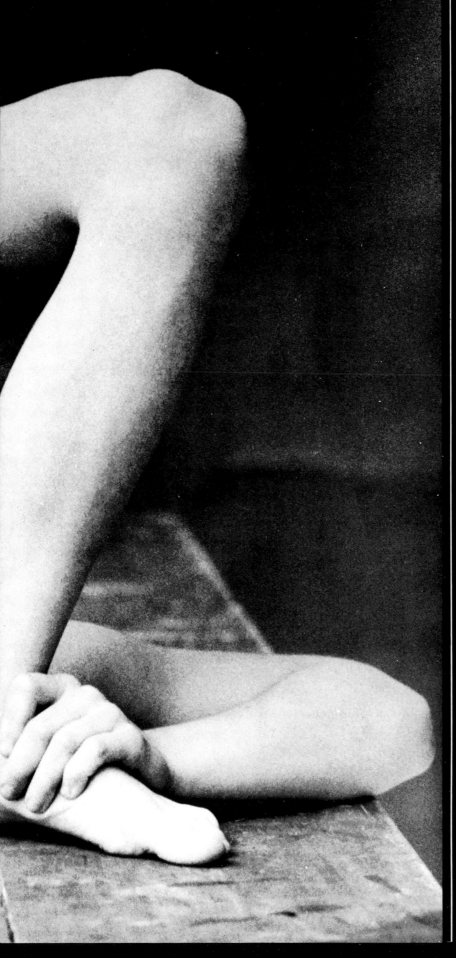

rejecting the mainstream of photography where visual images are valued primarily for their accurate representation of the subject. For example, our perception of everyday objects is regulated by familiarity, we do not have to examine them closely in order to identify them, knowing from past experience the shape, size, color and smell of each. Paradoxically it is often when something familiar is removed, like a piece of furniture from a room which upsets the normal arrangement of order, that our attention is drawn to its absence, and the space it once occupied. This kind of abstraction is apparent in many aspects of modern photography.

The freedom in painting that began with Cubism has also influenced photographers who have embraced the artistic movements of Surrealism, Symbolism and Abstraction. By manipulating images to create a desired effect, photographers are exploring a path started in the 1920s by Man Ray and Moholy Nagy. They seek to create a subjective vision by stressing the psychological or emotional elements of the picture. The images act as a catalyst to provoke an emotional response. This means that what the viewer sees is of less significance than what he experiences. The photographer as artist makes his own rules, imposes his personal viewpoint on his work, but the success of his pictures relies on the response the viewer has to them.

Photography has been emancipated just as the printing press once freed the written word, giving to many what was previously reserved for the few; negatives are capable of supplying an almost inexhaustible number of prints, and once the master print has been made it becomes a mechanical process — truly an expendable art. Photography has been given to all the people, which is where it belongs.

People are often pleased to show their skills in front of the camera, especially children, who are not self-conscious. This girl's extraordinary ability to contort her body makes an arresting picture without any attempt at "trick" photography. Unusual and exaggerated subjects are best presented in the most straightforward manner.

13

14

The photograph on the left shows how the camera can lie. The people are normal, but the room is abnormal. It was devised by the American painter, Ames, to demonstrate how the accepted manifestation of linear perspective can be distorted, psychologically and geometrically, to deceive the eye. The room is not the cube it appears to be but is an irregular six-sided form where the planes are not at right angles to each other. Deception occurs because the viewer's memory has preconditioned him to believe that rooms are usually rectangular, and regular in form. In fact, the perspective of the Ames room is distorted: the vanishing point on the right hand side of the picture is not at infinity, but has been moved closer, to exaggerate the planes. The room appears as normal and rectangular only when seen through the camera at a fixed point on a pre-established horizon line.

A sequence of pictures does not necessarily have to be in an expected or regular order, and the arrangement may be deliberately misplaced so that it conveys a particular mood or feeling. In the example left, the sequence illustrates the passage of time between the diver and the splash. The pictures attempt to convey the moment of tension immediately following the initial burst of action, and, just before the completion of that action, the tension that an audience experiences while watching the empty stage in anticipation of the performer's arrival.

Any photographs sharing a common denominator have an added interest because of their relationship to each other. I photographed these six similar rooms in an apartment block, one year after their completion. The rooms were 14 ft (4.3 m) square and illuminated by natural light. I used a Hasselblad camera with a 40 mm lens from the same position in each room, to show the individual environments to the best advantage and to reveal the character of the occupant.

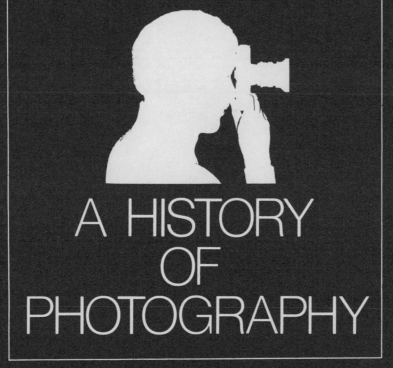

A HISTORY
OF
PHOTOGRAPHY

The First Photographers

Exclude as much daylight as possible from a room, but allow a single beam to enter through a small aperture the thickness of a pencil. Hold a sheet of white paper some six inches (15.2 cm) from the aperture, and the scene outside the room will appear on the paper, an inverted and blurred image, but recognizable. This device for forming "pinhole" images was first noted by Aristotle in the 4th century BC. It later became known as the *camera obscura*, a term introduced by the Italians meaning "a dark room."

Because light has the ability to transmit images, the natural laws that govern the art of photography were probably observed by primitive man. In prehistory, men lived in caves, or in small stone buildings that acted as natural cameras. A shaft of sunlight piercing the gloom of the cave through a crack in the rock could have projected images from the outside such as trees, the movements of other men, or the image of the sun itself. The fact that images were upside down added to the magic of the phenomenon, at a period in time when much in life was inexplicable.

this phenomenon by leaving a small object such as a key on poor quality paper in bright sunshine for a few hours. When the object is removed, its shape will be obvious on the paper.

The first great step in the history of photography was the practical application of the *camera obscura* as an aid to artists by the Italians during the 16th century. It is likely that most of the great painters of the Italian Renaissance used the *camera obscura*; certainly Guardi and Canaletto did in making their paintings of Venice. Leonardo da Vinci first noted the possibilities of the *camera obscura* in 1490 when he recommended viewing the image of a sunlit scene in a dark room where a small hole allowed light reflected from the subject to pass on to a thin piece of paper. Within the next 50 years two important refinements were added to the basic apparatus. The first was the lens. Originally mentioned by Girolamo Cardano in 1550, it was an invention used to correct poor eyesight. Italian lenses were bi-convex, and people noted their resemblance to the brown lentil with which they made soup – therefore, the word "lens" comes from the Latin for lentil. The second refinement was the diaphragm, possibly invented by Daniele Barbaro in the 1530s. Both devices were incorporated in the *camera obscura* to sharpen the image.

When artists realized that the *camera obscura* could assist them in solving the vexing problem of perspective, and the lifelike rendering of scenes and objects in two dimensions, the need for a portable "dark room" arose. The development of the portable camera was the next progressive step toward the modern camera, with which it shares basic elements: a lens, a diaphragm, and a sheet of material on which to make the image.

The idea was adopted and spread through Europe. A German scholar, Athanasius Kircher, illustrated a *camera obscura* that he had seen while traveling in Germany. Kircher's drawing shows a construction the

The portable camera obscura Athanasius Kircher, a German scholar, saw a portable *camera obscura* while traveling in Germany in the 1640s, and drew it for the *Ars Magna* of 1646, above. The camera was the size of a small hut, but light enough to be carried by two men – one was probably the artist who entered through a trapdoor in the floor. It consisted of a light wooden frame with canvas walls, and an inner box made of paper sufficiently transparent for an image to be sketched the correct way round although upside down, right.

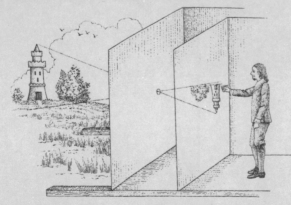

Since prehistoric times, men have observed and recorded those subjects that inspired them: the silhouette, cast on a rock wall by the rays of the setting sun, showed them how boldly and accurately an object might be conveyed on a flat surface. They undoubtedly noticed that some silhouettes were made permanent when subjected to bright sunlight. A leaf shape defined on the skin of an apple ripening in the sun is just one such example. You can observe

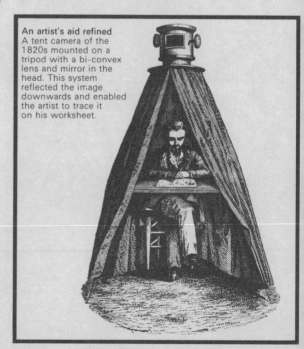

An artist's aid refined A tent camera of the 1820s mounted on a tripod with a bi-convex lens and mirror in the head. This system reflected the image downwards and enabled the artist to trace it on his worksheet.

Fox Talbot's box camera obscura
The *camera obscura* was still in use when Fox Talbot carried out his experiments to produce a permanent photographic image in the 1830s. This is probably the camera which took the famous picture from the window of his home at Lacock Abbey in 1835 (see p. 22).

size of a small hut and light enough to be carried by two men. One of the men was probably the artist who entered the camera through a trapdoor in the floor. Such a cumbersome device was possibly used to render large-scale pictures, for a smaller, tent camera had been invented some 20 years previously. The British diplomat Sir Henry Wotton was "much taken with the draught of a landskip on a piece of paper, methoughts masterly done," which an Austrian astronomer Johann Kepler had made in "a little black tent," in 1620.

A variety of camera shapes and sizes evolved: cameras which could be fitted over the head, others which were incorporated into the design of a sedan chair, and most important of all, a small box camera that could be carried under the arm. One of Kircher's pupils, Kaspar Schott, made a box camera based on a design he had seen in Spain in 1657. The camera had two lenses and adjustable focus, which functioned by means of two boxes, one sliding within the other. In England, Robert Boyle introduced a box camera which contained a sheet of oiled, transparent paper on which the image was projected. This idea was similarly employed by a German mathematics professor, Johann Sturm, in 1676, but he added a small mirror set at an angle of 45° to the lens, which reflected an upright rather than inverted image and a hood to improve visibility in the same way that the photographer's black cloth does now. Sturm's was the first portable reflex camera, and was marginally improved upon, a century later, by a monk in Würzburg, Johann Zahn, who replaced the oiled paper with opal glass, and added a telescope lens consisting of two elements (one concave and one convex) of different focal lengths to obtain an enlarged image. There was little more that physics could do to perfect the camera – it was the turn of the chemists.

The profile machine
The artist drew the profile, illuminated by means of a candle, on a screen between himself and the sitter. Goethe, a keen amateur profilist, helped to design the original machine.

Working indoors
A table model of the *camera obscura* was designed for use indoors. It was large, heavy and best used for static subjects. This illustration, drawn by George Brander in 1769, shows a table camera built in the Rococo style with extensions to give longer focal length for close-up work.

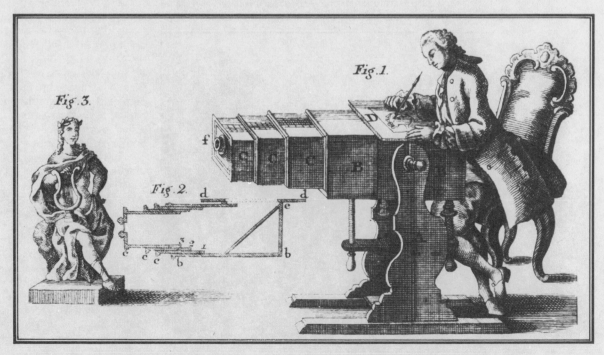

Fixing the Image

Using silver nitrate
Tom Wedgwood, son of the great potter Josiah, was the first to apply the idea of light-sensitive chemicals to the *camera obscura*. This silhouette of a fern was successfully reproduced on leather coated with silver nitrate.

The first photograph
The world's first photograph, below, was a view taken by the French experimenter Joseph Nicéphore Niépce in 1827. The exposure time was 8 hours so the sun can be seen shining on both sides of the picture! Light areas were rendered by hardened bitumen and dark areas by pewter plate.

It is unlikely that any of the 17th-century scientists who perfected the *camera obscura*, or the artists who used it, ever thought to obtain a fixed image. Why should they? Science had invented a novel optical instrument, and artists were achieving more lifelike renderings of subjects in two dimensions than ever before.

In 1727, a German professor of anatomy named Johann Schulze was experimenting with the manufacture of phosphorus. He made a precipitate of chalk in nitric acid and, to his astonishment, the chemical close to the laboratory window turned purple. Through a process of elimination, Schulze discovered traces of silver in the acid, and concluded that silver salts darkened when exposed to strong light. He decided that his observation was unique and important, but failed to use it for any worthwhile purpose.

However, other enthusiasts picked up Schulze's discovery. Jean Hellot applied silver nitrate to paper, in 1737. Some 40 years later, a Swedish chemist named Carl Scheele experimented with silver chloride, and discovered that it was particularly sensitive to the violet rays of the spectrum – he also found that blackened silver chloride was insoluble in ammonia, which acted as a fixing agent.

These early discoveries relating to the light-sensitivity of silver salts were little more than a novelty. Perhaps the term "photography" meaning "writing with light" can first be ascribed to the work of Hellot, as his experiments included "secret" writing with a solution of silver nitrate on white paper, which remained invisible until exposed to the sunlight.

First to apply the idea of light-sensitive chemicals to the *camera obscura* was Thomas Wedgwood, youngest son of the great English potter, Josiah. Josiah used the *camera obscura* to obtain accurate drawings for ornamenting china and pottery. Tom Wedgwood was, therefore, familiar with the camera – he was also interested in chemistry and especially in the effect of heat and light upon chemicals. He was aware of Schulze's discoveries related to silver nitrate, and carried out his own experiments making silhou-

ettes of leaves and insect wings on white leather coated with silver nitrate.

Wedgwood's dream of permanent pictures from a *camera obscura* failed, however, from the lack of a hardener to establish the image, and a fixing agent to preserve it, which even Wedgwood's friend and collaborator, the great chemist Humphry Davy, had failed to find.

The man finally credited with the invention of photography was a Frenchman, Joseph Nicéphore Niépce. Like Wedgwood, Niépce had failed to find a fixer for his pictures which were made on paper coated with silver chloride. Aided by his brother Claude, Niépce began his search for a solution to the problem by experimenting with a substance called bitumen of Judea, (then used for lithography), with which he coated glass plates. The exciting property of bitumen of Judea, as far as the brothers were concerned, was that it both bleached and hardened on exposure to light, while the areas protected from the light remained soluble and could be washed away.

Niépce made an engraving transparent by brushing it with oil, and laid it on a plate coated with bitumen. This was exposed to sunlight for about three hours, during which time the exposed bitumen hardened, leaving the unexposed areas under the dark lines of the engraving soft enough to be dissolved with lavender oil and turpentine. The resulting picture was found to be resilient and permanent. In his attempt to perfect the photograph, Niépce had invented photogravure, which he called "heliography."

After his initial success with bitumen of Judea, Niépce coated a pewter plate with the same chemical, and exposed it in a camera fitted with a meniscus prism to correct the laterally transposed image. He exposed the plate to the view from his workroom window in the Niépce family house at Gras near Châlon-sur-Sâone for some eight hours, and succeeded in producing the world's first photograph.

Another Frenchman, Louis Daguerre, was, like Wedgwood and Niépce, obsessed with the idea of fixing the image in a camera. However, his only invention until the time of Niépce's discoveries was the Diorama, an illusionistic, three-dimensional stage set involving the use of the *camera obscura*. He and Niépce went into brief partnership in 1829, in order to perfect the heliograph. Subsequently Daguerre embarked upon the search for the ideal fixing agent.

For several years he carried out experiments until one day in 1835 he put an exposed plate in his chemical cupboard. He was amazed to find, some days later, that the latent image had developed. Daguerre discovered that it was due to the presence of mercury vapor from a broken thermometer. In spite of this development, the images could not be rendered permanent until, in 1837, Daguerre succeeded in fixing them with a solution of common salt. He decided to call his invention "daguerreotype."

Daguerreotypes were positive pictures, and could not be reproduced; moreover they were fragile and difficult to view. For some time, Daguerre had been seeking financial aid to perfect his invention, and found an ally in the physicist and astronomer, Dominique Arago, who pressed the French Govern-

Development of the daguerreotype
The earliest existing daguerreotype, left, was a still life taken in a corner of Daguerre's studio in 1837. It was originally presented to the Curator of the Louvre but is now in the possession of the Société Française de Photographie in Paris. A later daguerreotype mounted in a presentation case is shown above.

Early photographers
A portrait of Joseph Nicéphore Niépce, top, painted by C. Laguiche in 1795. Niépce lived from 1765–1833. Daguerreotype, above, of Louis Daguerre (1787–1851), the inventor of the process by which this photograph was taken by J. E. Mayall in 1846.

The inventor's work
Boulevard du Temple, Paris – a daguerreotype taken by Daguerre c. 1838–39, and now in the collection of the Bayerisches Nationalmuseum, Munich.

ment to support Daguerre's experiments. He succeeded and the daguerreotype was finally perfected in the following manner: a silvered plate was sensitized with iodine vapor, which formed a layer of silver iodide. The plate was exposed in the camera, and the latent image developed by mercury vapor, the mercury adhering to those areas of silver iodide affected by the light. The plate was fixed with hyposulfite of soda, then dried over a flame. It was necessary for the final picture to be sealed beneath glass to protect the delicate mercury surface, and to prevent oxidation of the silver, but the daguerreotype was the most successful mirror of nature yet invented. Said the painter Paul Delaroche, on being shown a daguerreotype, "From today painting is dead!"

On August 19, 1839, at a public meeting of the French Academy of Science in Paris, Daguerre presented the photographic image and its process to the world. One hour later, it is said, every optician's shop in the city was packed with excited customers demanding the apparatus that would make the "new pictures."

Daguerre published a booklet, "The History and Description of the Process Named the Daguerreotype." Illustrated with scale drawings of the camera and equipment, the instructions enabled any instrument maker to produce the apparatus. More than thirty editions, summaries and translations were published within five months. The publications appeared in London, St Petersburg, Barcelona, Genoa, Berlin, Stockholm and New York. The medium which has become the major instrument of visual communication and documentation was established.

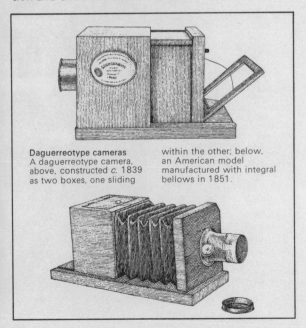

Daguerreotype cameras
A daguerreotype camera, above, constructed c. 1839 as two boxes, one sliding within the other; below, an American model manufactured with integral bellows in 1851.

The Negative Image

Fox Talbot
A portrait of Fox Talbot taken by the wet collodion process, which succeeded his own invention, the calotype.

Since 1833, the English mathematician William Henry Fox Talbot, had been pursuing the same idea as Wedgwood, Niépce and Daguerre, although totally ignorant of their achievements. While on holiday at Lake Como, Fox Talbot lamented the lack of a *camera obscura* to help him with his sketches. "How charming it would be," he wrote, "if it were possible to cause these natural images to imprint themselves durably and remain fixed upon the paper!"

Aware of the light-sensitivity of silver salts, Fox Talbot began his experiments which included coating paper with a solution of silver nitrate and common salt. He was able to make negative images of natural objects, as Wedgwood had done, by placing them in direct contact with the paper. From these he made positives by placing a piece of sensitized paper on the negative and permitting the light to shine through. At first the paper was not sensitive enough to obtain images in the camera but by trying different ratios of salt and silver in solution, Fox Talbot discovered that salt was an inhibiting agent. He prepared a paper coated with a solution of weak salt and strong silver and in 1835 he produced a negative picture with a *camera obscura*, of a window in his home at Lacock Abbey. It was the first paper negative. The image had been retarded and fixed with strong saline solution.

Meanwhile, in Paris, a civil servant named Hippolyte Bayard was experimenting with direct positives from a camera using silver chloride paper. He obtained his first successful picture in 1839 but was as unaware of Fox Talbot and Daguerre as they were of him. Both Fox Talbot and Bayard were independent inventors of photography who failed to establish the priority of their inventions with a public overwhelmed by the success of Daguerre. Furthermore, few were able to see the potential of Fox Talbot's negatives and poor-quality positives, or of Bayard's direct positive pictures that were, in some respects, preferable to daguerreotypes.

Early in 1839, Fox Talbot wrote to Dominique Arago, and claimed that his experiments had preceded those of Daguerre; he also showed examples of his "photogenic drawings" to the Royal Institution in London. In August of the same year, he exhibited 95 Photogenic

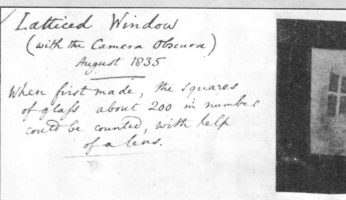

*Latticed Window
(with the Camera Obscura)
August 1835*

When first made, the squares of glass about 200 in number could be counted, with help of a lens.

Making the first negative
The world's first negative on paper was taken by Fox Talbot in 1835. It was a view of a window at his home, Lacock Abbey.

Negative into positive
Calotypes of Fox Talbot's photographic establishment at Reading in 1845. The two positive pictures shown above right, are a continuation, taken to include the complete subject. Part of the reversed negative for this print is seen, below right.

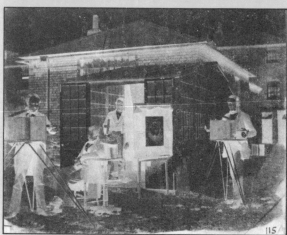

Drawings which included negative and positive superimposed pictures of objects, and negative and positive pictures taken with the *camera obscura*. Sadly, Fox Talbot's process failed to capture public imagination in the way that Daguerre had done with his speedily produced, large detailed pictures.

Bitterly resentful of such public indifference, and aware of the French competition, Fox Talbot intensified his experiments. He, like Niépce and Daguerre, was rewarded with an accidental discovery – the latent image. With a new camera made by the optician Andrew Ross, Fox Talbot took a number of pictures using paper sensitized with a solution of silver nitrate and gallic acid, valuable for its accelerating properties. When the paper failed to produce an image, Fox Talbot treated it with a further coating of gallo-nitrate of silver with the intention of re-exposing it. To his

The scientist who fixed the image
A photographic portrait, above, of the scientist Sir John Herschel, taken by the Victorian photographer Julia Margaret Cameron in 1867. Herschel described Fox Talbot's pictures as "childish" compared with those of Daguerre.

A calotype camera
Camera with an adjustable rack and simple microscope lens, used by Fox Talbot c. 1840 to make calotypes. The focusing hole could be plugged with cork and sensitive paper attached to the inside back of the box.

great astonishment an image appeared on the paper, which he fixed with potassium bromide; even today, many photographers are awed by the appearance of an image on a previously blank sheet of paper.

By 1841, Fox Talbot had perfected his process. It was as rapid as Daguerre's, capable of exposures of less than 30 seconds. By using silver iodide on writing paper, and coating it with gallo-nitrate of silver, the paper could be exposed and developed with an application of gallo-nitrate, gently warmed. Positive prints were made by the same superimposition process as photogenic drawings.

Fox Talbot swiftly patented his process which he called "calotype" after the Greek word *kallos*, meaning "beautiful." He fixed his calotypes with hyposulfite of soda, the fixing properties of which had been discovered in 1819 by the scientist Sir John Herschel, but failed to acknowledge Herschel's contribution or that of the Rev. J. B. Reade, who had discovered the properties of gallic acid. With Herschel, Talbot was almost certainly retaliating for his remark two years previously that Talbot's pictures were "childish" when compared to those of Daguerre.

In 1844, Fox Talbot set up a printing establishment at Reading, in order to print sets of calotypes for sale, and to deal with the growing demand for licences to practice the calotype process. Since its invention, the speed of the calotype had enabled photographers to take portraits commercially. Fox Talbot published "The Pencil of Nature," the first photographically illustrated book, in which he included the history of his invention. However, calotypes never became popular in the USA where daguerreotypes reigned supreme.

By 1842, a number of photographers had opened portrait studios in Britain, and some of the finest portraits were being taken by Robert Adamson in Edinburgh. Adamson met the Scottish painter David Octavius Hill, who was interested in using photography as a reference for his pictures, in particular for his group portrait of the Assembly of the Free Church of Scotland. Working as a team, Adamson and Hill took some of the finest photographs of the era, using Fox Talbot's calotype process.

In 1851, Daguerre died. It was symbolically the end of an era for, in the very same year, a new technique was invented which liberated the patent-bound processes of Daguerre and Fox Talbot – the wet collodion technique of Frederick Scott Archer.

By now, however, the ranks of photographers had swelled from mere hundreds to thousands. Photography had truly arrived.

Fox Talbot's invention – the calotype
A calotype, below, made by the distinguished Scottish photographic team, Hill and Adamson, of the Rev. James Fairbairn with a group of Scottish east coast fishwives, in 1845.

Permanence, Definition & Speed

Ambrotype of Scott Archer
Scott Archer, above, inventor of the wet collodion process. This portrait is an ambrotype, a thin glass negative on a black backing to create a positive effect.

The ambrotype method
Half the backing has been removed from the ambrotype, right, to show the positive achieved by placing the negative on a black background.

A portable viewing room
A dark tent for inspecting wet plate photographs as soon as they had been taken. Further exposures could be made if results were poor quality.

The work of Julia Cameron
Photograph of Maggie Thackeray, entitled "The Christ Kind," taken by Julia Margaret Cameron in 1868. This "artistic photography" was much admired by the Victorians.

The wet collodion technique resulted from experiments with the use of glass as a base for photographs, in place of metal plates. Glass, as with wax paper, had no overall texture and pattern and was lighter and cheaper than metal – in fact it was much more suitable for making negatives. Photography on glass was not a new idea but one of the main problems in using glass plates was the lack of a stable medium to hold the silver salts, which tended to float away during developing and fixing.

In 1847, Abel Niépce de St Victor, a cousin of Joseph Nicéphore Niépce, evolved a method of coating glass with albumen, the white of eggs, whipped-up and mixed with a little potassium iodide. When the coating hardened it was treated with a solution of silver nitrate, exposed, and developed with gallic acid. The French photographer Blanquart-Evrard adapted the emulsion to produce albumen paper, which was used in preference to silver chloride paper to such an extent that the factories engaged in its production were using 18 million eggs a year. The albumen on glass process eventually failed when Fox Talbot managed to patent certain modifications as a part of his own process, without acknowledging Niépce de St Victor.

Three basic factors occupied the pursuits of the early experimenters in photography: permanence, definition, and speed. Permanence had been gradually achieved by Niépce, Daguerre and Fox Talbot who had devised different means of fixing the prints. Definition came with improved lenses and, to some extent, improved emulsions. Finer quality lenses also helped to shorten exposure time.

The next advances were made by a London sculptor, Frederick Scott Archer, who had learned the calotype process to help him obtain more accurate likenesses of his sitters. Desiring a more sensitive paper than silver iodide or albumen, Archer began experimenting

with other emulsions. He tried a relatively new substance, guncotton dissolved in ether, originally used for dressing war wounds. It was called collodion, from the Greek *kolla*, meaning "glue." Paper was found to be a poor base for collodion, so Archer tried glass instead, coating it with an emulsion of iodized collodion. Others had experimented with collodion, allowing it to dry before applying a coating of silver iodide. Archer added potassium iodide to the collodion, dipped the glass into a bath of silver nitrate solution, and exposed it while still wet, since he had discovered that a considerable loss of sensitivity occurred as the plate dried. In fact, so highly sensitive was the new emulsion in its wet state that exposures of less than three seconds became possible. The plate was developed with pyrogallic acid or ferrous sulfate, and fixed with either potassium cyanide or sodium thiosulfate. The wet-plate process demanded not only photographic experience, but knowledge of chemistry as well.

Because exposures were rigidly linked to the darkroom process, it became necessary for location photographers to carry their equipment with them, including a tent, boxes of plates, and dozens of bottles. Huge "landscape" cameras producing plates of 12 × 16 ins (30.5 × 40.6 cm), and weighing up to 30 lbs (13.6 kg) were not uncommon, since these were the days before the introduction of enlargers, and big pictures were in great demand.

Fox Talbot, on learning about the new collodion process, claimed that Archer's invention was covered by his patent for the calotype. Archer was not personally involved in the fracas that followed, when Talbot tried to sue a Canadian photographer for breach of patent. Talbot lost, because the court supported the claim that the calotype and the collodion method were different. Scott Archer, a shy

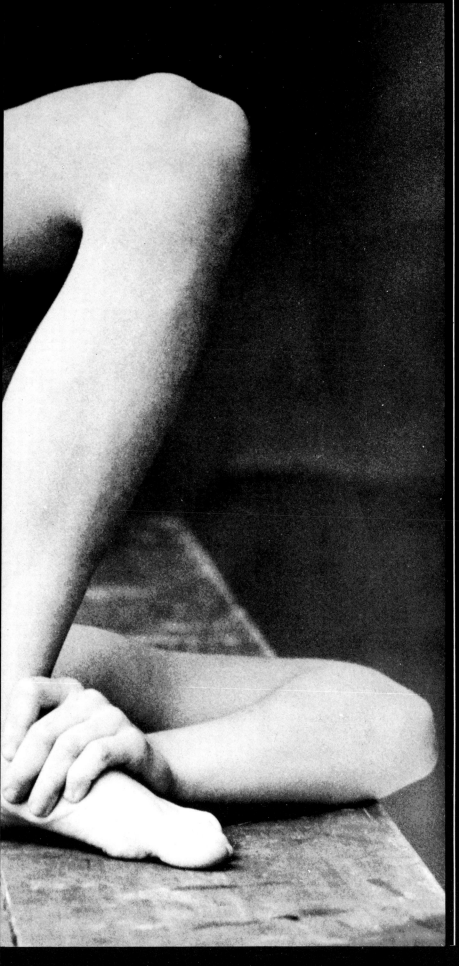

rejecting the mainstream of photography where visual images are valued primarily for their accurate representation of the subject. For example, our perception of everyday objects is regulated by familiarity, we do not have to examine them closely in order to identify them, knowing from past experience the shape, size, color and smell of each. Paradoxically it is often when something familiar is removed, like a piece of furniture from a room which upsets the normal arrangement of order, that our attention is drawn to its absence, and the space it once occupied. This kind of abstraction is apparent in many aspects of modern photography.

The freedom in painting that began with Cubism has also influenced photographers who have embraced the artistic movements of Surrealism, Symbolism and Abstraction. By manipulating images to create a desired effect, photographers are exploring a path started in the 1920s by Man Ray and Moholy Nagy. They seek to create a subjective vision by stressing the psychological or emotional elements of the picture. The images act as a catalyst to provoke an emotional response. This means that what the viewer sees is of less significance than what he experiences. The photographer as artist makes his own rules, imposes his personal viewpoint on his work, but the success of his pictures relies on the response the viewer has to them.

Photography has been emancipated just as the printing press once freed the written word, giving to many what was previously reserved for the few; negatives are capable of supplying an almost inexhaustible number of prints, and once the master print has been made it becomes a mechanical process — truly an expendable art. Photography has been given to all the people, which is where it belongs.

People are often pleased to show their skills in front of the camera, especially children, who are not self-conscious. This girl's extraordinary ability to contort her body makes an arresting picture without any attempt at "trick" photography. Unusual and exaggerated subjects are best presented in the most straightforward manner.

and diffident man, died at the age of 44, but "satisfied with the general recognition" of his work, which not only revolutionized photography, but had freed it, in England at least, from patent monopolies.

As a by-product of the collodion process, Archer introduced the ambrotype, in collaboration with a colleague, Peter Fry. Ambrotypes were thin, under-exposed collodion negatives on glass, bleached with nitric acid, and set against a dark background which reversed the tones and gave them the appearance of positives. They were comparable to daguerreotypes in that they were unique images of a similar size, and they became extremely popular as a technique for portraiture.

As far as photography was concerned, the Victorian era was one of intense activity and innovation. Following a craze for stereoscopic pictures, multi-lens cameras appeared hand-in-hand with the American invention of the tintype. Tintypes were similar to ambrotypes but thin, japanned-metal plates (i.e. plates coated with special lacquer) were used as a base for collodion instead of glass. The materials were cheap and the method of making tintypes was faster than the glass plate technique.

The most fashionable vogue of all began in Paris with the introduction of the *carte de visite* collodion portrait by the Paris photographer André Disdéri. In 1859, Disdéri, who used a multi-lens camera to produce ten negatives on one glass plate, was made famous overnight by the vanity of Napoleon III. Napoleon, who was leading his troops out of Paris to fight the Austrians, halted outside Disdéri's studio, and commanded him to take one of his multiple image photographs. He planned to have the images copied, mounted and distributed as visiting cards. The following day, the whole of Paris copied Napoleon's example, and Disdéri was besieged by sitters.

Cartes de visite have survived only as curiosities, however, whereas many of the larger-format "cabinet" portraits dating from the Victorian period have survived as excellent examples of the formative years of creative photography. Of particular repute are the portraits of a former caricaturist, Gaspard Tournachon, who called himself Nadar, and whose work was stark, simple and revealing.

In England, meanwhile, the poets Tennyson, Long-fellow and Browning were sitting for one of the most remarkable amateurs of all time – Julia Margaret Cameron. Her pictures are characterized by qualities and effects that are rare in early portraiture – namely, the use of the close-up technique, large plates, and adventurous lighting. She used an enormous lens and demanded that her sitters "freeze" for lengthy exposures of five to seven minutes, refusing to use a head clamp for fear that it would destroy the natural appearance of the pose.

Picture-making, in the Victorian era, could be a lengthy, painstaking and elaborate process, especially in the realm of "art" photography, which attempted to compete with meticulous painters. Photography was trying to imitate art, while artists were using photographs to obtain accuracy in drawing – then hotly denying it. Gradually, artists shunned realism and left it to the photographers.

Forgotten fashions
During the Victorian era many photographic techniques evolved but were quickly forgotten. This example of a crystoleum, left, fashionable during the 19th century, "especially among ladies," was made by gluing a paper photograph on to beveled glass with starch. When dry, the paper backing was removed with fine glass paper and the remaining image rendered transparent with wax. The "glass photograph" was then hand colored. This example is a photographic montage.

Recording the Victorians
A family on Clapham Common, below, being photographed by an itinerant photographer. The scene was recorded by John Thomson in 1876. "Gossip on the Beach," a combination print, bottom, by art-photographer Henry Peach Robinson made by taking two negatives, one of the beach and one of the people and superimposing them at the printing stage.

Pioneers of Reportage

A war photographer on wheels Roger Fenton, right, the first English war photographer with the converted wine merchant's van in which he traveled around the battlefields of the Crimea. Employed by the *Illustrated London News*, he specialized in landscapes and group photographs of soldiers, having been instructed to take pictures that would not be upsetting to readers. Working in desperate conditions and plagued by flies, dust and cholera, his van and huge quantity of equipment made an easy target for enemy guns.

Photography began to be a means of communication about 120 years ago when the *Illustrated London News* published engravings of photographs taken at the scene of the Crimean war.

The first war photographer was Roger Fenton, who moved around the Crimean battlefields in a converted wine-merchant's van, into which he had packed a bed, stove, food supply for himself and three horses, five cameras, 700 glass plates, a tent, tools, chemicals and 36 cases. The conditions in the Crimea were almost unendurable, so intense was the heat. Fenton was plagued by flies, dust, cholera and Russian guns for which his van was a conspicuous target. Fenton often lamented the difficulties of working with the large, wet collodion plates under such terrible conditions. He is reputed to have said "As soon as my van door was closed, perspiration started from every pore." The collodion began to dry even before it was spread on the plate, and Fenton could only work between dawn and 10 am to achieve any results at all. But he succeeded in taking 360 photographs during the war, mostly straightforward, unemotional group photographs of soldiers and landscapes, which had been requested by his employers on the magazine who were anxious that their readers should not be upset by pictures of battlefield slaughter.

When Fenton returned to England weak with cholera, his place was taken by James Robertson and Robertson's assistant, Felice Beato, who concentrated less on the portraits of soldiers than on the aftermath of the ravages at Balaclava. It was not possible to print photographs with the letterpress technique until 1880, so engravings continued to be made from their pictures, and published in the *Illustrated London News*. Sometimes sections of the photograph were distributed among blockmakers for speedier reproduction.

The pioneer in the technique of mass coverage of a war was the American photographer Mathew Brady, who is now almost legendary. Brady was a portrait photographer and daguerreotypist who correctly forecast the need for news pictures and financed a team of 20 photographers to record the American Civil War. Brady is often falsely credited with being the only photographer of the war, but there were others, several better than Brady. His assistants Alexander Gardner and Timothy O'Sullivan took some stunning and horrifying pictures including O'Sullivan's famous picture "The Harvest of Death." They worked, of course, with wet collodion plates in large-format cameras which required exposures of ten seconds or more. These, apart from their inherent technical problems, were too slow and cumbersome to take the action shots that became possible with the introduction of the dry-plate.

O'Sullivan was a photographer in the true pioneer spirit. He went to New Mexico, Arizona, Colorado and followed the 49'ers to Nevada where he photographed the famous Comstock Lode mines with the aid of magnesium flares. Gigantic areas of America were unknown to all but the Indians, until private or Government-sponsored explorers such as O'Sullivan visited them, burdened with cases of wet collodion plates and brass-bound cameras. The French photographer of landscapes, Auguste Bisson, climbed Mont Blanc with so much equipment that 25 porters were required to assist him. At a height of 16,000 ft (4,876 m), Bisson braved avalanches and intense cold to expose three plates which were then rinsed in melted snow. In 1864, the Englishman Samuel Bourne photographed the Himalayan range in Kashmir, accompanied by 40 porters, a staff of servants and six bearers. The result of this expedition was 500 exposed glass plates.

Publishers of landscape books often requested large pictures, which were printed and individually glued on to the pages. Since enlargements were not possible, it was necessary for the pictures to be full size inside the camera. Francis Frith took some famous pictures in Egypt with a camera that used plates as large as 16 × 20 ins (40.6 × 50.8 cm) on which the collodion appeared to boil in the intense heat of the Nile Delta. In those pioneer years of reportage photography, enthusiasts needed courage, endurance and passion.

Aftermath of battle A photograph taken in 1855 by *Illustrated London News* photographer James Robertson and his assistant, Felice Beato, during the Crimean War.

The Stereoscopic Craze

Part of the furniture
Stereoscopic photography became immensely popular by the time of the Great Exhibition in 1851. This pedestal holding a stereoscope is a fine example of the ornament and detail so loved by the Victorians.

Since at least the 2nd century BC it has been known that each of our eyes records a slightly different image, and that the two images combine to give us three-dimensional vision. In 1832, Sir Charles Wheatstone FRS found that by preparing two drawings from slightly different viewpoints, and viewing them through a device of mirrors and prisms which simulated the combination effect of human sight, the illusion of three-dimensions could be artificially produced. Wheatstone called his viewer a "stereoscope," and consequently became the founder of stereoscopy.

The application of stereo effects to photography was an obvious step, and stereo photographs were first taken in the 1840s. Daguerreotypes were impractical for use in the earliest stereoscopes because their shiny surfaces caused too much reflection. Portrait calotypes were also unsuitable because it was almost impossible for the sitter to remain totally immobile for the two photographs to be taken from slightly different viewpoints. Still life subjects taken by the calotype process could be used in stereo viewers, and several successful pictures were taken by, among others, Fox Talbot and Roger Fenton.

Stereoscopic photography became immensely popular by the time of the 1851 Great Exhibition in London. By that year, Sir David Brewster had introduced his lenticular stereoscope, a small box containing a pair of prisms in which two small pictures were mounted side by side. Antoine Claudet, a leading London daguerreotypist, holder of the first English patent, made numerous stereo daguerreotypes suitable for viewing in the new instrument, including many pictures of the Crystal Palace in south London taken with two cameras placed side by side. At this time the binocular camera had not been invented.

Typically of the Victorian period, equipment became highly ornate: pedestal and table stereoscopes were often built of elaborately carved wood, with adjustments for height, lens separation and focusing.

By this time albumen prints were mounted on card, and stereoscopes were equipped to be used with these as well as transparencies. The most efficient of

Stereoscopic cameras abound
Stereoscopy was made even more popular during the brief time it was in fashion by the huge quantities of cheap instruments available. The stereo camera illustrated here was made in 1856 by a Manchester optician J. B. Dancer.

the hand viewers for prints was made of aluminum, designed by the American writer Oliver Wendell Holmes in 1861.

The first binocular cameras were made by a Manchester optician, J. B. Dancer, although the idea had been suggested by Sir David Brewster six years before. Stereoscopy was further popularized by the huge quantities of cheap instruments and photographs produced by the London Stereoscopic Co., founded by George Nottage in 1854. In 1858, they manufactured a pocket stereoscopic camera that weighed little over 1 lb (400 gr.) and was available to the masses. Collecting stereo-picture pairs became a fashion but the widespread interest in stereoscopic photography was curiously short-lived. It was revived briefly in 1890 but had died by the outbreak of the First World War.

Victorians in stereo
A stereo daguerreotype and viewer, below, dating from c. 1854. The pictures were made by one of the leading London daguerreotypists, Antoine Claudet, who was holder of the first English patent for stereoscopic photographs. The stereoscopic photograph, right, shows a typical Victorian scene. Photographs such as this were often hand-colored for added realism and interest.

Photography for All

The creator of Kodak
George Eastman, inventor of the famous Kodak box camera. Eastman devised the word "Kodak" to be easily remembered and used in almost any language. He also pioneered roll-film to fit the camera, paper backed, and coated with a gelatin-bromide emulsion.

Kodak cameras for all
A page from the *Photographic Journal*, 1889, below, advertising the Kodak "detective camera" as all hand-held cameras were then called. Though mass-produced, the Kodak was a fine, precision camera, below right, incorporating unique features. By 1889 the first celluloid roll-film had been introduced and the stripping paper base previously used quickly became obsolete.

Great though the invention had been, there was a need for a simpler process than the wet collodion plate. It was the fastest method of photography yet devised, but it was messy, cumbersome and required considerable practice and dexterity. The problem of improving speed of exposure and processing, and method, occupied photographers for many years.

With this aim in view, photographers tried coating the plates with many substances in order to preserve them, including honey, beer, ginger wine and sherry. The results of the experiments were only partially successful: the plates could be kept for six months or more, but their sensitivity was reduced. A number of scientists and photographers, both amateur and professional, played their part in evolving the dry-plate process – it was not the work of a solitary genius.

It had often occurred to photographers that an emulsion of collodion and silver salts might be the answer, if only it could be preserved. An important step toward success was the invention of an alkali developer and a tannin preservative by Major Charles Russell. Two years later, a pair of young amateurs from Liverpool, William Blanchard Bolton and B. J. Sayce, made an emulsion of tannin, collodion and silver bromide, which allowed the commercial production of collodion dry-plates.

The other important aspect associated with the search for the ideal emulsion was to find a substitute for collodion. As long ago as 1847, Niépce de St Victor had suggested using gelatin, but found that it dissolved too readily, and was very slow to react. The first moderately successful experiments with gelatin were by an amateur photographer Dr Richard Leach Maddox, who used an emulsion of gelatin mixed with cadmium bromide and silver nitrate. Dr Maddox is generally considered to be the inventor of the gelatin emulsion, although it was improved by John Burgess in 1873 who developed it in alkaline pyro, and made it available commercially.

Soon, a dried emulsion was introduced, which was soaked in water, dissolved with heat, and poured on to the plate according to a technique invented by London amateur Richard Kennett. The plates reacted quickly because the heat "ripened" the emulsion and rendered it highly sensitive.

Another amateur photographer, Charles Bennett, arrived at the same conclusion but by an improved process. He ripened the gelatin silver bromide plates by keeping them at high temperatures for several days. In 1878, four firms in Britain were producing gelatin dry-plates commercially, and later an automatic machine for coating glass plates was patented.

It was now possible to take pictures with exposures of 1/25 second or less, fast enough to hold a camera steady without the use of a tripod. Speed and the dry-plate system led to compactness. In the 1880s, various hand cameras were marketed; many of them were novelties or curiosities designed to express the skill of the manufacturer. Those disguised as walking sticks, watches, books and other small articles were known as "detective cameras," the description having originated in 1881 with two cameras designed for police surveillance. For several decades, all small cameras were called "detective cameras," until the turn of the century when the name most associated with small cameras was "Kodak."

The ubiquitous box camera was developed together with the invention of celluloid film coated with gelatin emulsion. Alfred Pumphrey's magazine camera was the first to be operated by the now-familiar method of turning a knob which winds a frame of film into place. The system had been foreseen by Sir John Herschel, who wrote of the possibility of "taking a photograph, as it were, by a *snap shot*," in 1/10 second.

In 1888, George Eastman launched the "You press the button, we do the rest" camera – the famous Kodak. This marked the beginning of Eastman Kodak. Eastman devised the name Kodak as one that would

Pocket-sized cameras
The small size of miniature cameras only became possible when gelatin emulsion film had been perfected. The Ticka, below, was a "watch" camera supplied with additional spools which could be loaded in daylight. Each spool was sufficient to take 25 photographs such as those shown below center.

Detective cameras
Miniature cameras were very popular during the 1890s and became known as "detective cameras" after the London police force used them for surveillance. Many designs were evolved to disguise the cameras. The three shown — a book, a walking-stick handle and a revolver — all functioned well; the book and walking stick used roll-film and the revolver tiny plates which fitted into the cylinder. The rotation of the cylinder moved each plate into position and cocked the shutter, which was released by pulling the trigger.

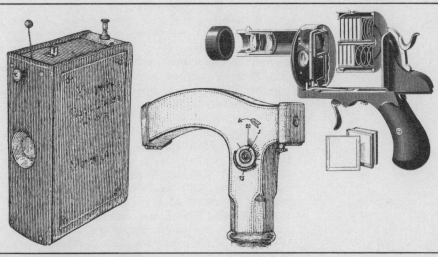

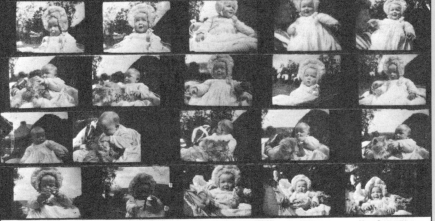

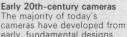

Taken with a "TICKA." These Pictures were all taken on a single spool, by an Amateur, almost the first time he used the Camera.

[P.T.O.

each negative on to a glass plate for contact printing. The camera was then re-filled with film and posted back to the owner along with the prints from the previous film.

The 1890s heralded the age of the small camera — the folding bellows camera, the twin-lens reflex ancestor of the renowned Rolleiflex, and a camera-processor called the "Nodark" where the film was processed inside the camera and not in a darkroom — hence the name. The trouble with the Nodark was its name. Kodak considered it a close anagram of their own trademark and sued the manufacturer for infringement, whereon the name was withdrawn. Nevertheless, the Nodark was the first camera to process its own film, an idea that was developed but only became fully practical with Edwin Land's invention of the Polaroid camera in 1947.

By the beginning of this century, anyone was a potential photographer. Kodak catered for the demand for cheap cameras by following their original success with the "Brownie" in 1900, and the folding-bellows pocket camera in 1903.

At the end of the 1920s the greatest improvements in small, precision cameras were made in Germany, where the monopoly was held for 60 years. The first and most beautiful of the German miniature cameras was the Ermanox (1924), the original model of which was built with a focal plane shutter and lens aperture of f2 and was ideal as an "available light" snapshot camera. The following year at the Leipzig Spring Fair, Leitz introduced the now historic Leica.

Early 20th-century cameras
The majority of today's cameras have developed from early, fundamental designs. This twin-lens reflex camera, right, was made by the London Stereoscopic Co., and took 4 × 5 ins (10.2 × 12.7 cm) plates which were loaded into the back of the camera. It was called an "artist camera" and was manufactured at the turn of the century. The two miniature cameras are an Ermanox, center right, and a model A Leica, far right. The Ermanox was a precision-made, German camera that only took single exposures on dry plates. The now-legendary Leica was designed between 1911—13 by Oskar Barnack, an employee of Leitz, the manufacturers. They built 30 models of his camera ten years after it was designed to test the market and by 1925 they were mass producing it.

be easily pronounced throughout the world. The camera effectively combined all the qualities required for mass production and world-wide appeal. It was light, compact and there was no need for the photographer to develop his own pictures. For the first time a camera could be loaded with roll-film, where paper which acted as a base for the emulsion was peeled off before printing, "stripping film," and was good for a hundred exposures. The camera was returned to the manufacturer who developed the film and transferred

Action on Record

During the early years of Victorian photography, portraitists had urged their sitters to keep still, and often employed head clamps to force immobility. A slight movement on the part of the sitter would have blurred the image, even with the wet collodion process. After the invention of fast, gelatin emulsions and improved papers, professional photographers became aware of the action picture.

The pioneer of action photography was Edward James Muggeridge, who rather eccentrically changed his name to Eadweard Muybridge. Muybridge was English but worked mostly in America, where he studied with Carleton Watson in San Francisco, eventually becoming his partner in 1867. In the same year he organized an expedition to the Yosemite Valley, to make whole-plate collodion negatives and stereoscopic slides of this largely unknown territory. Taking with him a tent, glass plates and bottles, and large-format cameras 22 × 28 ins (55.9 × 71.1 cm), on pack mules into the desert, Muybridge managed to return with some excellent landscape pictures.

Toward the end of February 1868, Muybridge advertised himself as "Helios, the flying camera," and offered a collection of 20 prints of the Yosemite region for 20 dollars a set. He attracted good press reviews, particularly for his cloud effects. These may have been achieved with the use of filters but more likely by printing two negatives together – one of the landscape and another of clouds.

The quality of Muybridge's work was considered so good that he was soon appointed Director of Photographic Surveys for the United States Government. Muybridge returned to the Yosemite Valley and took more outstanding pictures with his huge plate camera. The work of "Helios" became known throughout Europe, and he won a medal for his Yosemite pictures at the Vienna Exhibition.

Muybridge's interest and subsequent involvement

with action photography occurred as a result of an argument between the ex-Governor of California, railroad magnate Leland Stanford, and a friend, Frederick MacCrellish. MacCrellish refused to believe that a fast-trotting horse had all of its feet off the ground at the same moment. Stanford got in touch with Muybridge, who was working along the Pacific Coast, and asked him to make some action shots of a galloping horse. Muybridge chose the Sacramento racecourse, and borrowed all the bed linen in the neighborhood to use as a background.

The first day's work produced no results at all. The second day, Muybridge worked his shutter by hand, and was rewarded with a faint and blurred image. At the third attempt he used a spring-loaded shutter formed by two wooden blades with an eight-inch (20.3 cm) slit between them, sliding vertically in a grooved frame. With this shutter, Muybridge calculated that he was getting a speed of about 1/500 second but the quality of the final shot was very poor, and the result still open to argument.

After a period of five years, during which time Muybridge left America, killed his wife's lover, and returned to California, he continued the experiments on a farm at Palo Alto. A more ambitious program was arranged, and Stanford agreed to donate 40,000 dollars to cover the cost involved. The equipment included a rubber track, and 12 cameras arranged in a 40 ft (12.2 m) long camera house, each equipped with an electro-magnetic shutter operated by a clockwork timing mechanism, and an electric trip-circuit connected to the track. The results of the experiment in which Muybridge took sequence pictures of the horse's movement were conclusive, and showed that Stanford had won his argument. Muybridge then predicted that horse racing would benefit from a photographic technique, and ten years later the first photo-finish was recorded at a track in New Jersey.

Muybridge was not the first photographer to think of motion pictures, but his improved, fast shutter and a desire to show his horse pictures in rapid sequence led to experiments with a projector. At first he called his projector the "zoogyroscope," but in the spring of 1881 he changed it to "zoopraxiscope." It consisted of a lamphouse and lens from a normal projector with a revolving disk in the place of the usual slide mechanism. It was impractical and never developed.

However, it was not long before Edison, Marey, Friese-Greene and the Lumière brothers announced the birth of the cinema. In Paris, Professor Etienne Marey who was conducting experiments with animals in motion by a form of chronography, became influenced by Muybridge's work with the disk projector. In 1882 Marey devised a photographic gun, and in 1890 used the newly invented celluloid roll-film in a *ciné* camera of his own design, which was followed two years later by his projector.

The evolution of the high-speed picture meant that it was now possible for pictures to be taken of events of immediate importance for the ever-demanding news media. Until this time, the problem of printing technique had impeded progress, but in 1880 Frederic Ives invented the half-tone block, the first of which was used to print a news photograph in the *New York*

First proof
A sequence from the experiment made at Palo Alto with electrophotographic equipment in 1887 by Eadweard Muybridge. The original aim of the experiment was to settle an argument about whether or not all four feet of a galloping horse were off the ground at the same time. The second frame proved the point, and the experiment made history by marking the beginning of a new era – that of action photography. Thomas Eakins, an American painter, carried out similar experiments at the same time but received less recognition.

Capturing the event
One of the most famous of all news pictures, the explosion of the dirigible, Hindenburg, at Lakehurst, New Jersey, in 1937, photographed by Sam Sheere. A radio announcer wept as he broadcast the story over the air. Photographer Jack Snyder of the Philadelphia *Record* was so close to the mooring mast that the heat singed his hair. This picture was probably shot on a 4 × 5 ins (10.2 × 12.7 cm) dry plate camera, such as a Speed Graphic, a pressman's camera popularly known as the "Speed G."

Daily Graphic on March 4, 1880. Most editors, however, refused to disturb the austere design of their columns by adding photographs, believing that the printed word carried all the information required by their readers. Not so London's *Daily Mirror*, which ran a fully-illustrated photographic edition in 1904.

Curiously, the American press lagged behind until 1919, but the fashion magazines realized the potential of fashion photography. *Queen* magazine used society pictures in the late 1890s, and *Vogue* in America began printing photographs in 1913. Thus began the era of fashion photography and photo-reportage, when press photographers hefted plate cameras and used magnesium flash.

In the studios, all was calm. Photographers stooped beneath their squares of black cloth, while sitters stared fixedly at the lens; by the turn of the century most people had succumbed to the flattery of portrait photography. Few studios used panchromatic plates, preferring those types which could be constantly inspected under the dark room lamp. Certain forms of artificial studio light were introduced in the 1920s – the flexibility of mobile lamps was not appreciated until some years later.

Photography, hand in hand with modern art, began to explore new fields of expression. The Dadaist group of painters, including the painter and photographer Man Ray, experimented with photo-montages com-

History recorded
A great triumph for photography. Buzz Aldrin salutes the American flag on the moon and is photographed by equipment which traveled with the astronauts in the space module. This moment and many like it will be remembered for centuries with the help of photographic records.

Press photography and danger
The job of the press photographer in wartime is a dangerous one for he can be killed as easily as the troops – it has happened. Here, a youth wearing a gas mask in a Londonderry street is photographed with a home-made bomb in his hand.

bining pieces of photograph and newsprint with the painted canvas. Man Ray, the Hungarian Moholy Nagy and Kurt Schwitters of the Bauhaus extended this experimentation by making solarized and multiple images, using even radiography and scientific techniques to produce photographs notable for their abstract form and movement.

In America the photographic influence of the twenties was from a group of amateurs calling themselves photo-secessionists, headed by Alfred Stieglitz, and working as avowed pictorialists, mainly outside the studio environment. The group were influential and produced some outstanding work.

Perhaps the most significant type of photography to emerge from the period between the wars was photo-reportage, sometimes called "candid-photography." It led to the publication of several great illustrated magazines in different countries of the world including *Berliner Illustrierte Zeitung* and *Münchner-Illustrierte Press*, started in Germany in the 1920s, *Picture Post* and *Illustrated*, launched in Britain in the 1930s, and *Life* magazine, the most famous illustrated magazine to be produced in the USA. Most countries followed these leaders, but only *Life*, the grandest, was widely known outside its own country.

The Color Breakthrough

First step to success
Scottish physicist Sir James Clerk-Maxwell who first demonstrated the color combination principles upon which color photography was originally based.

It will surprise no student of photography to learn that both Niépce and Daguerre considered the idea of creating color pictures, and made a few unsuccessful attempts. Nature was colored, and the camera so faithfully captured reality, that it seemed the two should and could be united. It must also have occurred to photographers that the secret lay in the correct application and balance of chemicals, but because a great knowledge of chemistry was required, as well as a basic knowledge of physics, few were qualified to make any worthwhile attempts.

Probably the birth of modern color photography began with a lecture in 1861 by the Scottish physicist Sir James Clerk-Maxwell, in which he demonstrated that any shade of color could be made by mixing lights of the three primary colors (red, green, blue) in varying proportions. He demonstrated the theory by passing light through combined colored glass plates, and projecting the result on to a screen. This was the first additive system applied to color photography. The subtractive system was later described by a French pianist, Louis Ducos Du Hauron. In his book *Les Couleurs en Photographie; Solution du Problème* of 1869, Du Hauron laid down all the basic principles of modern color photography, both additive and subtractive. The subtractive method was based on the theory that pigments absorb or subtract from light all colors except their own, which they reflect.

For many years the dream of photographs in color remained theoretical. Then, in 1873, Hermann Vogel, Professor of Photochemistry at the Technische Hochschule in Berlin, discovered that the collodion plate, normally non-sensitive to colors other than blue, could be made more sensitive to green by treating it with certain aniline dyes. This led to the orthochromatic plate, found to be insensitive to red, still over-sensitive to blue, but a step in the right direction. It was not until 1906, that Wratten and Wainwright in London, introduced the panchromatic plate, which was sensitive to all the colors of the spectrum.

The first practical breakthrough came in 1891 with the invention of a color camera by Frederic Ives of Philadelphia, which followed Clerk-Maxwell's principles and could take the three negatives (each recording one primary color) on a single plate. Diapositives were made from the plate and viewed through an instrument that Ives called a "Photochromoscope." Further experiments were carried out by a number of scientists but none had great practical application until the developments made by Auguste and Louis Lumière, who patented the color screen process in 1904. There was little concern that exposures were 40 times longer than for black and white photography, and that the transparencies were rather dense. Color photography had arrived, and it seemed it could become commercially viable.

Of the two systems, additive and subtractive, the latter was more frequently used in experiments. Rudolf Fischer made a practical contribution when he invented dye-coupling in 1912, where three layers of emulsion, each with a different color sensitivity, are held on one support. The first practical film did not appear for 23 years, until Leopold Mannes and Leopold Godowsky produced Kodachrome film, at the Eastman Kodak Research Laboratories.

Color film has radically changed the world of photography and movie making, with one exception – use in newspapers. The latest and most remarkable development in color printing, first marketed in 1963, is the color picture produced automatically, by the Polaroid Land Camera.

In one respect, the new and improved processes have obsessed photographers for well over a century. Experimenting with chemicals was an intrinsic and all-absorbing part of the business when, as a French amateur remarked in 1839, "even the poorest proof gave me indescribable joy . . . ."

A color camera
Camera designed by Jospé in 1925 for taking color photographs. Only one shot could be taken before the camera had to be reloaded.

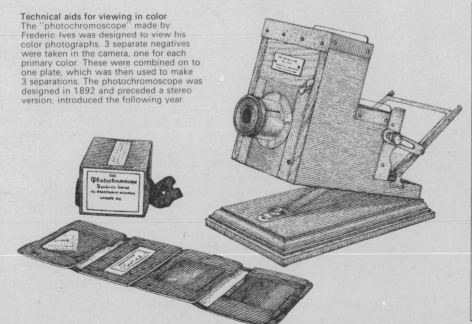

Technical aids for viewing in color
The "photochromoscope" made by Frederic Ives was designed to view his color photographs. 3 separate negatives were taken in the camera, one for each primary color. These were combined on to one plate, which was then used to make 3 separations. The photochromoscope was designed in 1892 and preceded a stereo version, introduced the following year.

HOW
THE CAMERA
WORKS

The Basic Camera

Every camera, from the very simple to the complex and sophisticated, is basically of the same fundamental design: a box or container carefully constructed to prevent extraneous light from entering except through the lens. The design incorporates the lens, an adjustable iris diaphragm, a shutter and a mechanism for holding the film. In addition, cameras have a viewfinder through which the subject/image can be seen and composed. An important aspect of camera design concerns the critical adjustments that relate the position of the lens to the *film plane*, the area inside the camera on which the image is focused by the lens. A rectangle of film, either part of a roll or in a single sheet, lies across this plane to receive the image transmitted by the lens.

Unexposed film can record a latent image on its light-sensitive, chemical emulsion layer. The camera is a mechanical device which permits light rays projected by the image to reach the film through the agency of the lens, controlled by the diaphragm and the shutter. The image is only made sharp and clear by adjusting the position of the lens in relation to the film plane, in other words by *focusing* – focusing makes all or part of the image sharp.

Because of the high sensitivity of photographic film a system is needed to control the light rays passing through the lens. The diaphragm varies the *strength* of the light by means of a variable aperture or hole, usually incorporated in the lens. In very bright light the aperture will probably require closing, or "stopping down," whereas in poor light conditions the aperture will need to be wide open. The action of stopping down improves the quality of the image, because reducing the aperture increases the *depth of field*, the area of sharpness of a three-dimensional subject upon which the lens is focused. Depth of field is not to be confused with *depth of focus*, the optimum distance between the lens and the film where the image of a flat object remains sharp.

The diaphragm's aperture is calibrated in *stops*, the symbol for which is "f" and can range from f1, where it is wide open, to f64 where it is closed to a mere pinpoint. The shutter controls the *duration* of time light is allowed to reach the film through the lens diaphragm. It is usually spring-loaded, and activated by pressing a button or small lever. Shutter speeds usually range from 1 second to 1/500 or 1/1000 second, and are set accordingly. A shutter can be set to remain open indefinitely, for long exposures. The simplest type of camera has a fixed shutter speed and fixed aperture, 1/100 second at f16, for example, and is designed only to take snapshots in bright light. The more expensive cameras are fitted with numerous controls, and offer a selection of accessories.

The *lens* is an essential component of any camera. Modern lenses are generally of compound construction, consisting of several elements of glass closely

A The lens of any camera is adjustable to permit focusing. The distance between the lens and film plane can be altered to bring different parts of the subject into focus.

B The aperture of the iris diaphragm can be manually or mechanically varied in size to control the strength of the light rays transmitted through the lens onto the film. It also controls the depth of field.

C The shutter speed determines the duration of light rays exposed to the film.

D The film plane is the area inside the camera on which the image is focused, and the film exposed. With roll-film, exposed sections are moved on by a winding mechanism. Flat or sheet film is mounted in slides, which are changed by hand after each exposure.

E The viewfinder system enables the photographer to view the subject area and compose the picture.

aligned and arranged together. Such lenses attain very high standards of focus sharpness, and are available in a variety of sizes, each with a definite function – wide-angle, close-up, long-focus, telephoto, and so on.

The *diaphragm* is usually an integral part of the lens, and works in conjunction with the shutter – an integral part of the camera – in order to achieve accurate exposures to light. In any given conditions of light the size of the aperture must relate to the speed of the shutter to maintain the same exposure; an f2 aperture in poor light will require a slow shutter speed, say 1/60 second, whereas the same aperture in bright light might need a fast shutter, perhaps 1/1000 second.

There are two main types of *shutter*: a diaphragm shutter set between the lens elements, and a focal plane shutter, working on the principle of a roller blind just in front of the film. Some systems employ both types; the kind of shutter used in a camera depends on the camera's purpose. The shutter on the average miniature 35 mm camera is automatically cocked by the action of the film-winding mechanism, a knob or lever mounted on the camera body. With plate cameras, large format cameras, and some types of twin-lens reflex, there is a special cocking lever to tension the shutter. A release sets off the cocked shutter at the appropriate time. When flash lighting is used, the shutter release closes an electric circuit and fires the flash. However, synchronization varies according to the type of flash. With electronic flash, synchronization is determined by a switch set to the "X" setting on the camera body, for bulb flash the "M" setting is used. These are exactly timed, and ensure that

the flash has reached its peak power by the time the shutter is fully open.

To enable the photographer to compose his subject, cameras have a *viewing system*. This can be separate from the lens and built into the camera body, or it can be designed to reflect the image through the lens onto a mirror and prism.

Large format cameras are designed for use with static subjects, where there is time to frame and compose the picture content. Small cameras offer greater facility and speed, and are therefore suitable for action photography and photo-journalism. In addition, small cameras are compact and easy to carry around, even with a range of accessories.

The Viewfinder Camera

Image and viewfinder

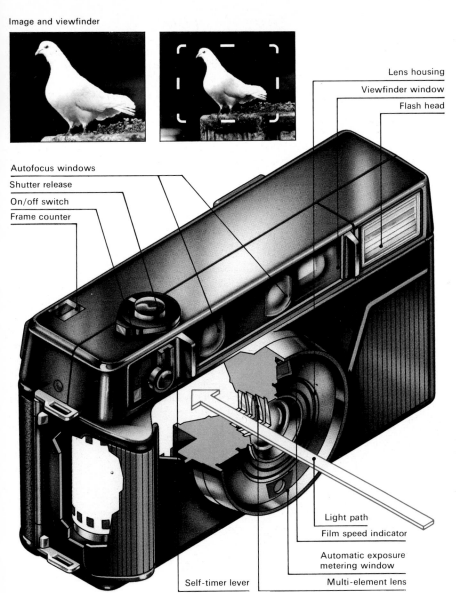

Lens housing
Viewfinder window
Flash head

Autofocus windows
Shutter release
On/off switch
Frame counter

Light path
Film speed indicator
Automatic exposure metering window
Self-timer lever
Multi-element lens

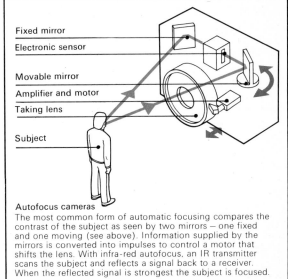

Fixed mirror
Electronic sensor
Movable mirror
Amplifier and motor
Taking lens
Subject

Autofocus cameras
The most common form of automatic focusing compares the contrast of the subject as seen by two mirrors — one fixed and one moving (see above). Information supplied by the mirrors is converted into impulses to control a motor that shifts the lens. With infra-red autofocus, an IR transmitter scans the subject and reflects a signal back to a receiver. When the reflected signal is strongest the subject is focused.

Viewfinder cameras use a small lens, often set behind a rectangular window, through which the subject area can be seen. There is one disadvantage of this system: the area seen through the viewfinder differs slightly from the area seen by the lens. Framing lines in the viewfinder correct for this except in the case of extreme close-ups.

The latest viewfinder cameras use sophisticated electronics and microcircuitry for nearly total automation. In the example on the left, infra-red automatic focusing will render sharp any subject positioned centrally in the frame (even in the dark). A built-in motor will control film loading, advance the film to the first frame, wind on after each exposure and, at the end of the film, automatically rewind the film. If light levels are too low the flash automatically pops up. The aperture is then automatically adjusted to ensure correct exposure over the effective flash range.

Modern viewfinder cameras

The compact and rugged *press camera* was designed to take 6×9 cm plates or sheet film which could be contacted directly into prints suitable for urgent newspaper work, thus avoiding the enlarging process. The camera has interchangeable lenses but no movements.

Film improvement and the development of smaller, precision cameras has led to the introduction of the *110 cartridge* camera. A distance-zone setting allows some focus control.

Subminiature cameras are by no means a recent invention — they were the rage of the 1880s. Modern versions include technical advances such as integral exposure meters, flash and close-up attachments. Subminiatures use 16 mm film, and the range of shutter speeds is limited to about five settings.

Designed mainly for commercial photography, the *technical* camera has a range of interchangeable lenses. The design incorporates basic movements. Technical cameras use either 120 and 220 roll-film, or sheet film.

Lightweight, compact, easy to use and to operate, the *35 mm* is the most popular camera size. Most makes have a remarkable range of accessories and lenses. Technical advances in press reproduction from 35 mm film has made the camera the essential equipment of photo-journalists.

Also lightweight and compact, but considerably less expensive and less sophisticated, the *126 cartridge* camera is designed for the mass market. It is simple to load and operate, and available in a range of specifications.

The Twin-Lens Reflex

The twin-lens reflex, popularly the "TLR", employs two lenses, both mounted on a moveable panel, one above the other. The top lens carries the viewing image upright and laterally-reversed, on a ground-glass screen. The bottom lens incorporates a diaphragm and shutter, and carries the image onto the film. Both lenses have the same focal length, and focusing is usually with a knob on one side of the camera body, which moves the lens panel backward or forward. A folding metal hood shades the viewing screen and holds a retractable magnifier for fine focusing.

The great advantage of the twin-lens reflex design is its combination of compactness and generous viewfinder. Introduced in the late 19th century, the camera is easy to operate and uses roll-film with a square negative format of the same dimensions as the ground-glass screen. This means that the camera can be held vertically for viewing, irrespective of the shape of the subject/image. Negatives make fairly large contact prints, and pictures can be cropped in the enlarger. The main disadvantage of the twin-lens reflex is its lack of interchangeable lenses, and a demand for a more flexible lens system has led to the development of an interchangeable system offering a range of lenses, bodies, backs and viewfinders. The standard twin-lens reflex cameras have a rapid-action lever for winding on film, and provision for eye-level focusing through a pentaprism, while some have built-in exposure meters.

Image and viewfinder

The twin-lens reflex screen, identical in size to the negative, shows nearly all the picture area. There is a slight degree of parallax error because the lenses are an inch or so (3–4 cm) apart; some models account for this with a moving correction mask.

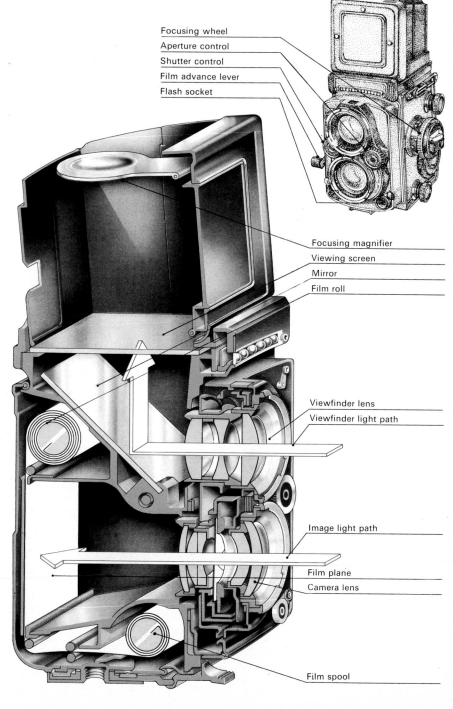

Focusing wheel
Aperture control
Shutter control
Film advance lever
Flash socket

Focusing magnifier
Viewing screen
Mirror
Film roll

Viewfinder lens
Viewfinder light path

Image light path

Film plane
Camera lens

Film spool

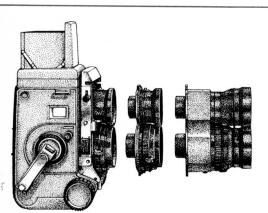

The twin-lens reflex interchangeable lens system
The 6×6 cm interchangeable lens system usually includes lens pairs of 55 mm, 65 mm, 80 mm, 105 mm, 135 mm and 180 mm. The lower lens on each panel has its own shutter, linked to the camera body. The focusing mount is formed by a bellows on the body front. Very close focusing is possible, and many accessories increase the camera's versatility.

The View Camera

The view camera system is designed primarily for professional photography and, though the camera size requires large format sheet film and tripod or monorail mounting, it is extremely flexible. For example, the front and back panels can be made to shift, rise and fall, tilt and swing making possible infinite corrections to the image. A ground-glass screen receives the image, and focusing is by means of bellows.

A wide variety of lenses of different focal lengths are made, each panel-mounted and with an integral shutter and diaphragm. The image is focused on the screen by leaving the shutter open with the aperture at its widest f stop. To avoid disturbing the fine focusing, you can rigidly secure the panels and bellows slide by tightening knurled knobs. After closing and tensioning the shutter, the aperture is set and the glass screen replaced by the film holder. Film holders are double-sided, each side having a thin panel shielding the film. This panel is removed when the holder is in place, so that the exposure can be made, and then returned to the holder after exposure. Sheet film, plates, roll-film and instant print film can be used.

Viewfinder and image
The focusing screen of the view camera shows a laterally reversed, upside down image. Film inserted into the back panel by means of a holder will record an image identical to that viewed on the screen.

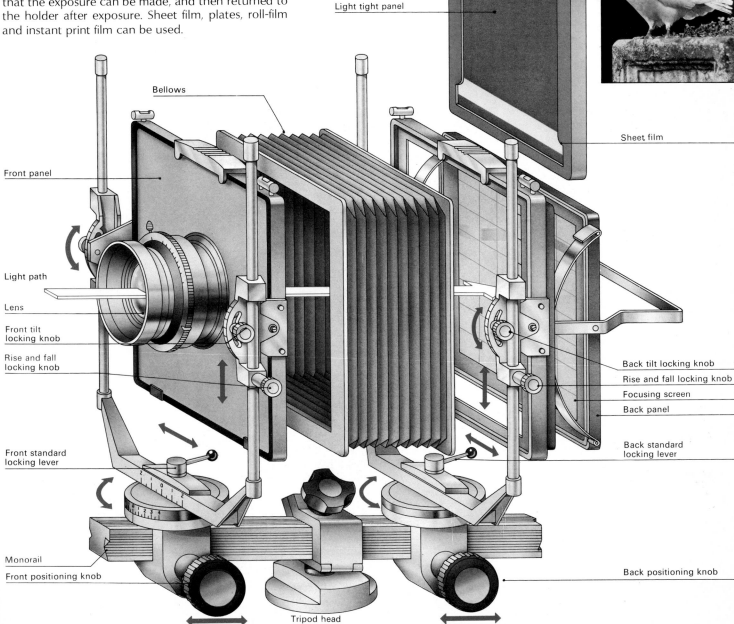

Film holder

Light tight panel

Sheet film

Bellows

Front panel

Light path

Lens

Front tilt locking knob

Rise and fall locking knob

Front standard locking lever

Monorail

Front positioning knob

Back tilt locking knob

Rise and fall locking knob

Focusing screen

Back panel

Back standard locking lever

Back positioning knob

Tripod head

The Single-Lens Reflex

Photography's future historians will probably conclude that the single-lens reflex – the "SLR" – is the most successful of all camera designs. This achievement has undoubtedly come about through the recent advances in design and technical innovation, coupled with the fact that photography is reaching a much wider and more prosperous market than before. The single-lens reflex fulfills many demands: it is lightweight, compact, easy to handle and operate, has eye-level or chest-level viewing, built-in exposure meter, an astonishing variety of interchangeable lenses, plus a host of other accessories. Furthermore, the 35 mm camera is accompanied by a fairly inexpensive system for projecting color positive transparencies; chemical advances in black-and-white film also allow bigger and better enlargements with finer grain.

The single-lens reflex receives the image through the camera lens, onto an angled, moveable mirror which transfers the image to a glass screen; the image is identical to the one received by the film, so there is no parallax error. A spring mechanism links the mirror to a focal plane shutter release, so that when the shutter is tripped the mirror automatically snaps out of the path of exposure. The small viewing screen of the 35 mm has lately been improved by adding a magnifying pentaprism for eye-level viewing of the upright image.

The principal components of the single-lens reflex are the viewing system and the focal plane shutter. The 35 mm cameras have a pentaprism viewer, while the larger-format types provide a screen and collapsible hood like some TLRs. The main difference between most models lies in the lens flange design. This can have a screw thread, breechlock or bayonet. Flange to film distance also varies. Integral light meters and automatic diaphragms and focusing devices are becoming commonplace with many manufacturers. Some have interchangeable film magazines and provision for instant picture packs, while some sophisticated 35 mm models have motorized film-winding mechanisms.

The 35 mm system
A typical 35 mm single-lens reflex system consists of lenses and attachments, close-up accessories, motor drives, remote control units, and flash equipment. Most systems offer bodies of varying degrees of sophistication; all can be used with the same range of accessories.

The interchangeable lens
The 35 mm single-lens reflex camera is supplied with a standard or normal lens but a variety of lenses are available to meet specific requirements – telephoto, fish-eye, soft focus, wide-angle, and so on. These can range from a focal length of 15 mm (or even less) to 1000 mm (or more).

Wide-angle lens
Any lens with a coverage of 60° or more can be called a wide-angle. Compact and light, they range from 35 mm focal length to such extreme types as 15 mm with a coverage of 180°

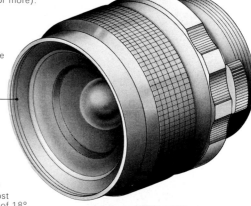

The large format single-lens reflex
The majority of larger SLRs are designed to take 6 × 6 cm roll-film, and the viewing screen is identical in size to the film negative as with many TLRs. These cameras are more bulky than the 35 mm, and viewing is usually at waist or chest level. Interchangeable lenses, viewfinders and film magazines are available.

Long-focus lens
Giving a greater magnification than the standard lens, long-focus lenses usually range from 85 mm to 1000 mm. The most popular is the 135 mm, covering a field of 18°. Bulk and weight increase with focal length.

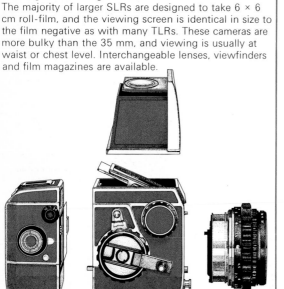

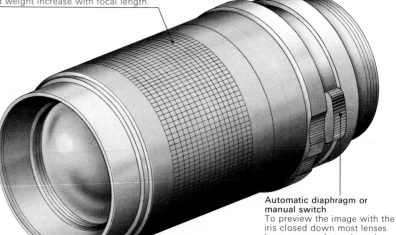

Automatic diaphragm or manual switch
To preview the image with the iris closed down most lenses have a manual stopdown lever or switch. This permits visual estimation of depth of field at a given aperture.

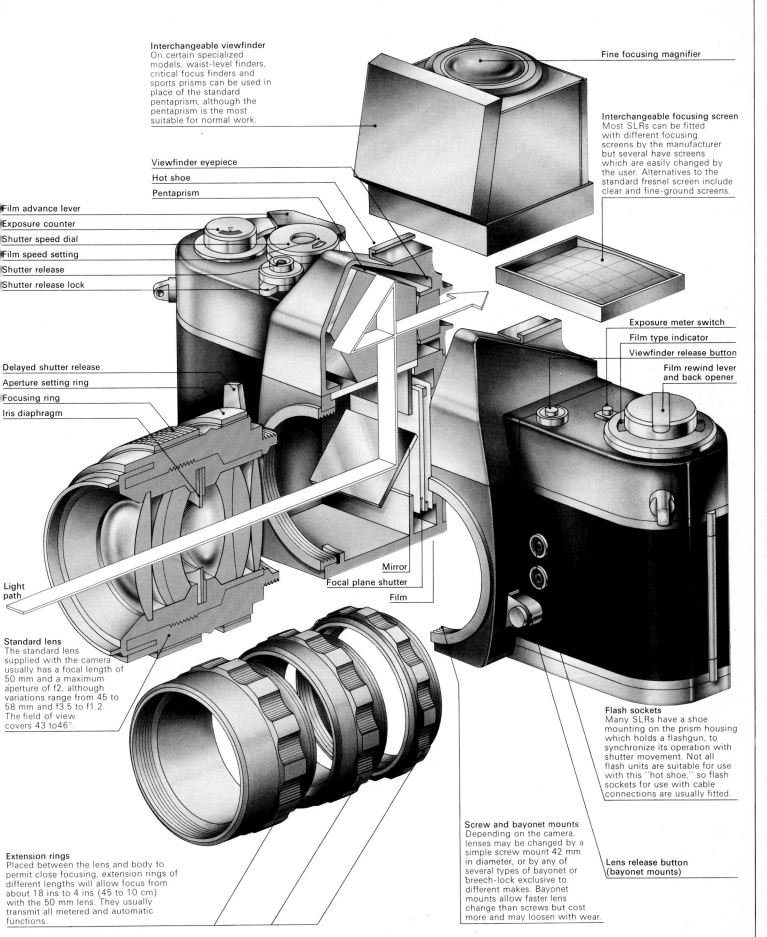

Interchangeable viewfinder
On certain specialized models, waist-level finders, critical focus finders and sports prisms can be used in place of the standard pentaprism, although the pentaprism is the most suitable for normal work.

Fine focusing magnifier

Interchangeable focusing screen
Most SLRs can be fitted with different focusing screens by the manufacturer but several have screens which are easily changed by the user. Alternatives to the standard fresnel screen include clear and fine-ground screens.

Viewfinder eyepiece

Hot shoe

Pentaprism

Film advance lever

Exposure counter

Shutter speed dial

Film speed setting

Shutter release

Shutter release lock

Exposure meter switch

Film type indicator

Viewfinder release button

Film rewind lever and back opener

Delayed shutter release

Aperture setting ring

Focusing ring

Iris diaphragm

Mirror

Focal plane shutter

Film

Light path

Standard lens
The standard lens supplied with the camera usually has a focal length of 50 mm and a maximum aperture of f2, although variations range from 45 to 58 mm and f3.5 to f1.2. The field of view covers 43 to46°.

Flash sockets
Many SLRs have a shoe mounting on the prism housing which holds a flashgun, to synchronize its operation with shutter movement. Not all flash units are suitable for use with this "hot shoe," so flash sockets for use with cable connections are usually fitted.

Extension rings
Placed between the lens and body to permit close focusing, extension rings of different lengths will allow focus from about 18 ins to 4 ins (45 to 10 cm) with the 50 mm lens. They usually transmit all metered and automatic functions.

Screw and bayonet mounts
Depending on the camera, lenses may be changed by a simple screw mount 42 mm in diameter, or by any of several types of bayonet or breech-lock exclusive to different makes. Bayonet mounts allow faster lens change than screws but cost more and may loosen with wear.

Lens release button
(bayonet mounts)

39

The Lens & Aperture

The three major controls on a camera lens system are the shutter speed setting, the f stop which indicates the size of the diaphragm aperture, and the distance scale which assists in focusing. Shutter speed settings are

Aperture
As the marked value of each f stop increases, the diaphragm closes and cuts the amount of light admitted in half. The exposure time must be doubled for every f stop closed down if exposure is to be kept constant.

1 sec.

1/2 sec.

1/4 sec.

1/8 sec.

1/60 sec.   1/30 sec.   1/15 sec.

f2   f2.8   f4   f5.6   f8   f11   f16

usually located on the camera body, sometimes on the lens mount. Normally aperture and focusing controls are in the form of rings set into the barrel of the lens. Each ring can be rotated within fixed limits and read off against an index.

Exposure is a product of the amount of light allowed to fall on the film (controlled by aperture) and the duration that light is allowed to act (controlled by speed setting). To keep exposure constant any change in the size of the aperture must be matched by a change in speed, and vice versa. Most speed settings are marked in seconds in the progression: 1 1/2 1/4 1/8 1/15 1/30 1/60 1/125 1/250 1/500. Each setting is thus about twice as fast as the previous one. Marked aperture settings follow the accepted series: f1 f1.4 f2 f2.8 f4 f5.6 f8 f11 f16 f22 f32 f45 f64. The series represents a strict geometrical progression, so for each increase in f number the area of the aperture, and hence the amount of light passing through it, is cut in half. (If the maximum opening of a given lens is not included in this series – e.g. f1.8 or f3.5 – the series nevertheless continues normally after beginning with the odd number).

The two scales of aperture and speed are therefore directly related. In changing the aperture by one setting (one *stop*), the amount of light falling on the film is halved or doubled; the time the light is allowed to act is similarly altered by the speed setting.

For example, light conditions call for an exposure set at 1/125 second at f16 but to freeze action a shutter speed of half that, 1/250 second, is preferable. To keep exposure constant with this speed the aperture must be doubled – that is, increased by one stop to f11.

The distance scale permits the lens to be focused on the correct point to form a sharp image. This scale begins at approximately 18 ins (45.7 cm) and continues in steps to infinity, marked with the symbol ∞. On either side of the focus index mark, most cameras have a series of numbers corresponding to the aperture scale either on the camera body or on the lens. This scale gives an indication of depth of field at a given aperture and distance setting.

The f stop
Any type or size of lens set at a specific f stop transmits an image of near identical luminance, because the diameter of the aperture is directly related to focal length. For example: an 80 mm lens used with an aperture 5 mm in diameter must be set at f16. Thus, the focal length of the lens, divided by the diameter of the aperture, gives the corresponding f stop number.

Depth of field scale
The depth of field scale reads off against the focusing scale and indicates the distance between the nearest point and the furthest point in the picture area which is acceptably sharp.

Focusing
The lens extends from the camera by means of a screw thread and is operated by a rotating ring so that the lens can focus on objects at different distances from the camera. The extension required becomes greater as subject-to-camera distance decreases.

| ft | ∞ | 30 | 15 | 10 | 7 | 5 | 4 | | 2.5 | | 1.5 |
| m | | 10 | 5 | 3 | 2 | 1.5 | 1.2 | 1 | | | 0. |

40

Depth of field

The distance between the nearest point and the furthest point of a three-dimensional subject that can be rendered acceptably sharp is termed the "depth of field." In other words, if you focus your camera on a building in the middle distance, and the foreground is also sharp, the objects that lie between will also be in focus: the picture will possess considerable depth of field. Although the depth of field increases as the distance between the camera and the subject increases, depth of field in closer subjects may still be achieved by stopping down the diaphragm. A picture taken with an f stop of 22 would give better depth of field than a setting of f4, but the shutter speed would need to be correspondingly slower at f22, to permit a greater amount of light to penetrate the small aperture. A good guide, except when focusing on close subjects, is that depth of field extends 1/3 in front of the focused point, and 2/3 behind it. Most cameras or lenses provide a depth of field scale, by which you can relate the depth of field to the aperture size and the distance of the subject. As we have seen, depth of field is not to be confused with depth of focus. What it really means is "the area or field of observation in which the subject lies that gives a good illusion of depth, since all the objects in that area are acceptably in focus through the lens of the camera." Depth of field was an intrinsic part of early photographs, since most lenses had small maximum apertures; a landscape lens with an aperture of f14 was not unusual. The rules governing depth of field apply to any lens, but by using lenses of different focal length, depth of field will change. Lenses of short focal length have a greater depth of field than lenses of long focal length, although *all* lenses give the same depth of field if f number and image size are constant.

Using depth of field to advantage

As shown top right, it is often possible to emphasize one item in a photograph by using a shallow depth of field. Greater detail is obtained, see middle right, by stopping down. By increasing the depth of field still further it is usually possible to render everything sharp, see right.

By keeping the same focus but stopping the aperture down to f8 the scale shows that depth of field exists from 7 ft (2.1 m) to 15 ft (4.5 m) from the camera.

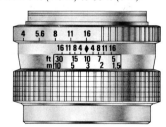

With the aperture stopped down to f16 and the lens still focused on 10 ft (3 m) the depth of field extends from 5 ft (1.5 m) to 30 ft (9 m).

Changing aperture
By stopping down (i.e. increasing the marked value of the f stop), you reduce the aperture. The smaller the aperture, the greater the depth of field obtained. For example, a greater depth of field is achieved with an aperture of f16 than with f2.

Changing subject-to-camera
The further you place your camera from the subject the greater the depth of field will be. As the subject gets closer to the lens, depth of field diminishes. For example, depth of field is greater when the lens is focused on 15 ft (4.5 m) than on 5 ft (1.5 m).

Changing focal length
The shorter the focal length of the lens being used, the greater the depth of field. For example, for the same f number and subject distance a 28 mm wide-angle lens will allow a greater depth of field than a 135 mm long lens.

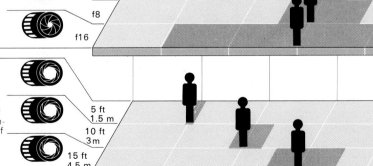

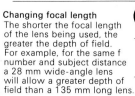

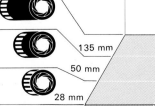

The Lens & Focusing

As a general rule, objects reflect rays of light from a light source, although some substances – glass, for example – transmit light rays, while others actually absorb light. All objects are seen by both the human eye and the camera lens according to the effect of light, which shows shape, substance and size.

Light rays travel in straight lines, and through the agency of a small aperture can cause an image to form on a screen, as can be seen by the example of the simple pinhole camera. A very small hole made in a thin piece of card will pass the image of a subject which can be projected onto a screen. The image will be upside-down, since the light rays from the bottom of the image pass through the pinhole in a straight line, traveling upwards, reaching the upper area of the screen. The rays from the top of the image travel through the pinhole in a downward direction reaching the lower area of the screen – the image is therefore inverted. Quite acceptable photographs can be taken with a pinhole camera but although they have almost infinite depth of field (because of the tiny aperture) really sharp definition is impossible, and you need to make long exposures, limiting the choice of subject.

A simple lens in place of the pinhole will considerably improve the quality of the image, because of the lens's power to control the path of light rays, to concentrate the image. The lens is the eye of the photographer and the most important part of any camera. A simple lens – or indeed *any* lens – behaves as if constructed from prisms, pieces of angular glass so shaped as to refract or deflect light rays, changing their direction of travel. The angle of re-direction depends on the angle at which the light rays strike the surface of the glass, and the curvature of the lens surface. The object of a lens, then, is to improve the flexibility of the camera and the quality of the photographs.

To have the freedom to photograph and exploit any subject you will need a basic selection of interchangeable lenses of varying focal lengths. There are a bewildering selection of lenses available, but unless you

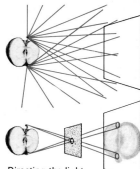

Directing the light
Light rays reflected from an object diverge and do not form an image. A sheet of card or paper pierced by a very small hole will limit and direct rays from the subject to form an inverted image of moderate quality.

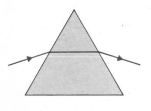

Focusing the image
A prism has the ability to bend light, left. Rays diverging from each point on the subject converge to a point when passed through a convex lens, below left. The point of convergence is termed the focal point. A focused image consists of an infinite number of points.

Focal plane
A line drawn through the focal point at right angles to the optical axis is called the focal plane, see above right.

Focal length
Focal length relates to the angle at which a lens bends light rays. It is measured as the distance between the lens and the focal point when the camera lens is set on infinity, as shown right. A lens with a short focal length has a sharp angle of bend, bringing the rays to focus just behind the lens.

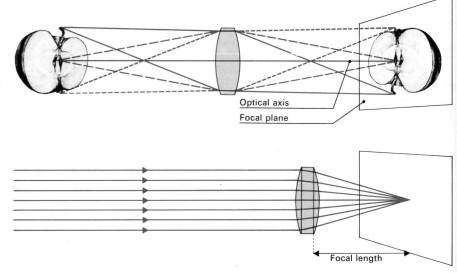

Optical axis
Focal plane

Focal length

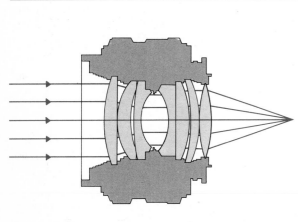

Compound lenses
A compound lens can be described as a lens containing two or more elements of shaped glass, either concave or convex. Such constructions offer a greater degree of freedom for lens design and overcome, or at least diminish, many of the aberrations found in simple lenses. Compared with simple lenses, image quality is greatly improved, maximum apertures are more variable and covering power is enlarged to suit a variety of requirements.

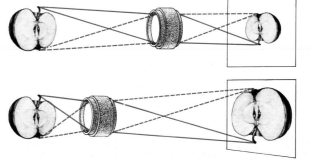

Angle of view
The angle of view indicates the limits of the subject area filling the picture format. It is directly related to the focal length and the dimensions of the picture the camera is designed to produce.

Image size
To change image size without moving subject or camera, a lens of different focal length must be used. To increase the size of the image, a longer focal length lens is necessary; to decrease the size, a shorter focal length. A lens with twice the focal length of another will produce an image of twice the size, as shown left. All lenses, however, must be related to the negative size for which they were designed.

wish to specialize there is no need to have more than three. The normal lens which usually comes with the camera, has a focal length about equal to the diagonal of the negative, i.e. 50 mm for a 35 mm camera; it gives an angle of view of about 45° which is roughly equivalent to that of the human eye.

A *long* lens gives a larger image and has a narrower angle of view. Its focal length is usually greater than 85 mm for a 35 mm camera. It is most useful in preventing distortion of perspective, which can happen if you are too close to the object you are photographing. This is particularly significant in portraiture and architectural photography. Lenses of 180 mm or more on a 35 mm camera will give very large images and have an extremely narrow angle of view.

The *wide-angle* lens has a short focal length, usually less than 35 mm on a 35 mm camera and will give a wide angle of view, greater than 60°. It is very useful in confined areas and because of its great depth of field is much used by photo-journalists.

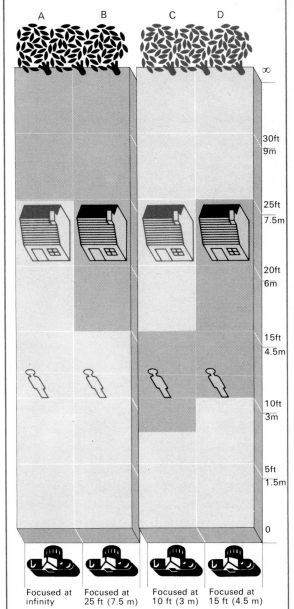

Focusing for maximum advantage
Except when using very close focusing, depth of field extends 1/3 in front and 2/3 behind the point upon which the lens is focused. **A** When focused on infinity, it is logical that 2/3 of the depth of field, supposedly beyond infinity, is wasted. **B** By refocusing on the nearest limit of depth of field, all objects to infinity remain in focus but the depth of field has been brought forward to include closer objects as well. **C** When focused on close subjects the depth of field is shallow. **D** By refocusing on the furthest limit of the depth of field, the depth of field can be increased to include not only the closest subject but also subjects further back.

Focused at infinity | Focused at 25 ft (7.5 m) | Focused at 10 ft (3 m) | Focused at 15 ft (4.5 m)

Sharpness
The sharpness of picture detail depends on the fineness of the countless points which make it up. These points are finest when they are in perfect focus. Areas in a picture in front of or behind the points in sharp focus become blurred as the points increase in size until they appear as overlapping disks or "circles of confusion."

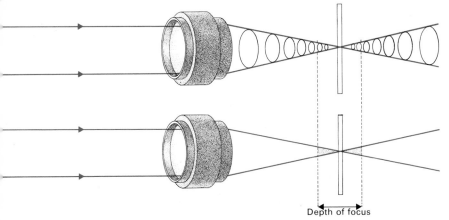

Depth of focus

Depth of focus
A lens focuses light rays to a point on the focal plane. In front of and beyond the focal plane the light rays are formed not into a point but into a disk (or circle of confusion) which increases in size as it moves further away from the focal plane (shown in the top diagram). The disks closest to the focal plane are not perceived by the eye because they are so small; they also appear as focused points. Depth of focus is the distance the lens can be moved from the film while keeping the subject image in acceptable focus, and within the range of disks too small to be perceived (as shown above).

The Shutter

In the early days of photography long exposures were needed to record a reasonable image on the plates or paper negatives then used. Exposures of several minutes were required on dull days, and even in sunlight 20 seconds was not unusual. Exposures were made by simply removing a cap that fitted over the lens. As more sensitive materials were invented, exposure times became shorter and by the late 19th century it was necessary to provide exact exposures between 1/25 second and one second.

The first mechanical shutter was the guillotine or drop shutter, a metal plate with a hole in it which fell past the lens. By varying the size of the hole, different exposure times could be achieved. Many shutters were developed but none could reach the speeds demanded by the 20th century. By the 1920s a top speed of 1/200 second or 1/250 second was achieved; by the 1930s this advanced to 1/500 second or 1/1000 second. Only two shutter types, the focal plane shutter and the leaf shutter, were capable of such high speeds. Today many focal plane shutters supposedly reach 1/2000 second although marked speeds shorter than 1/500 second may suffer from inefficiency because of the high tensioning used and the problem of shutter inertia. It can usually be assumed that the actual speeds obtained are slower than the speeds indicated.

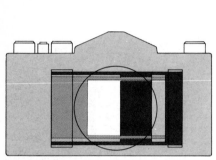

Focal plane shutter
This shutter, fitted to most SLRs and interchangeable lens viewfinder cameras, is positioned as close to the focal plane as possible. It consists of a system of blinds and tensioning drums. The primary blind has a rectangular aperture similar in size to the film gate; the secondary blind, attached to tapes, is used to cover part of this aperture to form a slit. The narrower the slit, the shorter the exposure. For speeds between 1/125 sec. and 1/1000 sec. the slit itself exposes the film whereas for speeds lower than 1/60 sec., the primary blind uncovers the entire frame before the secondary blind begins to cover it.

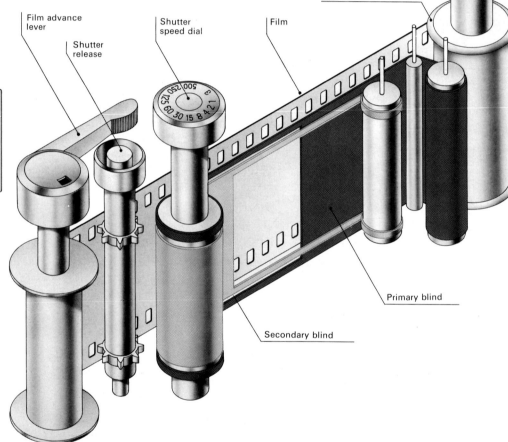

Film rewind

Film cassette

Film advance lever

Shutter release

Shutter speed dial

Film

Primary blind

Secondary blind

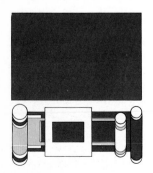

Before shutter release, the unexposed film is covered by the primary blind.

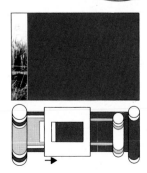

As the primary blind begins to travel, a section of the film is exposed.

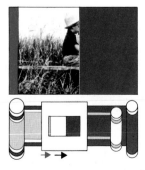

The primary blind continues, then the secondary blind is released. The width of the slit relates to shutter speed.

The established width remains constant as it moves across the film.

By the time the slit has passed across the film a local exposure time equivalent to the speed selected has occurred.

The effect of using a focal plane shutter with flash at the wrong speed setting; the flash has fired with the frame half-covered by an advancing shutter-blind, exposing only a portion of the picture.

Flash synchronization with shutter speed

To synchronize the correct exposure with flash and a focal plane shutter, the entire frame area must be uncovered at the moment the flash reaches maximum efficiency — the selected speed must be one at which the second blind does not begin to travel until the first blind has stopped. Fairly slow shutter speeds are used to meet this requirement. At the instant the first blind reaches the furthest edge of the frame, a contact fires the flashgun, and exposure is completed before the second blind is released. This is at a speed of 1/60 sec. or more when the shutter runs horizontally or 1/125 sec. or more when the shutter is designed to move vertically. With leaf shutters, there is no direct covering of the film area and hence no risk of part-frame exposure. However, synchronization is timed so that the flash is producing maximum illumination at the stage when the shutter blades are fully opened.

Controlling movement with the shutter

A very fast shutter speed will "freeze" a moving object giving overall definition. The slower the shutter speed the more blurred and undefined the object will become. The definition of an object depends on its distance and speed, the speed of the shutter and the direction in which the object is moving, and its distance from the camera. You will require a faster speed if the object is moving left to right than if it is approaching at an angle.

A car moving obliquely is blurred when photographed at 1/60 sec.

If a car moving obliquely is shot at 1/125 sec., the image is less blurred.

If a car is moving across the frame, the image is blurred with a speed of 1/125 sec.

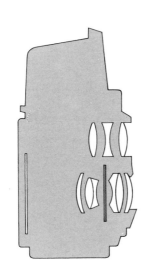

Shutter speeds

With a focal plane shutter, changing high speeds involves altering the width of the shutter-blind slit in direct proportion to the shutter speed selected. The blinds then travel at a constant rate to maintain the width of the slit. The narrower the slit, the faster the shutter speed.

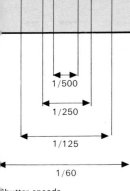

By the end of the cycle, all the film has received equal exposure, although traveling time has exceeded exposure time.

Leaf shutter

The modern leaf or blade shutter, below, is usually positioned next to the iris diaphragm inside the lens unit, above. For this reason it is also called the interlens shutter. A complex mechanism opens and closes a set of thin metal blades, right; for fast speeds between 1/30 sec. and 1/500 sec. the

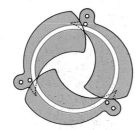

tension of the operating spring is changed, and for slow speeds between 1/15 sec. and 1 sec. a timed escapement is used. In addition "B" and "T" marked settings are found on most cameras. In both cases this enables the shutter to be opened for any required duration. The "B" setting allows the shutter to stay open so long as the release is pressed while the "T" setting requires the shutter release to be depressed for opening and again for closing of the shutter. The shutter release is light and simply releases the tensions of a mechanism "primed" by a separate setting lever or during film advance.

If a car moving obliquely is shot at 1/250 sec. the resulting image is sharp.

A car moving across the frame shot at 1/250 sec. produces a partially blurred image.

To freeze the movement of a passing car a shutter speed of 1/500 sec. is necessary.

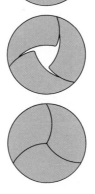

The Exposure Meter

Electronic exposure meters are recent developments in photographic history. Before their invention various methods were used to calculate exposure but none could reach the degree of accuracy found in the systems used today. Nevertheless, they were perfectly efficient when applied to the types of emulsion and methods of development used at the time.

With the advent of films which were reasonably consistent in speed, and the need for comparatively short exposure times, the measurement of light intensity had to be made more accurate. The first exposure meters were clumsy and inefficient. Some incorporated small offcuts of film to make what was, in effect, a trial exposure; others used the sensitivity of the human eye, the accuracy of which is only relative to existing light conditions and could lead to inconsistent results.

The earliest electronic exposure meters worked by comparing the available light with an artificial source of fixed brightness, a small electric bulb. The greatest advance was made when it was discovered that a metal called selenium generated an electric current when activated by light. The current generated was also found to be directly proportional to the light falling on the selenium. A new type of exposure meter was designed. It was very accurate by past standards, and used no batteries. The "selenium cell" as it was called, became universal.

Unfortunately the current generated by the selenium is weak, and large quantities of the metal are needed to register low levels of luminosity. Attempts to build meters into cameras resulted in large cameras with relatively insensitive metering systems. An alternative had to be found. This came with the development of the photo-resistor. Unlike the photocell, the photo-resistor generates no current, but when light falls on it, its electrical resistance increases in proportion to light intensity.

The photo-resistor most commonly used in meters is cadmium sulfide (CdS). It requires a current, usually between 1.3 and 6 volts, produced by a small battery. It is important that this battery can maintain a steady, unvarying voltage until the end of its life, otherwise false readings would be given. The circuitry can be made on a smaller scale than that for the selenium type. It is sufficiently sensitive to record very low light levels, and can be used inside cameras, or incorporated into automatic exposure systems.

The final and most logical development of the exposure meter has been its incorporation into the camera; this has ranged from uncoupled selenium types simply added to cameras, to completely integrated automation. Most single-lens reflexes have through-the-lens metering, which sees the viewing screen just as the eye does, but some meters intercept light in other ways. Usually the meter is coupled to the shutter dial and aperture setting, and the user merely centers a needle in the viewfinder. In automatic models, either the aperture or speed is pre-set, and the meter completes the sequence by setting the other. In some simple automatic cameras the meter sets both aperture and speed according to a built-in program. Some through-the-lens systems use silicon (Si) cells instead of CdS as these have better color response.

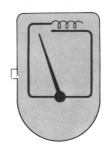

The selenium photocell meter

This electronic exposure meter uses a simple circuit, left, requiring no battery. Light falls on an area of the metal selenium, which generates a small but measurable electric current in proportion to the amount of light falling on it. This current moves a galvanometer needle against a scale of values which can be translated by using a calculator. This calculator is fitted to the meter but is used independently to translate the galvanometer readings into f stops and shutter speeds for the ASA speed of film in use

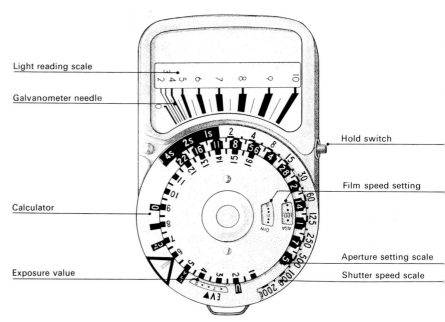

Light reading scale

Galvanometer needle

Calculator

Exposure value

Hold switch

Film speed setting

Aperture setting scale

Shutter speed scale

Using the meter

For use in bright light a baffle (A) covers the selenium cell. By pointing the meter at the subject, the light level can be read from the scale; a hold switch locks its position. In low light levels the baffle is dropped down and a lower scale of values automatically moves into position (B). In order to read light source intensity or incident light, a diffuser cone is placed over the cell (C).

A   B   C

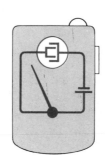

The CdS photo-resistor meter

More sensitive than the selenium cell and requiring less precision in manufacture for acceptable results, the CdS photo-resistor works on a different principle. The cadmium sulfide cell generates no current; instead, its resistance to electricity varies with the amount of light falling on it. The brighter the light, the higher its resistance. Current is supplied by a small battery — between 1.3 and 6 volts. Unlike the selenium cell meter, the CdS type must be switched on, and can fail because of weak batteries, but as it provides a much stronger current and includes a power source low level readings in particular are more reliable. As an alternative to a calculator a pair of light diodes which blink or cancel when the dial is moved to the correct point is also available. Sophisticated CdS meters, unlike selenium types, have attachments for use with other optical equipment such as enlargers and microscopes. The reading area can be very selective — as low as 1° — and the cell itself is very small.

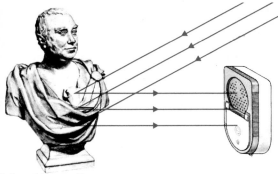

Reflected light reading
The normal way of metering the brightness of a scene to be photographed is to measure the light bounced off the subject area, i.e. the reflected light. This takes into account the color and reflectivity of the subject as well as the brightness of the illuminating source. It follows that a very dark subject will "recommend" more exposure than a light one, even when they are identically illuminated. For this reason, take careful readings of areas which are important to the main subject.

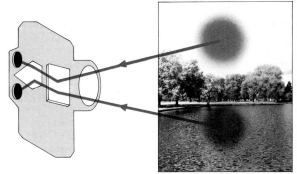

Built-in metering systems
Many cameras now have built-in metering systems, often referred to as behind-the-lens or through-the-lens (TTL) metering. Some systems are semi-automatic, others fully automatic. It is important to understand the method by which light is measured by a meter since it can affect camera handling. The main methods incorporated in modern cameras are explained below.

The overall method
A cell in the pentaprism records from a moderate area of the subject but normally two cells need to be used to give a reading covering the whole image. These are angled for good coverage of both halves of the subject. The result is an integrated or overall reading but with increased sensitivity in the two areas marked right.

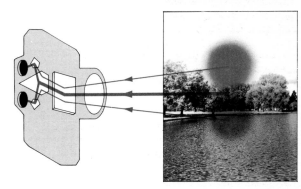

The center-weighted method
To overcome the disadvantages of an overall reading system, camera designers angled the meter cells inward or used deflectors to bias them. The overlap of the sensitivity areas creates an even zone of response from the central area of the subject, usually the area of importance in a photograph.

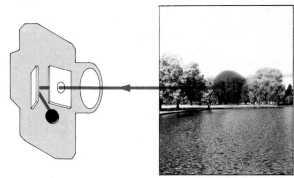

The spot method
The spot metering method may employ a cell probe, a deflector in the mirror or any one of a number of other devices to read a small section of the screen. The metering device must be aimed at a medium-gray tone in the subject for a direct reading; separate highlight and shadow readings can also be taken and the mid-point used for exposure. This system requires careful handling, but gives accurate results.

Incident light reading
Technically more accurate than reflected light metering, incident light reading involves measurement of the brightness of the illuminating source, regardless of the subject. A reflected light reading is taken from camera position, but an incident light reading involves aiming the meter, fitted with an incident light adapter, toward the light source from subject position. On this basis, subjects reproduce as dark or light in the picture according to their natural reflectivity. This method is best for color reversal work or the photography of very dark or light subjects.

Taking an average reading
Most scenes contain a wide range of tones from deep shadow to bright highlight. If these are evenly distributed and a meter reading records the whole area, the exposure will be roughly correct. Should the dark and light areas be broad masses and the meter reading a selective one, it is likely that exposure will be biased too much towards "evidence" from an excessively light or dark patch. Some meters — for example most selenium cell hand-held meters and many in-camera CdS meters — work on this overall system. But many meters, particularly hand-held CdS types, take in a narrow angle (under 20°). It is therefore advisable to take two readings, one from the highlight area and one from the shadows, and to use an average setting. This can be biased slightly toward the light or dark areas according to their importance.
Another averaging method which can be used with meters incorporating viewfinders, is to aim the cell angle of coverage toward both areas at once. This is less accurate and often difficult to achieve.

It exposure is based on a dark ground area only the foreground is reasonable while other areas are light and lacking in detail.

When an exposure reading is taken for bright sky only, the resulting photograph is under-exposed with a dark foreground and a fairly dark sky.

Correct exposure is achieved by metering the sky and the ground separately and using the average setting.

The Basic Equipment

Many great photographs have been taken by photographers who own only one camera and a single lens, but with a selection of additional lenses and equipment the scope is considerably widened. It is unlikely that any photographer would need every piece of equipment in a system. There is, however, a range of basic equipment that meets the majority of requirements.

The most valuable additions to a camera body, fitted with a normal lens, are probably a wide-angle and a long lens. A wise choice would be a 28 mm and a 135 mm respectively. Neither causes excessive distortion and their range of application is enormous. Lenses should always be used with lens hoods for protection and to reduce flare. Yellow and orange filters are useful lens attachments to add contrast in black and white photographs, while an ultra-violet or haze filter helps to penetrate haze when photographing in color. The UV filter can be left on the lens for most photography; in this way it also protects the lens surface.

Extension tubes increase the versatility of lenses and are a worthwhile investment for close-up work. They are often sold in sets of three to allow different degrees of extension.

Although modern cameras can be hand-held and excellent results obtained, a tripod is a necessity for static work and long exposures. If used with a cable release camera shake is kept to the minimum.

Many cameras are built with integral exposure meters but in situations where exposure times are critical, it is useful to check a reading with a separate hand-held meter. This, of course, is an essential piece of equipment when calculating exposures for cameras without built-in meters. An electronic flashgun can supplement available light and allows photographs to be taken in situations where lighting is poor.

Care is vital if a camera and equipment are expected to function well for a long time. The cleaning of all pieces should be carefully carried out using tissues and brushes specially made for this purpose. Afterwards the equipment should be packed in well-fitting cases with all protective linings, caps and lids securely in position. Keep it all in a strong, light case.

1 Normal lens on camera body
2 Tripod
3 Cable release
4 Electronic flashgun
5 Exposure meter, cases and accessories
6 Notepad, pencil and adhesive tape
7 Filters and filter case
8 Camera care equipment
9 Lens hoods
10 Long lens and caps
11 Wide-angle lens and caps
12 Extension tubes
13 Equipment bag and lens cases
14 Spare film

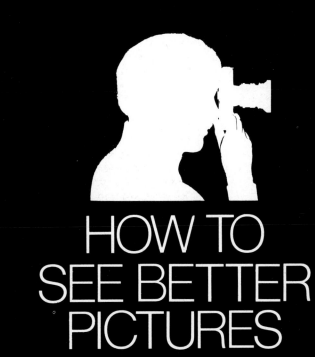

HOW TO
SEE BETTER
PICTURES

The Essential Elements

When we isolate the three essential elements of photography, we can see how photographs work. The first is *shape*, followed by *tone* and *color*. We can combine these elements to yield three further qualities: *pattern*, *texture* and *form*. All photographs must contain some of these regardless of subject matter, and you will probably choose to stress one more than others. The result of this emphasis will be pictures that express your individuality as a photographer – your own personal way of *seeing* things.

The pictures in the following section, beginning on the opposite page, are arranged so that you can examine each of the essential elements and qualities separately. When we take a photograph we are trying to capture the effect of a three-dimensional world, translating it into two dimensions on the photographic print or color slide. *Shape*, more than any other element, helps us to identify the subject of the photograph. When tone or color are suppressed, or when form is excluded – you are left with an outline, with a shape, or silhouette.

Tone is a word used to describe the degree of contrast between the light and dark areas of the subject. *Color* can be used to create contrast as well – a brilliant orange, for example, set against a somber blue. Color is the element in pictures from which we derive the most direct emotional response. Everyone can say whether or not they like a particular color.

We also respond to tone in much the same way as we respond to color, especially the scale and relationship of those grays that range between the two extremes of black and white. A certain mood is created by these elements even before we begin to notice and identify the subject.

Amateur photographers usually take better pictures in color than in black and white because black and white demands a more restrictive approach, a more selective eye.

We see most things in terms of color. We are extremely receptive to color changes, to the intensity of a particular color, and its relationship to others adjacent to it. Color describes a scene in its fullest sense, leaving less to the imagination than do the abstract qualities of black and white.

Black and white is "abstract" in that one real element, color, is missing. In photography, the use of black and white requires paying careful attention to composition, and to the juxtaposition of the other essential elements and qualities in order to make a good picture. Many professional photographers prefer black and white prints, and regard the esthetic effects to be obtained by techniques of printing and processing as a challenge.

By adding tone and color to shape, we try to give a sense of *form*, that most elusive of the essential qualities of a photograph. Tone describes the form, giving it solidity, creating an appearance of fullness, or of roundness and depth. Form is extremely important to a three-dimensional effect. For example, the milk churn on the right could be immediately identified by its shape, even if it were flat and devoid of color. But the light from one side has created gradations of tone, producing form. It is real enough to be recognized as a milk churn, and convinces us that it now has volume.

Shape, with the addition of form, reproduces the illusion of solidity on a two-dimensional sheet of paper. We can now heighten this illusion in our two-dimensional photograph by adding *texture*. Texture in a picture conveys the tangibility of a subject; it makes the viewer want to reach out and touch, and is inherent in all subjects, whether they are rough, shiny, pitted or sharp.

The effect may be enhanced by the viewer's own experience and memory – he is aware that canvas is rough-textured, so the piece of cloth hanging next to the milk churn is very real to him, as is the grainy, unpolished wood.

All but one of the essential elements and qualities have now been integrated, and intensified by mood. But the final quality, *pattern*, has the power to destroy this carefully-constructed picture. Pattern is repetition and accentuation of shape, either organized or accidental. It is not necessary for shapes to be identical to make a pattern, and indeed they can be quite dissimilar, but pattern seeks to establish a motif.

As we shall see in the following section, pattern can confuse form. It can cheat and distort our vision by demanding our attention, and by breaking up form and emphasizing the flatness of surfaces.

Each of the elements and qualities is revealed by light. The character of form depends on lighting, from bright sunlight to soft, diffused directional lighting. It also depends on the selection of viewpoint to record the light falling on the subject most effectively.

Establishing these qualities depends on recording the fine detail of the subject, for which photography affords us every opportunity. It is the camera's *forte* and part of its great versatility.

The fundamentals of photography
In this simple still-life picture I have combined all the essential elements and qualities – color, tone, shape, form, texture and pattern. The picture also possesses subsidiary factors, including color-contrast, composition, design and atmosphere.
Linhof, 1/30 sec., f32, Ektachrome EX.

Shape through Silhouette

Watch the sun set over a landscape on a clear evening and you will notice how the scene gradually changes with the movement of the light. Texture, form and depth remain clearly defined, until the sun falls behind the horizon. Then all form vanishes, and you are left with an image of stark outlines or profiles, silhouetted against the sky. The effect can be startling – an ordinary scene transformed into a two-dimensional pattern of almost abstract shapes. The ability to see and use such shapes and outlines is vital in composing any photograph.

In a composition where shape is of primary importance, the photographer can make use of back-lighting to produce an image silhouetted against any background. Most interesting forms will look powerful in silhouette, because of the simplicity and economy of detail. This is an important point: if too much information is included, the picture will be reduced to a confused image.

Silhouette may emphasize delicacy. It may, for example, transform the winter branches of a tree into an intricate and beautiful pattern, a dark tracery against a light background. A shape or silhouette can contain a wealth of information without revealing any detail in the mass. The profile or silhouette of a person might show the character of the sitter in a more revealing way than the conventional portrait. The shape of the head, the outline of the nose and mouth, help to create a strong image.

To produce a semi-silhouette where some detail is discernible but subordinate to shape, use a carefully-placed side-light or reflector. This will give a slight degree of form to the subject, and help to convey a feeling of reality, provided that it doesn't interfere with the purity of the shape or line.

Shape is the most fundamental of all the pictorial elements, more so than tone, pattern or texture, because it forms the structure of a picture. Look around you and notice how shape can dominate a given area, especially when viewed through the camera lens. Although a picture composed entirely of irregular patterns might be arresting, or one that shows coarse texture might tempt you to reach out and feel it, a simple silhouette in black and white will probably have the most impact.

The reason for this is because shape is the principal element of identification. The shape of something is usually the first thing we recognize – before its form, its tone or its smell. If we close our eyes, a particular object might easily be identified by its smell alone – an orange for example – but we need to know its shape to confirm our impression.

Creating silhouette in the studio

Simple back projection
The lighting in this set-up is similar to that used by the early profilists. I used an old picture-frame covered with wax paper to capture the image on a screen, projecting the shadow by means of a light 3 ft (0.9 m) behind

the sitter. The screen was at an angle of 90° to the light source, to prevent distortion of the silhouette. Always remember in silhouette photography to expose for the highlight, which is invariably the light background.
Rolleiflex, 1/15 sec., f8, Kodak Tri-X.

Lighting the background
This more complex type of silhouette is great fun to compose and photograph. You light the background rather than the subject and because of the greater area involved, several lights will probably be required to illuminate it evenly. Try to select objects with interesting shapes that relate in a harmonious way.

This set-up covered an area about 12 ft (3.7 m) wide, the objects were placed 6 ft (1.8 m) away from the background, with the camera 9 ft (2.7 m) from the objects. If several groups are made they can be printed together on a sheet of photographic paper, or mounted to form a frieze. *Hasselblad, 1/60 sec., f8, Kodak Tri-X.*

Natural background light
This type of profile is the simplest of all. The photographer simply places the sitter or object in front of a brightly-illuminated background where no light can fall on the subject from the direction of the camera – a window is the most obvious choice. Exposure, as in all silhouettes, is for the highlight or background.
Rolleiflex, 1/125 sec., f11, Kodak Tri-X.

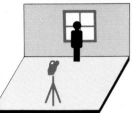

Outdoor silhouettes

At night
Extreme contrast between darkness and artificial light can produce startling outlines. Here I focused the camera on the middle distance and turned off the car lights. The cat was released on to the focused spot in front of the car. As the headlights were turned on, it froze. A brief exposure on very fast film was sufficient. The meter reading taken from the headlights was reduced by two stops, since most of the scene was required to print black.
Hasselblad, 1/30 sec., f8, Royal-X.

At midday
To outline the horse and cart against the sky at noon, and at the same time to record the texture of the sand, I placed the camera at ground level.
Rolleiflex, 1/250 sec., f16, Kodak Tri-X.

On a misty morning
Early morning mist accentuates the soft shapes and the delicate tracery of trees by suppressing background detail. The exposure in misty conditions is critical if the full effect is to be captured.
Hasselblad, 1/250 sec., f8, Kodak Tri-X.

Adding a reflector
A portrait of artist Edward Ardizzone, taken with background lighting. Slight rim lighting was added to the front of the face by means of a silverized reflector which reflected light from the background. This procedure gives some detail and form without destroying the silhouette image. Silverized reflectors can be made with aluminum foil mounted on cardboard. The white background was lit by two 500 watt floodlights, and the reflector placed 5 ft (1·5 m) from the face.
Hasselblad, 1/30 sec., f11, Kodak Tri-X.

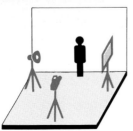

Shape within shape
Henry Moore silhouetted against the canvas of his deck chair
by the powerful Mediterranean sun — a natural form of back
projection. Note the slightly lighter areas of the silhouette,
particularly the face, where the body is not in contact with the
chair. The structure of the chair is an intriguing shape and
provides an interesting frame for this unusual portrait.
Hasselblad, 1/500 sec., f22, Ektachrome EX.

Selecting the viewpoint

These two pictures of a Canadian granary were taken within minutes of each other. They show how different viewpoints alter the direction of light and radically change the mood and feeling of a picture. The viewpoint chosen for the large picture gives the scene great depth, dramatic light quality, and creates a silhouette against sharply contrasting planes. I chose a low camera angle looking into the sun, to achieve harmony between the sharply-receding lines of the railway, and the imposing bulk of the granary framed against the sky. The exposure was calculated for the highlight.

Leicaflex, 1/125 sec., f16, Ektachrome EX.

The Tonal Range

In simple terms *tone* is the strength of grays between white and black. It relates to brightness, lightness and darkness, and varies according to the direction and intensity of illumination. Variations of colors include hues, tints and shades but monochrome can vary only according to its tone. We can say that a picture has light tones, and is "high-key," but tone, in real terms, is conditioned by surfaces and the amount and direction of light reflected or absorbed by them.

Any picture, whether black and white or color involves a tonal scheme, since the grays making a tonal range may also be mixed with color.

With tone, as with color, do not seek the "perfect exposure" that will result in a picture using every degree of tone. What, anyway, is perfect? It is certainly true that professional photographers frequently avoid using the "perfect exposure" according to textbook rules, to add interest to their pictures.

Light and the angle at which it strikes the subject are of primary importance to tone. Only you, the photographer, can decide how to manipulate this basic factor. You can under-expose or over-expose, pushing the flexibility of the film to its limits in order to capture atmosphere but your choice will ultimately depend on how you wish to interpret your subject.

It is important that tones in a picture relate to the subject, especially where the intention is to create a strong emotional response. In using this relationship tones can be compared and likened to mood: dark tones are often associated with mystery or menace, light tones with freedom, space and softness.

There are occasions when the existing quality of light induces the photographer to base his picture or series of pictures on it, perhaps exaggerating the quality and atmosphere by making a soft light even softer, a weak light dark and somber. In this way, you can capitalize on the effects of light, turning them to your advantage. If a scene is lit by a harsh light, you may choose to make a high-key picture where the concentration is on the highlights, possibly eliminating the shadows entirely.

The final result, though, and the success of any picture, will be due to your own intuitive response and your ability to be selective.

Tonal separation
This photograph contains a range of sharply separated tones, which give it a crisp feeling and staccato rhythm. Increased contrast between the tones was achieved by using high speed film for a grainy result.
Hasselblad, 1/250 sec., f16, Royal-X.

An example where all tones from 0–9 have been used.

Here contrasting tones from each end of the scale have been used with mid-tones.

A soft diffused picture composed of tones in the range from 3–6.

Tones from the high end of the scale give this photograph the desired atmosphere.

A low-key picture containing tones from the lower end of the scale.

9   8   7   6   5   4   3   2   1   0

The gray scale
The range of tones from white to black where each tone is described by a number. Each change in tone is equivalent to changing one f stop at the exposure stage. Reflected light meter readings from a subject record as tone 5, so by taking readings from light and dark areas, the photographer can control his results.

High contrast

A limited number of highly contrasting tones used in conjunction with shape and careful lighting emphasizes the expression and character of the conjuror. Mood is heightened by the variation between the black clothes of the man, and the white fur of the rabbit.

Hasselblad, studio electronic flash, f16, Kodak Tri-X.

High key

This is a high key picture containing a wide range of light gray tones, taken under soft and hazy lighting conditions. The low key (dark) tones have been further eliminated by printing on soft paper, to give greater prominence to the figure of the man.

Hasselblad, 1/125 sec., f8, Kodak Tri-X.

Low contrast

This picture contains overall gray tones, which flow gently from one to another. The mist subdues strong or dominant tones, allowing the softer tones to merge and create tonal harmony.

Hasselblad, 1/125 sec., f11, Panatomic-X.

Low key

The low key effect and harmony of tones was obtained by using a red filter to darken the sky and foliage and at the same time, to lighten the path which was reddish-brown in color, for pictorial effect.

Hasselblad, 1/125 sec., f8, Kodak Tri-X.

Understanding Color

Color and tone are very closely related. When applied to shape they are the elements that give it solidity and substance. Color, of course, has an emotional content – the reds and greens and blues of everyday life please us or repel us, particularly in certain combinations. Color conveys information about our surroundings, as well as creating mood and atmosphere; we register color according to our experience and associations – a brown tree in winter, a green tree in spring.

Nature relates color to form, using it to convey shape, by employing tones and hues of color to describe three dimensions. Really convincing pictures can be made with a restricted use of color and a full range of tone. Do not be misled into thinking that color photography demands color accuracy – there is no such thing as "accurate" color, in spite of what you may have read to the contrary. Daylight is always changing color, and we readily accept this change in nature, the reddish glow of sunset that sometimes changes to purple, and the pink flush of dawn.

Here, we are speaking of being perceptive, which comes through practice and experiment. The degree of perception which we can use to make our pictures stand out in an individual way will never be fully explored if we stick to the rules.

Ideally, color pictures should have one main subject and one main color – with any additional colors being supporting and subordinate. Thus a dominant color, broken down into different hues and tones, will give a feeling of depth to a picture.

More often than not, harmony is achieved through the use of tones of the same color, and a limited range of colors might have as much power as might a contrast of bold, primary colors. Bold colors, those of equal weight and contrast, can sometimes confuse form – by flattening it into a pattern, as we can see in the picture of canoeists opposite. As a general but not invariable rule, a bold color will balance with a weak one – a brilliant green can be placed next to a pale pink. However, the use of color depends on the photographer's personal taste, so these rules should only be used as a guide.

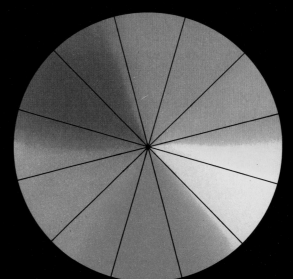

Color harmony
The early morning atmosphere is fully evoked by the use of restricted color – here mostly hues and tones of green – creating color harmony. Misty atmospheres with naturally soft lighting tend to mute strident colors, and scenes that would be harsh in bright sunlight become more harmonious. Great care should be taken with the exposure. Readings of both highlight and shadow areas will be required, and the exposure selected accordingly.
Leica, 1/125 sec., f11, Ektachrome EX.

Harmony on the color circle
Isolate any quarter of the color circle as shown above and the changing colors within that area will be in *harmony* with one another.

The color circle
This circle, shown left, is based on color pigments where the *primaries* are red, yellow and blue and the *secondaries* are orange, green and purple. It can be broken down into even smaller sections of intermediate colors such as blue-green, orange-yellow and so on. Each section on the color circle is known as a *hue* which is a pure, *fully-saturated* color to which no white, gray or black has been added. All the hues make a complete color spectrum.

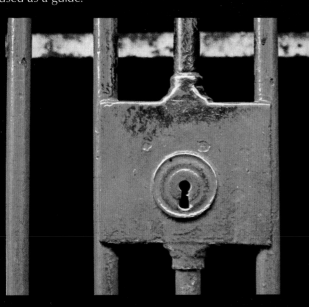

Design with dominant color
Pictures showing one dominant color rely very much on the strength of the composition or design; these railings would have been just as striking had they been blue or green. The area of color chosen has to correspond to the design. If such pictures are to be effective, careful selection is required. Here, the area of the red bars, and the dominance of the color, is balanced by the shadows and tones.
Pentax, 1/125 sec., f11, Ektachrome EX.

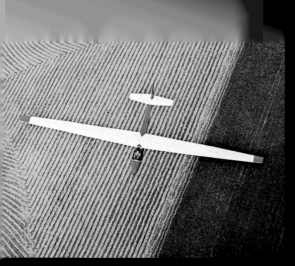

Color contrast

A contrast of color tones in a simple, almost abstract design, left. This picture is effective because of the geometric, angular pattern made by the glider, and the red areas which contrast with the two shades of green. The view from above, and the flat lighting, destroy the illusion of space and movement, and increase the emphasis of the pattern.

Leicaflex, 1/250 sec., f16, High-Speed Ektachrome.

Discordant color

Pure, intense color is usually described as being "fully saturated." In the picture, right, the juxtaposition of fully saturated colors has tended to confuse the image. The bold color contrast relies entirely on perspective to create a feeling of depth; you can see how effectively the combination of pattern and color contrast destroys form. To ensure depth with strong colors, a careful adjustment between the area of one to another is essential — a big area of blue, for example, against a tiny proportion of yellow.

Leicaflex, 1/125 sec., f8, Ektachrome EX.

Complementary colors

A primary color, e.g. red, and a secondary color composed from the other two primaries, e.g. blue + yellow = green, are said to *contrast* with one another and are called *complementary* colors. They always appear opposite each other on the color circle.

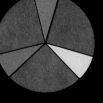

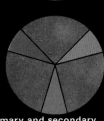

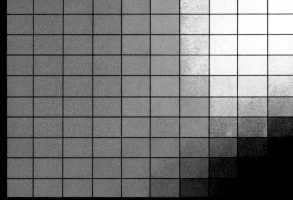

Primary and secondary colors

Primary colors, top, are separated on the color circle by secondary colors, above. Secondary colors are made by mixing two primary colors.

Chroma, shade, tint and tone

Any fully-saturated color can be changed by the addition of white, gray or black, as shown above. This reduces its intensity or *chroma*. As the color becomes blacker, it moves through a range of *shades* and conversely, as it moves toward white, *tints* are produced. Shades and tints are all *tones* of a color. Chroma is at its strongest on the left of the grid and weakest on the right.

Subdued color with strong tonal contrast

This picture has limited hues of cool blue-gray that supplement the full range of tone and emphasize the roundness and fullness of the form. They help to direct the eye to the sculptured quality of the stone.

Leicaflex, 1/125 sec., f16, Ektachrome EX.

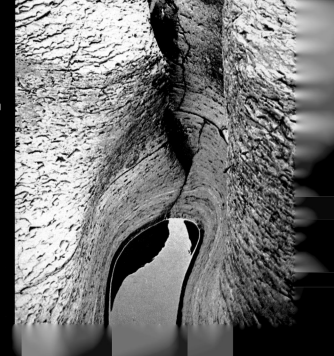

Subdued colors with limited tonal contrast

Foggy conditions have completely obliterated primary color in the shot, left, of Norwich Cathedral, so that the picture consists mainly of color tones. A subdued range of color tones often gives beautiful though muted effects that can be more evocative than a scene of bold colors. Weather and lighting conditions such as rain or mist deter many amateurs from taking pictures, but the professional or more experienced photographer welcomes such opportunities. I am constantly amazed at the amount of subtlety and detail which color film can record in seemingly impossible conditions.

Hasselblad, 1/60 sec., f5.6, Ektachrome EX.

Discovering Pattern

Pattern is an important aspect of photography because it can enhance pictorial effects by arranging components to make them more pleasing to the eye. It can make harmony from chaos. Having established a motif, pattern emphasizes it by repetition, and this the eye finds reassuring. When we find pattern visually agreeable, we are inclined to make considerable use of it in our pictures. This is true even of disordered patterns, for there is strength and unity in numbers, the more so if the numbers are identical in shape, size and color, but irregular in design. The harmony of a colored pattern may be disturbed by the presence of clashing colors such as bright green and red. The addition of such colors is often intentional, especially in abstract art and textile design.

Pattern can decorate an area, or emphasize the flatness of a surface. The eye rests upon and then moves over a pattern, and is forced beyond it only when some other pictorial element is introduced, such as perspective or form.

The photographer has every opportunity to explore the world of pattern and to draw attention to the frequently unnoticed wealth of detail that surrounds us all. You will discover pattern in rows of houses, and in the branches of trees. Autumn leaves scattered across the surface of a pond make a pattern. Brick-work makes a pattern, so does a window full of bottles, a shelf of books, migrating birds on a telegraph wire.

Photographing an existing pattern, whether man-made or natural, is mainly a problem of selecting the angle and the lighting. To convey more than just the image, consider the function of the pattern, and how best to present it. A small area or portion might have more impact than a pattern as a whole. Judge which is the vital element and include enough of it to make it work.

The lighting should be carefully considered in conjunction with the area selected. If you choose a two-dimensional pattern, you will need an evenly-distributed frontal light to exclude any emphasis of texture or form. Only if the pattern is part of a building can the image be looked at as having depth, possibly including texture and form. In this case, a strong side-light could create the most balanced effect.

The aim of creative photography is to make an interpretation of a visual experience, and not just to record an image. The key word is *interpretation*, and so your choice of a pattern in a photograph should not be a random one, but a calculated effort to convey something that excites and interests you, something that you wish to share.

Selecting existing patterns
Looking at this spiral staircase from below gives greater prominence to the pattern than to the architectural form. Having discovered a pictorial aspect that interests or excites you, explore the many possibilities by which the aspect can best be conveyed. In this shot I have concentrated on the pattern and rhythm of the structure. Using existing light, I mounted the camera on a tripod, as a fairly long exposure was required. *Rolleiflex, 1 min., f22, Kodak Tri-X.*

Introducing pattern for emphasis
Here pattern has flattened an otherwise three-dimensional picture, making the figure of the man appear to be sitting above the entrance hall, rather than within it. Daylight from an overhead skylight was used to light the composition. Including architectural features provides added interest to a straightforward portrait. *Hasselblad, wide-angle lens, 1/15 sec., f22, Kodak Tri-X.*

Depth destroyed by pattern
An overcast sky provided the perfect light to photograph this pebble path, with its complex but orderly arrangement of stones. If the path had been lit from one side by by strong sunlight, it would have emphasized the form of the pebbles but destroyed the pattern. Diffused frontal light evenly distributed over the whole area, helps to flatten existing depth.
Hasselblad, wide-angle lens, 20 secs., f32, Panatomic-X.

Use of disordered pattern
This is an example of deliberately confused pattern, where objects lose their identity and become part of the overall design. Only on close scrutiny can each be identified.
Hasselblad, wide-angle lens, 1/30 sec., f8, Kodak Tri-X.

Pattern revealed by light
The strong, harsh sunlight and the camera angle gave me an opportunity to stress this example of pattern, where light and shade contrast in these factory roofs. The use of a long lens compresses perspective and helps to emphasize pattern. There is a great variety of pattern subjects to be found in any urban environment, especially when the source of light is coming from a low angle.
Leicaflex, 1/500 sec., f16, Kodak Tri-X.

Pattern within patte...
Pattern is all around us,
particularly in street mar...
where groups of objects
attractively arranged. He...
the vegetable marrows e...
pattern upon pattern, si...
the vegetables are patte...
within the display. They...
similar qualities of shape...
color which are repeate...
Pentax, 1/250 sec., f8,
High-Speed Ektachrome

Isolating pattern.
The driving wheel of a
locomotive, right. By cr...
in closely on the wheel,
carefully selecting this a...
from the whole of the er...
I was able to imply the
powerful force that a rai...
engine generates. The d...
color in no way diminish...
this force. The patch of
color on the drive shaft
to direct the eye to the ...
of thrust.
Leicaflex, 1/30 sec., f8,
Ektachrome EX.

Man-made pattern
The seaside provides an
immense wealth of patte...
where the sun and sea c...
turn the crudest colors in
subtle hues. Here I conce...
trated on the pattern ma...
the row of beach huts ar...
their changing decoratio...
The important point is to...
concerned with the patte...
alone and not the object...
make it possible. Take c...
use the correct exposure
to allow for reflected lig...
from the sea and sand.
Leicaflex, 1/250 sec., f1...
Ektachrome EX.

Pattern by repetition
Although the boots on th...
wall, far left, are not arra...
in a precise order, the
monochromatic range of
and the repetition of thei...
shapes, help to create pa...
Pentax, 1/125 sec., f8,
High-Speed Ektachrome

Pattern in nature
An example, left, of one...
nature's patterns — a sma...
area of bark on the trunk...
plane tree. A soft frontal...
is best to record and emp...
patterns of this type, whe...
shadows are not needed.
Natural patterns such as...
are limitless, but it is imp...
to select the area to be
photographed with care....
fact that it is possible to...
photograph several hun...
in a single day does not
diminish the esthetic val...
each one.
Leicaflex, 1/125 sec., f1...
High-Speed Ektachrome

Revealing Texture

Used in a descriptive manner, texture plays an important role in almost all successful photographs. Texture adds a tactile quality to the elements shape, color and tone. It describes the character of a surface, and often tells us more about its substance. From past experience we may appreciate the feeling of a surface without actually touching it. We know the skin of an apple feels smooth, while the crust of a loaf is usually rough.

Texture can suggest depth, without giving volume, and in photography it will increase the illusion of a three-dimensional image. One of the ways in which we can emphasize an object's character is to enlarge it photographically to larger than life-size. Seen in this way, the texture may catch us unawares with its deceptive appearance. Photography can magnify and record textures which, although familiar to us, will be made unrecognizable: the skin of an orange seen in this way relates more to lunar landscape than to a citrus fruit. By using the fine focus mechanism of a close-up lens we can completely change the appearance of surfaces.

The majority of surfaces are quite rough and pitted, even those that normally seem smooth and shiny. With an acute, raking side-light, the textural character of a surface will betray hidden qualities. In portrait photography, for example, you should attempt to include texture, rather than concentrate on the sitter's pose and expression alone. By emphasizing the roughness or smoothness of the skin, you can often reveal more about the sitter. This rule can also apply to inanimate objects where texture can reveal the substance or the erosion of a surface. It can suggest the passing of time, and will display previously hidden subtleties.

Only when you wish to emphasize shape or pattern may you decide to eliminate texture, to prevent the surface clashing or conflicting with the motif. Texture is not usually a quality to include in a silhouette, for example, or when you desire to convey contrast in color. The value of texture as a quality of photography is to enhance the feeling of depth and form and to reveal to a greater degree the nature of surfaces.

Lighting for texture

Texture in portraiture
Portrait of the cartoonist, Illingworth, lit by a strong side-light, thereby revealing the texture of his skin. This lighting technique lends an interesting quality to the picture, tells us more about the age of the person, and adds drama to the close-up.
Rolleiflex, 1/125 sec., f11, Kodak Tri-X.

Texture in nature
Natural forms such as vegetables offer a wealth of textural surfaces which are particularly attractive when combined with color or tone. Weak winter sunlight gave balanced emphasis to the tone and texture of this cauliflower and leaves. It is better to err on the side of under-exposure to give added depth to a texture.
MPP, 1/125 sec., f16, Kodak Tri-X.

Texture with diffused light
Rugged surfaces are best lit with a soft, diffused, directional, side-light, so that shadows do not hide too much of the surface area. This stone foreshore was photographed with the sun behind a thin layer of cloud at a time when the light fell obliquely across the rock.
Linhof, wide-angle lens, 1/15 sec., f32, FP4.

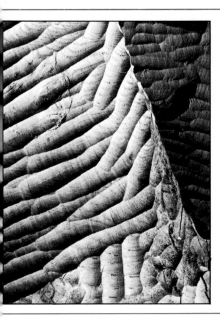

Using a reflector with existing light
This detail of a Henry Moore wood sculpture was lit by side-light from a window, and a reflector (see diagram below) to give detail in the shadows. By carefully selecting the camera angle, the direction and the amount of light, I show the surface in a three-dimensional way. It is hard to decide if it is concave or convex. Turn the book to change the effect.
Hasselblad, 1/30 sec., f16, Kodak Tri-X.

Comparing textures
Strong, oblique light reveals the interesting qualities of surfaces on this old barn wall. Although both are painted with pitch, the characters of the metal and wood are clearly defined because each surface absorbs and reflects different quantities of light.
Sinar, 1/125 sec., f8, FP4.

Effects of corrosion
The photograph, opposite,
expresses strong contrast
between the delicate cobweb
and the brittle texture of the
rust and flaking paint. It has
depth, form and color harmony,
all of which are part of a good
composition. The picture was
taken in weak sunlight.
*Leicaflex, 1/125 sec., f8,
High-Speed Ektachrome.*

**Texture emphasizing
movement**
A shaft of sunlight from one
side illuminates the girl's body
and reveals the folds on her
clinging wet dress. To arrest
this fleeting moment I used a
fast shutter speed.
*Leicaflex, 1/250 sec., f8,
High-Speed Ektachrome.*

Capturing Form

Form is the quality where tone – or the apparent "shading" of an object – describes its solidity. It can be a most exciting aspect of photography, because the camera is able to record the infinite gradations of tone which, when added to shape, bring your picture to life. Tone added to shape does not necessarily create form, where the tone is flat and uniform. But when the tone is gradated into areas of light and dark and cast shadow, and then added to shape, the illusion of solidity occurs. Tone describing form can be subtle and elusive where soft, diffused light falls on a nude figure; it can be powerful and geometric where harsh sunlight falls obliquely on to a building. Very often, amateur photographers destroy form by over-lighting the subject, in the hope that a greater degree of solidity might be achieved.

A fleeting light cast on a shape at once enriches it with a three-dimensional quality which the camera can record in great detail. On a flat sheet of paper the photographer can produce an illusion of life that arrests attention, and suggests innumerable associations. By creating a continuous tonal range from light to dark, the form appears in the two-dimensional photograph to curve on the paper, to gain depth, volume and space.

Since we cannot see a round object, form is limited by our vision. The manner in which form in photography is able to suggest life in three dimensions depends on the viewer's memory and experience. If you photograph a simple object, such as the basket of eggs on p. 71, the camera can record the image only from one angle and according to the amount of light falling upon it. Our imagination supplies the missing areas and details.

By lighting an object in a certain fashion, the photographer is able to convey his way of seeing to the viewer, using the medium of the camera. He may concentrate on a particular aspect of form, perhaps in close-up, where he might arouse curiosity or imagination. Using form and shape to describe a novel or unique way of seeing familiar objects is one of the basic principles of art, and thus of photography.

Remember that the photograph must be conceived through the camera's simple, single eye. The position of the camera in relation to the angle of light must be carefully judged. A good light to work with is a large, soft, directional light, such as a bank of four 500 watt floodlights, diffused with a white, opaque sheet. But as every form varies one from another, so must the light, and with practice you will be able to see and use form to make increasingly interesting pictures.

Using tone to describe form
A single source of diffused light was used to achieve the subtle gradations of tone that describe the form of the human body so accurately.
Linhof, 1/30 sec., f11, HP3.

An exercise in lighting for form

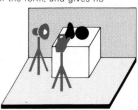

Using one diffused light
This photograph of fruit was lit by a single, diffused, side-light which shows only a part of the form, and gives no detail in the shadows. Harsh contrast between the light and dark areas is distracting.
Linhof, 1 min., f11, Plus-X.

Adding a reflector
Using the same camera position, and the same light source I added a silverized reflector to reveal more of the form by giving detail to the shadow area.
35 secs., f11.

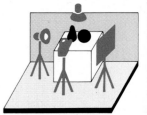

Including overhead light
The primary light source and reflector were not changed but for this example I added an overhead light to increase the tonal range and the modeling of the form.
35 secs., f11.

Retaining modeling in glass
Glass bottles lit by side-light from a window and a white reflector to give added expression to the shapes and translucent form. Great care should be used in judging the exposure when photographing glass as accuracy is needed to retain the delicate modeling.
Linhof, 1 min. 20 secs., f16, Ektachrome EX.

Natural form
Eggs, imprisoned in a wire basket, and lit by light from an overhead side window on an overcast day to provide perfect modeling. Natural forms are often satisfying to the eye, as their simplicity and perfect lines help to emphasize their esthetic value.
Linhof, 1 min. 45 secs., f45, Ektachrome EX.

Composition

Pictorial composition is the deliberate arrangement and juxtaposition of separate elements, establishing an arrangement between them to create a unified effect. The elements may be few, or varied, but, as we have seen, they can include shape, tone, color, pattern, texture and form. To these we may add the elements of depth and perspective. They can all be arranged to give balance and harmony, or to stress a particular area of a picture. You can make a composition with a single spot of color on a white rectangle of paper. Where you decide to place the spot in relation to the boundaries imposed by the shape of the paper depends on the most important aspect governing composition – that of personal choice.

The composition of a picture may be eccentric, an off-balance design where the stress is in an unexpected place, or it may be the arrangement of shapes in a rhythm designed to guide the eye around the picture.

One can only follow general guidelines. It is usual to have a main subject in a picture against which other elements are subordinate, a main theme supported by other, less important themes; where two or three subjects of equal importance are seen together, the pictorial result is likely to be confusing. Having said this, it is possible to have a picture where three equally dominant subjects create the interest by virtue of their equal status. In the majority of pictures, the subject will be the first thing to attract the viewer's interest and, if the arrangement is well-composed, the eye will be led around the picture, away from the main subject, to explore the subordinate elements before returning to the main subject. In such a picture there will probably be a marked degree of balance and harmony between the subject and the subordinate elements. For the photographer, the elements of a composition can be arranged and re-arranged according to his position in relation to the scene, and the conditions of light.

In the following section we will see how these guidelines may be applied to our pictures: how to arrange areas of mass to balance with each other, how the eye might be best led into the picture, and how to frame the subject. There are various theories relating to the natural path of the eye upon studying a picture, but it will invariably look for the subject and main focal point. For example, in a landscape this might be a tree, a distant church spire, an animal or a human figure. It is important, therefore, for you, the photographer, to move around and to try different viewpoints, since the position of the focal point in relation to the other elements can enhance or mar your composition. A picture that is badly composed, however effective the individual elements, will quickly confuse and then lose the viewer's interest.

Having selected your main subject, consider its balance against other areas of mass – how effectively each corresponds or interacts. Arrange your composition in relation to the foreground, the middle distance or the background. One or all of these areas will assist as a foundation for the composition.

Directing the eye
A well composed photograph needs a main point of interest, with all other components subsidiary to it. They should help the scene but should not impose on the principal subject. In the picture opposite the eye is directed toward the children by the use of a low camera angle, by the converging lines of the wall, and by their position at the brow of the hill, framed between the dark shapes of the chimney and the wall. The figures of the two children are further emphasized by their relationship in scale to the vast chimney and to the light expanse of sky beyond.
Rolleiflex, wide-angle lens, 1/125 sec., f8, HP3.

Framing the subject
This picture is divided into two large areas; the out-of-focus foreground, where rider and horse frame the subject, and the light background on which the focal point and action are imposed. The large, dark area balances the light, detailed area. The eye is led to the jumping horse and rider by use of sharp focus, and by the strong vertical and horizontal lines that help to isolate the subject. Further interest is created by the mirror which reflects the foreground. The picture was taken in an indoor riding school in restricted light.
Leicaflex, 1/500 sec., f2.8, Fast Recording (ASA 1000).

Depth & Perspective

Depth in a picture is expressed by the spatial relationship between the foreground and the background, and by the diminishing size of those objects on the ground plane, as they recede into the distance. Depth can be further emphasized by the presence of perspective, and by the deliberate use of the foreground to lead the eye into the picture. Intermediate and distant features in a landscape give an illusion of depth; so do the converging lines of *linear* perspective. Linear perspective is seen in terms of diminishing size and lines or planes that converge to a distant "vanishing point" on the horizon. The volume of space between the viewer and the far horizon is described by *aerial* perspective, where objects, features and colors lose detail and intensity as they recede.

While depth is not a vital element in a picture, most pictures possess it to some degree. It is likely that you will wish to create an illusion of great depth when the subject is in the middle distance or on the horizon. When photographing, say, a large building in the middle distance, it is often necessary to relate it to the foreground and to the background, in which case a considerable depth of field is the best choice.

The camera lens can be used to distort or emphasize linear and aerial perspective for particular effects. The distance from which a subject is photographed affects the image size in relation to the focal length of the lens. If a telephoto lens is substituted for a wide-angle lens, it appears to alter the distance between your viewpoint and the subject. In this way, even far distant objects can become the center of interest if a long lens is used. Linear perspective can be accentuated with a wide-angle lens, and diminished with a long-focus lens. Although tone and color intensity can indicate distance, depth is most frequently achieved by selective focusing. If you focus on the foreground, and use a wide aperture, you will lose depth. If you keep the foreground in your picture, but focus on the middle distance or far distance, you will achieve a greater degree of depth.

Depth, with form, are the elements that most create the illusion of three-dimensionality in your pictures, but depth can cause an imbalance if too greatly stressed in one area of the picture.

Depth and perspective
By standing in the center of the drive and using a wide-angle lens, I was able to emphasize the perspective in the picture, above right, and lead the eye to the house, the main point of interest. The photograph was taken in subdued light to mute the colors and to prevent strong, overpowering shadows from obliterating parts of the composition.
Nikon, wide-angle lens, 1/30 sec., f16, Ektachrome EX.

Using selective focus
To stress the perspective and balance the depth against the mass of the wall, right, I focused at a point in the wall calculated to coincide with the center of the picture area. The use of a wide aperture gave shallow depth of field, which further emphasized the feeling of depth.
Leicaflex, 1/500 sec., f2.8, Ektachrome EX.

Classic composition
A classic composition, opposite, where converging lines lead the eye to the main point of interest — the patch of light reflected on the sea. The eye continues to scan the horizon and to absorb information about the sky. The sun was almost hidden by a cloud, giving the picture a continuous recession of tones which help to emphasize the depth. Exposure was for the highlight.
Leicaflex, 1/125 sec., f8, Ektachrome EX.

Balance & Proportion

The large areas of a picture, or the areas of mass, should be proportionately arranged to give a feeling of balance – dark areas contrasting with light areas, simple shapes used in conjunction with complex shapes, highly detailed areas relating to large, empty ones and so on. Furthermore, these areas may be linked to each other, and to the main subject, by other elements, including perspective, color, texture, vertical or horizontal lines. In this way, the emphasis can be changed to another part of the picture.

A much used pictorial device is to place the main subject one third across and one third up the picture. Although a central focal point can often be used to good effect, it normally leads to a very formal arrangement. Diagonal lines can often lead the eye out of a picture, but this tendency can be counteracted by the introduction of horizontal or vertical lines, such as those imposed by trees and walls. These must be used carefully, however, as vertical lines used in the foreground can act as a barrier to the eye, especially if they stretch to the full height of the picture.

If you can photograph the subject of the picture from a position where it is framed by a foreground device – for example, an archway, a door or a window frame – this adds emphasis to the focal point. The format of your photograph is equally important but must depend on the content of the picture which will suggest a shape to give unity of both mood and structure to the composition.

Introducing scale
The natural scale provided by the trees and church is completely dwarfed by the cooling towers. The aim of the composition was to show how grotesque and overpowering modern industry has become and the low viewpoint was chosen to emphasize this.
Hasselblad, long lens, 1/125 sec., f11, Kodak Tri-X.

The subject and proportion
Here, the main subject – the dog – only features in a small part of the picture. The surrounding area of door sets the scene; it is simple, well-balanced against the more detailed subject, and gives meaning to the dog's expression.
Leica M2, 1/60 sec., f8, Kodak Tri-X.

Balancing mass against detail
Although the old lady is the subject of the picture, she occupies only one-sixth of the area. By including the surrounding brick wall a bleak, urban environment and sense of loneliness is implied. This is strengthened by positioning the focal point of the picture off center, allowing a greater concentration of mass to balance the detail.
Hasselblad, long lens, 1/125 sec., f8, Panatomic-X.

Balancing powerful shapes
A photograph of artist Graham Sutherland drawing in South Wales. Two powerful shapes, the tree stump and the figure of the man were carefully chosen to echo one another and to work together to create a unified subject. The tree stump seemed particularly relevant since it symbolized the contorted shapes in nature from which Sutherland derives his inspiration. The tone of the picture was darkened with the aid of a yellow filter, in order to strengthen the sky.
Rolleiflex, 1/125 sec., f11, Panatomic-X.

Using the foreground
The man's face was in shadow and the background in brilliant sunlight. By deliberately keeping the background out of focus to prevent it dominating or competing, the foreground subject stands out. By eliminating depth, I have given greater importance to the detail in the head.
Hasselblad, 1/125 sec., f4.5, Panatomic-X.

Selection for Effect

Elements in a composition can be used to express mood or atmosphere, to convey a particular pictorial structure or aspect in a scene. For example, you may be impressed by the way a subject can be arranged in relation to its surroundings to promote a feeling of drama or mystery. By composing the picture in order to emphasize this you must decide which elements are dominant and consider the degree of priority each should be given. It is unlikely that you will give the dominant elements equal status, although sometimes the situation will suggest it – for example, when the repetition of an element is the factor which creates the sense of drama or mystery.

As in all picture-taking, your perception and selectivity will lead you to choose those components which most please, excite or inform. According to your experience, taste and consideration of subject-matter, you will choose a particular point of view, length of lens and type of film.

When you aim your camera, frame the image to exclude any area or detail that interferes with, or is extraneous to the main subject. Sometimes you can arrange the subject in relation to the surroundings, where items of furniture or props can be moved around until the best result is achieved. Unusual or remarkable characteristics in a scene may lend themselves to exaggerated or eccentric composition. Whatever the approach, composition must always be considered from the camera's position, taking into account the type of lens used.

Once the photograph has been taken, you can crop the picture during the enlarging and printing process, to stress the subject even more. Some photographers claim that they never crop their photographs, as though cropping were some kind of deceit, but there are occasions where, in scenes of activity and movement, there may be little time to compose with care.

When picture composition was first formulated as a science, it was founded on rules similar to those applied to sentence structure. Images, like words, need to be arranged into some sense of order if they are to be communicated successfully.

Verticals to counteract diagonals
Diagonals in any picture are inclined to lead the eye away from the center of interest and out of the picture. In the composition, left, the vertical lines of the trees counteract the diagonal lines of the hill and allow the viewer to concentrate on the church, the focal point. Further contrast is provided by the solidity of the church compared with the filigree texture of the branches, and the restricted color gives a sense of isolation.
Leicaflex, long lens, 1/125 sec., f8, Ektachrome EX.

Evoking atmosphere
In this picture, above, the subject, artist Graham Sutherland, has been placed in the middle distance and the objects in the foreground and background arranged to evoke atmosphere and mood. Each area has interest, but none is more powerful than the subject, which is strongly related in tone to the rest of the scene. The subdued lighting was carefully chosen to relate to the mood and to encourage closer investigation of the scene.
Leicaflex, wide-angle lens, 1/60 sec., f8, Ektachrome EX.

The dominant focal point
The building at the bend in the wall would have been the focal point wherever it occurred in the picture. It dominates because of its intensity of color and detail, balanced against the simple green area of the fields. The wall and pale green tracks in the fields also contribute to make a pleasing design.
Leica M3, 1/250 sec., f8, Ektachrome EX.

Balancing light and shade
The viewpoint for this composition was chosen to convey the atmosphere caused by a vast, flat area of water enclosed and overpowered by the monumental Rocky Mountains. Light was striking areas of the subject in different ways, so that some were strongly lit, and others were in shadow. Because of the variation in lighting, parts of the picture appear to be more detailed than others.
Leicaflex, wide-angle lens, 1/125 sec., f8, Ektachrome EX.

Changing the Emphasis

When we compose a picture we arrange and re-arrange certain elements within the frame in order to achieve a desired effect. We may wish to show balance, harmony, symmetry and rhythm. Conversely, we may arrange elements that contrast, clash, are eccentric or asymmetrical.

The photographer who points his camera at a landscape or urban scene can only compose his picture by moving around and exploring the various angles of view: scenes rarely compose themselves to fit the camera format. The influence that the photographer has upon his subject depends on his ability to take all factors into account. He can alter depth by using different lenses – select a specific area by using a long-focus lens.

Sometimes it is impossible to compose a picture with any degree of deliberation and care. There simply isn't time, especially when shooting fast-moving objects, changing scenes and candid subjects. In such cases it is best to allow an extra margin of background around the subject, which can then be more carefully positioned within the picture area by enlarging and cropping in the darkroom. Cropping a picture – that is cutting out the extraneous detail – further helps direct the eye to the focal point.

A really good, strong image can be rendered even more powerful by cropping, perhaps revealing unforeseen possibilities. Apart from the actual taking of a picture, the enlarging and printing process is often the most exciting and rewarding part of photography. When possible, try and visualize the final picture, even before you've got your subject in focus.

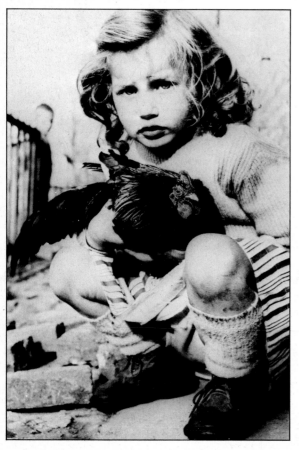

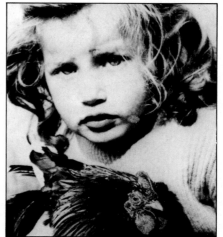

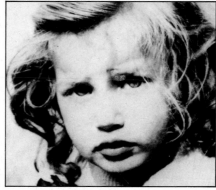

The pictures on this page show how you can concentrate on vital areas within the frame, emphasizing one or two points of interest while creating balance and harmony by cropping. In this manner, even the mood and the "message" of a picture can be altered. The first picture is the whole, uncropped frame. The subject is a child holding a chicken, and in the background a boy stands watching. By cropping the edges of the frame, taking out the fence and the brick wall, we still retain the main areas of interest; in fact, we emphasize them — the girl, the chicken and the boy. Moving in closer we eliminate the background entirely, only showing the girl and the bird: the background has gone, the boy has gone and with them goes some of the atmosphere of the scene; the little girl might now be in the photographer's studio, the chicken a studio prop. In the final picture we have cropped to a close-up of the child's face, eliminating the bird so that no hint of the location or atmosphere remains.

Cropping alters the interest and dictates the shape of the picture. By trimming the finished print made from the whole negative you cut away unwanted areas but reduce the size of the print, so it is best to alter the size and shape of the image by adjusting the head of the enlarger, "blowing-up" the image to the size of the printing paper, then trimming the finished print if necessary.

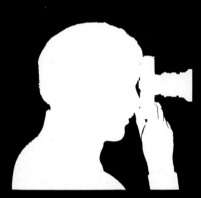

HOW TO
TAKE BETTER
PICTURES

People

In the days before photography, successful portrait painters were those gifted with the ability to capture a likeness, while at the same time flattering the subject, usually by exaggerating those qualities that he or she wished to project. With the introduction of photography, portraiture was freed from the tyranny of having to get a likeness, for accuracy was practically guaranteed. What photographers had to contend with was a certain stiffness of pose, due to the long exposures and the use of head clamps to hold the sitter still. The stiff pose was complicated by the unflatteringly self-conscious look of the sitter.

However, after 1851, and the invention of the wet collodion plate, followed by the gelatin dry-plate, photographers were free to capture the fleeting moment of a gesture, the natural attitude, the "candid" shot. Although portraiture continued to dominate as the most important branch of photography – by 1866 there were 284 portrait studios in London alone, and photographing people was (almost) a respectable profession – the formal pose was out-of-date, except among those photographers whose clients equated formality with dignity and manners.

The rendering of a likeness on a piece of paper is now a skill available to anyone who can hold a camera, and a likeness that may be endowed with humor, sadness, anger, determination, cunning, and so on. When taking a portrait, decide on the mood you wish to create, the one that best reveals the sitter's personality. The mood might be entirely relaxed, or extremely formal, but this should be determined at the start of the session, and is brought about by the relationship established between you and the sitter.

The popularity of portrait photography lies in its ability to describe far more efficiently than words, what someone looked like at a given time. It also records, swiftly and permanently, the person in his or her environment, or a group of people during a special occasion – a family gathering, office outing, a wedding or a birthday. The scene will never be quite the same again, and it is a memory that only the camera can capture with such accuracy. On the whole, photographs of people elicit greater response from viewers than any other kind of subject, except perhaps pictures of animals. "The proper study of mankind is man." Had Alexander Pope been alive today, he would most certainly have been carrying a camera.

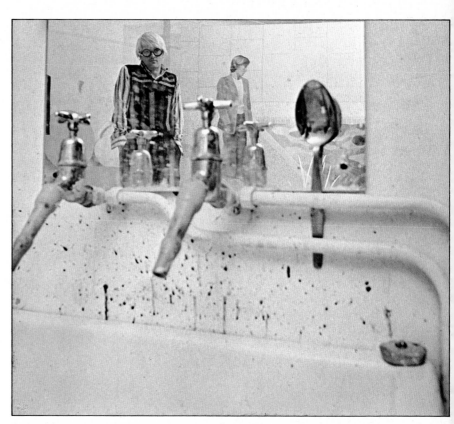

Variations on a theme

These three portraits of artist David Hockney show how one subject can be treated in different ways. The top picture is an unconventional view of an unconventional painter, reflecting the imagery he uses in his pictures. Hockney had to stand on a pair of steps in order to fit into the picture frame. The resulting picture has a flattened perspective with isolated images like the figure in his background painting. His unusual, eccentric character demanded a more liberal approach to the subject. In the picture below I was attracted to the chair, which reflects Hockney's taste and says something about his personality. I looked for a pose to increase the geometrical and rather theatrical qualities of the chair. Here it appears as if the chair is draped from the artist's outstretched arms, making a really stylized photograph. The portrait on the right shows the face of a versatile, mobile person. It was not necessary for me to have to animate or relax this sitter. It was more a matter of selecting the right expression. Here, the circular shapes in his face all work well together to make a complete composition.

Top: Hasselblad, 1/60 sec., f11, Ektachrome EX. Bottom: Hasselblad, wide-angle lens and extension tube, electronic flash, f16, Ektachrome EX. Right: Hasselblad, long lens and extension tube, electronic flash, f16, Ektachrome EX.

Single Portraits

A good portrait photograph should try and tell us something about the subject's character, for the portrait is a visual biography in a sense, and can capture the essence of one moment that may be worth more than a thousand formal poses. To become a good portrait photographer requires careful and studied use of the camera and lighting, and an understanding of the particular problems involved in photographing people.

The first consideration is who to use as a subject. Something about the subject's appearance should capture your imagination – the lines and creases on an old man's face may tell the story of a lifetime. A pretty face that holds your attention may have some added distinguishing quality – arrogance perhaps, or vivacity; we have come a long way from the time when beauty was defined in strict terms of proportion.

A well-thought-out background should be determined before you begin to arrange your subject. The background must always relate, wherever possible, to the subject and his or her environment, but must never dominate the total composition by being too intricate, or too strong in color. Selective focusing can be used to reduce the clarity and importance of the background, thus directing the eye toward the subject.

The whole setting must have a relaxed atmosphere. Try to understand your subject, and put him at ease. Conversation is usually the best softener; if you talk to the sitter constantly, he may forget that you are a photographer. Above all, do not force your subject into a pose, because your principal aim is to make him feel relaxed, and to feel that he is a valuable part of the creative process, rather than a helpless puppet. If your subject is particularly restless or tries to conduct the proceedings himself, give in to his whims for a while – use the film as a means of putting him at his ease. When your subject seems relaxed you can begin to expect a good portrait. Don't minimize on film – in an informal atmosphere the face is constantly changing, and each subtle shift must be captured.

If the aim of the picture is to flatter your subject, find a camera angle which hides the weaker or less attractive parts of the face. The nose will be lengthened and a broad forehead diminished if the camera is tilted upward, but in doing this a weak chin will be emphasized. A broad nose looks broader with the camera taking a full-frontal view; a high camera position foreshortens the head and is unflattering. As a general rule, focus on the eyes and then adjust depth of field accordingly. If the eyes are sharp the portrait is almost certain to be acceptable.

Lighting plays a very important part in the flattery of a face, by helping the photographer define bone structure. Strong, diffused light accentuates texture and gradations of tone. A much used form of lighting is a concentrated beam from a photo flood or spot, placed at 45° to the side and 45° above the subject's head. A backlight, overhead light, and low-level sidelight, which puts half the face in darkness, can cause dramatic shadow effects if well used. The main point in portraiture is that the interest of character lies in the many delineations of the face and its individual assets. Some of the best portraits are not mere likenesses, they are interpretations of an individual's character.

Capturing facial expressions

Cecil Beaton, an urbane, fashionable, fastidious man who shows self-confidence and no trace of shyness in front of the camera. A photographer himself, Beaton knows what is expected of him.

On children's faces emotions are undisguised. This child is showing a number of emotions simultaneously, including frustration, confusion, and above all, anger.

The contemplative, almost dreamy, expression of Stanley Spencer is further emphasized by the position of his hand.

The use of extra characteristics
Face and hands combined add an extra dimension of expression to this portrait. After the face, the hands are the most expressive feature. Henry Moore's hands, right, reflect the nature of his work as a sculptor. He is using them to frame and scale a piece of sculpture, to isolate it from its surroundings.
Hasselblad, long lens, 1/250 sec., f11, Kodak Tri-X.

Capturing the personality
The lively, mobile face of Germaine Greer, opposite, shot in harsh light to bring out its full expression.
Leicaflex, long lens, 1/250 sec., f8, Kodak Tri-X.

Finding the dominant feature
When taking portraits, especially for publication, look for interesting rather than flattering features. Here, the profile of Francis Bacon, the inventor of the fuel cell, was the most interesting angle of the face, and a diffused light was used to give good modeling. The sitter was looking toward the light.
Hasselblad, long lens, 1/125 sec., f8, Kodak Tri-X.

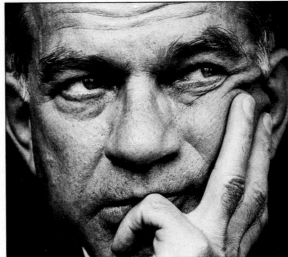

The unposed expression
The picture, left, was one of four, taken during a three-minute session. During this time Senator Fulbright was in conversation with two other people in the room, and he was almost totally unaware of my presence. Politicians are used to the attentions of photographers and tend to ignore them. It allows the photographer greater freedom because of the lack of self-consciousness in the sitter.
Hasselblad, long lens and extension tube, 1/250 sec., f5.6, Kodak Tri-X.

Photographed during a practice session, Vaughan Williams, the composer, shows us that he is crusty, irascible, and impatient.

Igor Stravinsky, a man totally involved, poised and concentrating, absolutely at one with the orchestra and the music.

The camera has arrested a fleeting expression of suspicion and alarm on the face of the artist, Augustus John.

The revealing face of this child shows that he is obviously enjoying himself. He does not notice the camera and is totally involved with the source of hilarity.

An Australian miner's face, as rough and craggy as the terrain and just as weatherbeaten. So great is the erosion of the face that it is quite difficult to guess his age.

Single Portraits

Using light to complement a pose
Barbara Hepworth's delicate and almost oriental expression has been heightened by the use of soft, evening light. This is a carefully posed, almost formal picture, with a high viewpoint to enhance the fragility of the subject.
Leicaflex, 1 sec., f5.6, High-Speed Ektachrome.

Dramatic lighting to enhance color
The hair and its powerful color was one of the most outstanding features of this girl, so I concentrated on a head portrait, all other information being suppressed to achieve intense contrast. To emphasize shape, profile and color, I used rim-lighting against a black background.
Rolleiflex, 1/250 sec., f8, High-Speed Ektachrome.

Using two types of lighting
This portrait of a student was taken on artificial light film, where both artificial light and weak daylight were used for illumination. The daylight gives the blue tinge to the floor and the window. I decided on a full-length pose, which I carefully composed so that the "V" of her neckline echoed that formed by her crossed legs. This helped to add strength to the design.
Leicaflex, 1/15 sec., f11, Type-B Ektachrome.

Selective use of shadow
For this portrait of the artist Richard Hamilton, I left half the face in shadow to create interest and to give an expressive gleam to the eyes. This method of lighting the far side of the face in a three-quarter view is useful to avoid emphasis of unflattering features. There is little color in this picture, blue being dominant, though the touches of red provide contrast.
Rolleiflex, 1/125 sec., f8, High-Speed Ektachrome.

The use of reflected light
Actors are normally easy to
photograph because they
instinctively know how to
pose for the best effect. In this
example, I chose to take the
picture in the cloisters away
from the fierce Mediterranean
sun; the reflected light came
from the white walls and
arches. The light being soft
and diffused gave strength to
the color in the photograph.
Noel Coward's relaxed pose
complements his relaxed
expression.

*Leicaflex, 1/250 sec., f8,
High-Speed Ektachrome.*

Group Portraits

The first portrait group that broke away from the conventional arrangement was Rembrandt's "The Night Watch." He didn't care that some of the participants could not be recognized, nor that they refused to pay him. While photographers are at liberty to experiment with groups of people, the aim of large, formal pictures is that all of the faces should be seen to their advantage. This method is used to record functions, social groups, teams and so on, where the object is to identify each member of the group.

Usually, groups have something in common and, because the members outnumber the photographer, are fairly self-possessed and easy to handle. In fact it is often difficult to attract the attention of everyone at the same time, so the photographer may have to employ such tactics as telling a story, or asking them to sing a song together; asking them to look at the camera may result in fixed stares and glazed expressions. Again, don't minimize on the use of film. The larger the group, the more shots you may have to take before you achieve one where *everybody* is playing their part; of a group of twenty-five people, twenty-four may be smiling while the twenty-fifth is scowling or closes his eyes as the shutter opens.

The expressions of the individuals touches on another point, that of light, especially if the group is photographed out-of-doors. It may be an advantage to the photographer to have the sun behind him, but if it causes the group to screw up their eyes because of the glare, then it is better to re-arrange the positions. Remember that light falling from more than 60° – the approximate angle at which the sun falls on a clear midday – casts shadows in the eye sockets and stresses the forehead lines. The best outdoor light is when the sky is slightly overcast, or when the sun is low.

When arranging formal groups the photographer should try and compose the individuals as the occasion demands. There is invariably an order of precedence at weddings, in military groups and school groups. The traditional group usually has the most important figures in the middle and often in the front row, in other words, the focal point of the picture. The tallest people are placed at the back, the smallest in the front row, the rest in the middle row sitting on a bench or chairs. The alternative is to arrange the group on a slope, or to photograph from a high point.

With informal groups, the photographer is free to arrange individuals in an unconventional way, perhaps suggesting that people look in different directions or look anywhere but at the camera. Even so, it is important to be able to identify each individual, whose place within the group isn't merely arbitrary, but forms a part of the whole composition.

The lighting technique can also be unconventional, perhaps using backlighting to throw the shapes of the group into prominence, and then placing the accent on certain areas of the group by use of spotlights to give depth within the composition. So conventional and stylized have group photographs become that photographers should be encouraged to break the rules, and to attempt unusual compositions, backgrounds and lighting techniques. The use of props helps to break up the regular symmetry, and create an additional focal point within the picture.

Photographing a small group
When photographing two people it is best to make one person dominant, the focal point. These two old ladies, right, have been photographed in a gesture which suggests a close, friendly relationship — the lady in the front looks protective towards the frail lady in the background. They were thrilled at being photographed, but felt rather self-conscious. This was a spontaneous shot, and in no way was I made to feel that I had intruded on their private lives.
Leica M3, 1/250 sec., f8, Kodak Tri-X.

The informal group picture
I invited the participants to arrange themselves into what they considered a suitable pose for the picture, left. They were proud to be the owners of new motorcycles, and the emphasis on the machines features clearly in their arrangement.
Linhof, 1/125 sec., f8, Kodak Tri-X.

Composing a formal arrangement
The group and their instruments, left, suggested a very formal and carefully posed picture, while the composite shape allowed plenty of scope to arrange a good figure composition, with the instruments in the foreground. With large groups of this type, it is important that all their faces should be seen, and seen to the best advantage.
Hasselblad, 1/125 sec., f11, Kodak Tri-X.

Arranging groups
To photograph a small group, place the tallest at the back and the smallest at the front. If people still can't be seen, make some sit on the ground, others on chairs and leave the rest standing, as shown far left. An alternative is to stagger them on stairs or on an incline, as shown middle left. A useful method for photographing large groups involves elevating the *camera* so that it looks down on the people, as shown left.

Using the Environment

The early portrait photographers liked to pose their sitters against studio backgrounds, often of a romantic or sentimental nature, instinctively realizing that a person removed from any environment seemed to be lacking a dimension. The studio background was in imitation of paintings, while the sentiment was a reflection of the times. The early photographers were further influenced by the traditions of portrait painting, where the sitter was usually depicted against the background of a landscape or distant house, perhaps to show that he was a landowner. A background is added information to a picture of a person, particularly where the surroundings form his natural environment, and can tell us something about his social status, his job perhaps, his interests, much of which he might shed on entering the studio.

When photographing a subject in any given environment, be careful not to allow the background to dominate, even though it is generally true that the human element, however incidental, will invariably be the focal point of any picture. A great deal of interest can be added to a picture by placing a person in relation to his natural surroundings, even by exaggerating those surroundings. The photograph of sculptor Henry Moore on this page is enhanced by the confused and cluttered studio background; extra pieces of sculpture and equipment could have been added without detracting from the atmosphere of the picture, or confusing the focal point – the sculptor himself. The priority of your picture must, however, not lead you astray. If you wish to make a portrait of a person in his or her natural environment, you will probably want to place them in the middle distance or the foreground. It wouldn't be much use photographing a farmer, say, at the far side of a field of corn. The aim would be to photograph him with the field or the farm in the background, perhaps just out of focus so as not to confuse the composition.

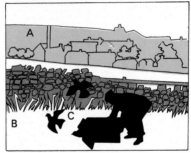

How the environment tells the story
Every element of the picture above, which was not previously arranged or set up, tells us something about the man. The background, A, shows that he probably lives and works in an industrial environment, but then escapes to the nearby country, B, where he can practice his hobby – pigeon racing, C. I deliberately chose a slow shutter speed to capture the burst of flight and feathers in an otherwise static scene.
Rolleiflex, 1/30 sec., f8, Ektachrome EX.

The working environment
Henry Moore's environment was entirely dominated by his work, by his pieces of sculpture and the tools of his trade – he looks like a traditional craftsman, and could easily have been a carpenter or cobbler. The figure is the central focal point, surrounded by a wealth of detail for the eye to explore.
Hasselblad, extra-wide angle lens, 1/30 sec., f16, High-Speed Ektachrome.

The center of interest: the surroundings
The pose is not blatantly seductive, but the combination of girl and bed is suggestive. By using a center focus lens attachment, the sharp corners and edges of the picture were softened. The subdued colors and the girl's frank expression further contribute to the atmosphere. The lighting, right, was soft, diffused and directional and was achieved by using four lights behind a sheet and a reflector.
Hasselblad, wide-angle lens, 1/80 sec., f5.6, Type-B Ektachrome.

The nude as a formal subject
I based this picture on the painting "Les Poseurs" by Seurat. I chose props to harmonize with the subject and reflect the period. The soft effect of the picture was achieved by breathing on the lens, and then taking the photograph before the lens cleared. Electronic flash was used to light the scene, right, but I bounced this from the ceiling and into two umbrella reflectors for a soft effect.
Hasselblad, electronic flash, f16, Ektachrome EX.

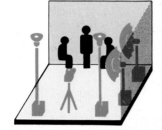

Aspects of the Figure

When you pose and light your model, and when you choose your viewpoint, you should have in mind a theme around which you wish to work. The nude body can be as expressive as the face: a curvaceous pose suggests softness and sensuality, an upright pose is often static and solemn, an angular arrangement of limbs gives a sense of agitated movement. You may decide to select certain areas of the body to stress form or texture, creating an abstract study by isolating relevant parts, as in the photographs on this page.

Limitless experimentation is possible in terms of light falling upon the figure and showing form, especially where the abstract shapes have an added element of mystery and/or eroticism. The combination of the nude figure and the dark background creates a sense of intimacy, especially since it attempts to conceal, and to draw the viewer into the depths of the composition. The technique of using dim lighting has the added benefit of concealing faults, and allowing you to stress the qualities of the particular model.

Just as you should never force your model into a pose, remember not to make her contribute to a picture where the mood is not her own – an extrovert personality may overpower a soft, romantic environment, one more suited to a model with an introspective or more modest appeal. A distinction can be drawn here between "nude" and "naked." The first implies a confident awareness of her body, while the second suggests vulnerability. If the nude model is fairly indifferent to the camera the resulting pictures will tend to be more authentic than those in which the model is embarrassed and "naked."

Enhancing form with light and shadow
Since this model, left, was not very tall, I used a wide-angle lens to make her legs appear longer and her body more sleek and elegant. A fairly strong light cast dark shadows, giving prominence to her stomach and breasts and making her legs look slim. Leaving half the face in shadow creates a theatrical effect.
Hasselblad, 1/30 sec., f16, Plus-X.

Combining texture and form
In this picture, above, I posed the model by a window, to photograph the contours of her body accentuated and revealed by the direction of the light. The lighting also gives a velvety texture to the skin. A white reflector placed about 3 ft (1 m) away gave sufficient detail in the shadows, but not enough to soften the contours.
Hasselblad, 1/30 sec., f16, Plus-X.

Concentrating the area
The model, far left, remained in the same position as in the picture on the right on the opposite page, but I moved in for a close-up of a particular area, taking the shot from a different angle so that no outline contours were visible.
Hasselblad, 1/30 sec., f16, Plus-X.

Lighting abstract form
Concentrating on the abstract shapes of various isolated areas of the body, I introduced a harsh spotlight to emphasize the outline and shape, and exposed for the shadows. The shots of buttocks and cleavage were printed to retain the outline of the shadow area. The breast contours have more detail and texture, since some light was reflected back from the body. All three pictures were taken with a wide-angle lens to distort the shape slightly and increase the effect of the design.
Hasselblad, (top and middle), 1/250 sec., f11; (bottom), 1/250 sec., f22, Plus-X.

Selective use of light
Photographers should always try to match the quality of light with the quality of the subject matter. I chose a spotlight to illuminate the model's arm, and I exposed to give detail in the highlight areas, retaining the soft quality of the skin, which complements the elegant shape of the arm and hand.
Hasselblad, 1/500 sec., f32, Plus-X.

Exaggerating the idea
The semi-naked model wears clothes and make-up usually associated with eroticism. But by getting the model, left, to avert her eyes I have eliminated the intimate relationship that might exist between viewer and model. Also by using a strong, angular, graphic pose with heavy shadow, the background area becomes an integral part of the picture, and the viewer can look at the composition as a whole.
Leicaflex, 1/30 sec., f11, Type-B Ektachrome.

Elements to emphasize the erot
The suggestive appeal of this shot, right, is helped by the clinging clothes and shiny skin. The girl's face and her dark eyes attract the viewer to explore the rest of her body. The picture was taken by daylight, in a swimming pool and under a fountain. I used a slow speed to catch the falling water, and the side-light shows well the shape and form, also the texture of material and skin.
Leicaflex, 1/15 sec., f16, Ektachrome EX.

The casual pose
Candid picture of a nude model off-duty, during a photographic session, relaxing among the studio props. A nude shot but a very unglamorous pose — even models can be caught unawares.
Leica M2, 1/60 sec., f8, High-Speed Ektachrome.

Children

Children can be remarkable actors. The process of photographing them is made easy by their natural tendency to perform. The photographer may be rewarded and entertained by the entire range of human emotions during a session – from rage to disarming frankness – but he should avoid those pitfalls of sentimentality inherent in many types of child and animal pictures, that mawkishness that the Victorians so enjoyed portraying. This is evident in the work of photographers who seek to emphasize characteristics which children are supposed to possess, namely a certain vulnerability, shyness and a tendency to appear wistful.

Once a child is used to the camera, he will forget it while being absorbed in something else; children are less concerned than adults with their image on paper. Because of this unconcern, they can only be expected to remain moderately still for a few minutes at a time. Also, they won't like sitting under hot, bright lights so the use of electronic flash is recommended, though very tiny children might be frightened by it.

The photographer must be patient, and try to understand the children he is working with. Even if you are working for a formal picture, the results may turn out to be informal, unless you use cunning, guile, bribery and similar tactics to achieve the desired result. Informal pictures full of spontaneous action can be expected with the majority of children because they can be persuaded to join in the fun of being photographed, if only for a limited time. The photographer will have to work fast in order to capture the essence of a child's performance – it is highly unlikely to be repeated.

Children in their environment
Children are naturally drawn to certain types of environment and location – the school playground, play areas in parks, sports grounds, fairs, zoos, or even the street. In fact, they will often ignore a designated playground to favor the street. You will almost certainly achieve some wonderful shots of spontaneous action if you wait until the children have accepted your presence in their own territory. The weather rarely affects this spontaneity, and rain, sun or snow can add to the excitement and atmosphere. Obviously, you will get the best results with a hand-held camera, and preferably a 35 mm, while the ideal would be to have two cameras, since you are likely to run out of film before you realize it. Because you will have to work fast, don't waste time focusing, but use the distance scale on the lens and judge by eye. Anticipate children's actions by thinking of all the things they do. Pre-set your camera to at least 1/125 sec., and set the aperture before you begin shooting, only altering it if you are shooting in rapidly changing light conditions such as at dusk.

This series is the result of watching a street and the movements of the people who lived in it. I began by photographing the old man in the doorway.

The group of approaching children became interested in what I was doing. Across the street a little girl was also watching with mild interest

Importance of the viewpoint
Although this boy was photographed in the same vicinity as the children in the series below, he was aloof and wanted no part of them. He didn't respond to the camera at all, but he did want to see the picture when it was developed. I used a low camera angle to increase the feeling of aloofness and isolation.
Leicaflex, 1/125 sec., f8, Kodak Tri-X.

The unguarded moment
The shot opposite was taken just after a session with the mother and child in the house. As I was leaving I turned round and caught the mother holding up the child, reassuring him that he could relax. I was thus able to capture the instinctive relationship of love and affection between the mother and her child.
Rolleiflex, 1/250 sec., f11, Kodak Tri-X.

The advantage of distraction
The picture on the right was one of a series taken in a children's home. Only one little girl seems aware of the camera, while all the others have been momentarily distracted. A picture full of different expressions and poses.
Hasselblad, electronic flash, f8, Kodak Tri-X.

When the children saw the camera they began to play up to it without any prompting — most children are natural actors, and it is often difficult to capture them in more relaxed moments.

The more familiar the photographer the less notice they take of the camera. By the time the performance of these children was in full swing, the girl across the street had started taking more interest in the action.

The considered snapshot

The considered snapshot
An obvious place to find a contented child is in water — provided it isn't the obligatory bath. This picture, left, was simplified by the use of the blue bowl, the blue hat and the blue-green background. I used a fast speed and aperture to capture the ever-changing expressions and poses.
Rolleiflex, 1/250 sec., f6.3, High-Speed Ektachrome.

The unposed pose
The picture below tells more of a story than if I had carefully posed the girl and her cat in comfortable positions. The simple background helps to emphasize the pose and the huge size of the cat.
Leicaflex, 1/250 sec., f8, High-Speed Ektachrome.

The technique of guile
I told the children that I would photograph the first one to reach the swing. They all rushed at the same moment and fought to be first. I panned the shot above to keep movement to a minimum. The photographer must always be ready with the camera set for fast, quick-changing events; there is no time to change focus or aperture.
Leicaflex, 1/30 sec., f16, Ektachrome EX.

Matching the pose with the mood
I chose a position and stance to match the age and development of the child, who has reached the age of self-awareness, and is a little shy. The picture was taken in a corner of a ballet practice room, and I used the weak available light, which gives strength to the form, and a gentle feeling of mood.
Hasselblad, 1/15 sec., f4.5, High-Speed Ektachrome.

The family portrait
A nicely-posed and well arranged family group, opposite, which, although static, is animated by the children's expressions. I used limited props, only a chair, plus a dark background so that the clothes became a vital part of the picture.
Hasselblad, electronic flash, f16, Ektachrome EX.

Still Life

A still life is an inanimate object, or group of objects, arranged as the subject for a picture. It can serve as an exercise in skill and creativity, to show an artist's understanding of composition, his ability to depict color harmony, form, texture, and the effects of light upon the objects. A still life can also be an exercise in taste, restraint, and decoration. The still life pictures painted by great artists in past history prove a point: it's not what you do but the way that you do it. Like the painter, the photographer can express color and tone, form and texture, composition and decorative taste. Because his subject is inanimate, the photographer is able to concentrate more than is usually possible on lighting and composition.

Still life groups may either be found as a single entity, or set up by the photographer – an arrangement of fruit and flowers perhaps, or a jug and a few half-filled glasses left on a table. Setting up your own still life can be very rewarding since you have total control over the choice and arrangement. It is advisable to begin with one object and gradually build up a composition in which various parts relate to each other. The items used in the group should not be selected arbitrarily; choose a theme and work things together to fit that theme, which can be based on a number of things, such as objects chosen from a certain period, or a particular place. The essential point is to collect as many props as possible. Professional photographers employ a stylist to do this, and it can take several weeks to find all the things needed for one picture.

Before you begin to arrange your objects, look for a suitable background, one that relates to the subject, but doesn't dominate it. The background should harmonize and help to enhance the atmosphere of the theme. For example, a collection of Victorian antiques would relate to a surface of scrubbed pine, but not to a surface of plastics.

Begin by setting up your group with the most important object, always viewing it through the camera and adjusting its position until you are satisfied. Add the second object, and check through the camera again. In this manner you can build up your still life one piece at a time. Balance must be judged in relation to the total proportion and shape; you must take into account the strength of colors, the highlights against the shadows, the fine detail against large, simple areas. The objects should complement each other in some way, but should be so organized as to emphasize rather than detract from the focal point. When you are building up the arrangement, concentrate not only on the predominant objects, but on the shadows cast by them and, unless you are working in black and white, the reflections of color. The spaces between the objects are as important as the objects themselves, and the areas of shadow can be controlled by lighting techniques in such a way as to provide visual links with each object. Remember with still life photographs to arrange your lighting so that the shadows all fall in the same direction. You should never have conflicting shadows in a composition of this kind.

Composing a still life group
Objects were added that related to the "Traditional farmhouse" theme. Each picture is successful but the enlargement is perhaps the most harmonious.
Linhof, 1 sec., f32, Plus-X.

Seeking Impact & Atmosphere

Lighting for atmosphere
This arrangement of antique
cook books, left, was lit by a
single shaft of light, weak
and diffused for just enough
detail while allowing the
remaining area to disappear
into shadow. The aim was to
create an atmosphere of
ancient and valuable
knowledge that had just been
discovered, perhaps hidden for
centuries within the leather
bindings of these books. The
open pages lead the eye from
the foreground into the
background area.
*MPP, 4 secs., f32,
Ektachrome EX.*

The natural still life
Vigilant photographers become
quick to perceive interesting
and powerful images in
everyday life, by constantly
searching for them. I found a
strong design of color and
composition in this view, right,
of a telephone and directories
in a Vancouver phone booth.
*Leicaflex, 1/250 sec., f11,
High-Speed Ektachrome.*

Using photo-montage
A picture, right, taken for a
magazine spread on jewelry.
The model was first photographed in black and white,
and a matt bromide print made
from the negative; the matt
finish eliminated reflections.
The objects of jewelry were
arranged on the print and then
re-photographed in color,
with the light bounced from
the ceiling to avoid shadows.
*MPP, 5 secs., f16, Type-B
Ektachrome.*

The subjects all around us

Still life pictures like these *objets trouvés* are everywhere. With this kind of shot I usually underexpose 1/2 stop to intensify color. All taken with a Leicaflex camera on High-Speed Ektachrome.

Reflections photographed in a window, showing an advertisement of the 1930s combined with a number of show-cards. *1/250 sec., f6.3.*

Memorabilia, flags, photographs and Victoriana give a kind of chauvinist theme to this "Royalist's" mantelpiece. *1/30 sec., f16.*

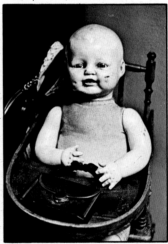

A showcase of French variety stars who wax and wane along the Rue Pigalle, Paris. Photographs within a photograph. *1/30 sec., f8.*

In the window of a Paris antique shop, a Jumeau doll in a baby's high chair. *1/60 sec., f5.6.*

A life-size image of the Pope flanked by gondoliers' straw hats, at a street vendor's stall in Venice. *1/250 sec., f11.*

Food

Those artists who painted still life groups were inclined to choose objects which were "still" yet contained life – flowers, fruit, or an item of food such as bread, cheese or a piece of ham. These were arranged, with loving care, in juxtaposition to a glass of wine, a bottle, a plate or two, and sometimes a dead game bird or a hare. This kind of still life had many advantages: the flowers were attractive, the fruit nicely colored, the wine translucent, and the whole thing could be set against a convenient indoor background, such as a table or sideboard.

The photographer has considerable advantage over the painter in that he gets his picture before the flowers wilt, the fruit shrivels, the meat begins to smell. Professional photographers use techniques in food photography that might shock the average consumer: food painted with oil or glycerine to promote shinyness, luscious "meat" pies with nothing under the golden crust except reconstituted potato, wine watered down to prevent it photographing too densely, food dyed and painted to look inviting in the picture, peas where the indentations have been picked out with a pin, ice made of glass that doesn't melt, beer with a head of detergent, cold tea in a brandy glass – there's no end to the iniquity.

The non-professional photographer will probably be less concerned with deception than with expression, composition, color and form, and lighting.

Light and shade are of primary importance in still life composition. With a studio light, or a source of daylight, you can bring out texture, pattern and form; through careful control of reflected light you can place an accent on individual objects by introducing highlights, adjusting the lights and the objects so that the shadows merge with the reflections. Notice how various textures take on different types of shadow, and how shadows are inclined to become darker if there is a dark object opposite. The sort of lighting you choose will depend entirely on your subject and the desired effect. If your composition is large and detailed you will probably want to use a diffused light, and avoid strong shadows which might confuse the overall shape and detail. When lighting to bring out the detail, it is best to place your light at about 45° to the group, with a reflector – to fill in shadows. An alternative method is to bounce your light from walls and ceiling, especially in a small room, and one with white walls. It will give you a certain amount of form and gentle shadow. When lighting for mood and atmosphere – dark and mysterious, or light and fresh – there are a number of techniques you can use. A gauze over the lens or lights can impose shadows; colored filters on lights concentrate patches of warm or cool light; shooting through wire netting or a hole in a piece of card gives a vignette effect.

As in any composition, your choice of viewpoint is extremely important. Always arrange through the camera viewer to avoid discrepancies between your eye and the lens level. A straight-on viewpoint makes the most of form, reflected light and rhythmic spacing. A slightly higher viewpoint is needed if you want to give a sense of volume and depth. An old and well-tried device for emphasizing depth is to arrange one or two objects so that they project over the edge of your table, or into the immediate foreground; then crop your picture into the object. A high viewpoint is effective in stressing design. Any composition which uses geometrical shapes looks most striking from this angle. Of course, your still life group will take on a slightly different character each time you change your position, so move around the subject until you have found a position which best suits your purpose.

A still life group can be austere, monumental, mannered, or it can sprawl as a jumble of informally assorted shapes and colors. Either way it will demand patience and precision, but the results will be rewarding. It's up to you, for in a still life, you, the photographer, have total control. You choose the objects, the camera, the lenses, the viewpoint and the lighting. If your picture is not a success, start again.

The art of technical effects
Another period piece, this time a Victorian larder in an English country home. The grapes and the harvest loaf were painted with glycerin to give shine, the black ham was relieved by the fork which breaks its heavy shape, and a silverized reflector was used to highlight the fork. I lit the entire group by diffused light, with a gauze screen on the light, and used a large format camera for maximum definition and quality with the smallest possible aperture. As in all food still life groups, the individual objects should always be of the finest quality. Props, especially for antique and period pictures, must be accurate. The picture on the right would have been unconvincing had I used one of the commercial honeycombs where the wooden frame is bright and new.
MPP, 10 secs., f45, SG Pan.

Adding human interest
A still life picture of food can often have the added interest of an accompanying figure – perhaps the person who prepared the food, or who is about to eat it. This device is used in advertising and magazine pictures, and is often used by photographers at weddings or birthday parties.

Left: taken for an "Edwardian" cook book, to show a kitchen and gamekeeper of the period. Center: this composition of a chef with food was shot in weak sunlight, because strong light would have cast strong shadows and destroyed detail. Above: Christmas spread complete with cook, taken for a magazine. The cook obviously enjoys both eating and cooking, and conveys the feeling of the festive season.

Arranging Food for Effect

Simulating a location shot

Above, an example of an "exterior" cafe scene, set up in the studio as illustrated, left. I used the studio to avoid the possible distractions of a real-life situation and to enable me to control the foreground, middle distance and background more easily. The shot was taken through a sheet of engraved glass.

MPP, 2 secs., f11, Type-B Ektachrome.

The face of food

A vegetable "portrait," opposite, in the style of the artist Guiseppe Archimibaldo. The diagram, right, shows how I constructed the piece using a chicken wire frame mounted on a wooden foundation. The frame was covered with modeling clay and the vegetables fastened to it with pins.

MPP, electronic flash, f22, Ektachrome EX.

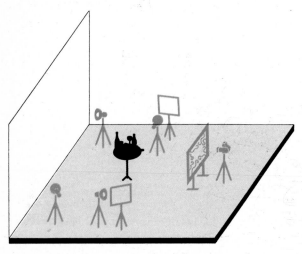

Creative Still Life

Art, as a means of self-expression, has always strayed into areas which the general public have found hard to follow. For artists use a visual language and you have to be sensitive and sympathetic to respond at the same emotional and intellectual level. The artist manages to convey emotions, feelings and ideas which cannot easily be put into the layman's language. What we like to call "modern" art has forced art critics to spin webs of descriptive prose in the hope that the artist's message might thus be more easily grasped. The artist however is not communicating with words but with his art, an emotional and intuitive response to his intellectual ideas.

In commercial art the image and message are usually obvious and superficial. In popular art, the aim is to reinforce traditional and fashionable ideals. These areas are of importance to photography. Equally important is the current trend towards the abstract and the unconventional, where the viewer is invited to make his own interpretation; the artist poses the question to which the viewer provides possible answers. This type of photography chooses as its subject objects that are not in themselves important. The viewer is free to regard the picture in the abstract, so that the picture is no longer the artist's vehicle for self-expression alone, but the viewer's also.

The still life in time . . .
The picture above deals with the aspect of time. The objects in the picture — the chair and cushion, the moving tree — seem to pose questions about time, past and future. What occurred before the picture was taken? Who sat in the chair? Why is it empty? What happened when the photographer went away? The imagination is touched, an individual response is inevitable.
Hasselblad, long lens, 1/4 sec., f16, Kodak Tri-X.

. . . and in space
The fence may have been put there to keep people out, or to keep cattle in, but in the photograph, left, the fence itself is important only as an influence. It is less a picture of a fence than a picture of a geometric exercise in space. Because of the placing within the frame of the picture it creates a feeling of depth on a flat plane, creating a foreground, a middle distance and a background. Without either linear or aerial perspective it manages to convey a three-dimensional illusion.
Hasselblad, 1/250 sec., f16, Kodak Tri-X.

The selective viewpoint

"Festival Reclining Figure" was the first piece of Henry Moore sculpture where "space and form were completely dependent on and inseparable from each other." The pictures on this page attempt to show this by isolating and emphasizing certain parts and shapes that are perhaps not apparent at first glance. Depending on the point of view, a part can sometimes be more interesting or revealing than the whole, especially in the work of Moore, which reveals sculpture within sculpture. My contribution to the piece was to try and interpret the sense and meaning of the work, not only in itself, but in relation to its surroundings and to other contemporary works. When photographing pieces of sculpture, wait for the right light, explore all the angles, take care in selecting the film and the lens. Consider how it might best be portrayed, either by shooting against the light for bold silhouette, or using a raking side-light for texture, or a soft, diffused light for detail. Photographing sculpture should not only be a record of the artist's work, but also the photographer's interpretation of it.

113

Landscape

For the photographer, attracted by a scene that is dramatic, or colorful, or serene, landscape is a subject that invariably promises good results. Landscapes offer limitless interpretation, because the photographer has a number of very influential factors to help him. The time of year is one major factor, because each season suggests special feelings – rejuvenation in spring, abundance in summer, melancholy in autumn, bleakness in winter, and so on. The time of day is also influential, because the mood of a landscape will be constantly shifting between dawn and dusk, the more so if the weather conditions are changeable. Add to these the factors of space, light, unusual or varied terrain, natural phenomena, an imposing building or object, and we can see why landscape is one of the most photographed of all subjects.

Yet landscape photographs frequently prove disappointing. An inspiring, panoramic view, for example, that you were certain you captured on film fails to convey the scene as you had visualized it. Everything seemed perfect – a good, strong light to give adequate depth of field, brilliant color, trees, hills, a river, clouds – even a ruined castle, ivy-clad. What went wrong?

A few basic rules can help explain the problems often encountered in landscape photography. One is that by selecting and concentrating on a small area, you can be more successful than if you were just to point your camera across the broad expanse and hope to encompass the whole scene. When looking at a landscape pictorially, concentrate on the dominant feature. Placing the emphasis on one area of the picture establishes a structure and helps to guide the viewer's eye, which might otherwise wander around looking for something to settle upon. You should aim to have a central feature, with other elements subordinate to it.

The second rule regards space. As shown earlier (in the section on "Composition"), space in a landscape can be described in terms of perspective: *linear* perspective, where lines diminish and converge toward the horizon; *aerial* perspective – the volume of space between the viewer and the distant horizon separated by areas of tone – where colors lose their intensity as they recede, and objects lose their definition. Perspective might include the foreground, the middle distance and the background, but a shot of a wide-open space will be unconvincing if you fail to relate the foreground to the horizon by utilizing the middle distance. This can be done by including a stone wall perhaps, or a clump of shrubs.

A third general rule is that a scene lit at midday, with the sun directly overhead, is the worst possible light for photography, as it destroys form and diminishes texture. Think of the landscape as a vast still life, imagine the sun as a spotlight and yourself photographing for texture or form. Choose a time of day when the sun is low, either at dawn or sunset.

It is usual to have the main subject matter in the middle distance, so select a position and angle that will make the foreground interesting, but where the eye will be guided into the middle distance. It takes skill to construct a picture with a recession of shapes, tones and forms to produce a harmonious balance, creating order out of the disorder of nature.

The Time of Day

Weak light conditions
An atmospheric shot taken in moonlight, diffused by a thin layer of cloud.
Hasselblad, extra-long lens, 1/2 sec., f4, Royal-X.

As we have seen, two of the principal conditions affecting the appearance of a landscape that we might wish to photograph are the weather and the time of day. The weather conditions may influence the photographer's choice – depending on how uncomfortable or severe they are. The time of day depends on the amount of light available; pictures can be taken in remarkably poor light conditions with great success. Remember that a piece of film is extremely sensitive to light, and will record images contrary to our expectations where light is feeble and misleading to the human eye.

Because light is constantly changing, and shifting its position and intensity, a single scene will undergo a remarkable number of changes during the day. One of the principal aims in landscape photography – but by no means the only aim – is to combine the scene with mood and atmosphere. This is usually best achieved by early morning or evening light. Much depends on the photographer's individual requirements. You may deliberately set out to emphasize particular qualities in a particular scene, or you may have been struck by the effect of light at a certain moment in the day, in passing so to speak – the inspiration of a moment. A desert scene of sand dunes, shot by early light, will reveal the texture of the sand, and the contours of the dunes, creating a soft, ethereal quality. But perhaps you want to state "desert" in a more positive and striking way, in which case you will take your picture in the heat of noon, when the light is hard and there are few shadows.

Because landscapes are always taken with available light, and you cannot "fill in" shadows as you might in a studio, an accurate balance in exposing for light and shadow is essential. As a general rule, give two-thirds of your reading for the dark areas of the picture, and one-third for the highlights. In some cases though, you may choose to expose only for the shadow, leaving the highlight to take care of itself, as in the yacht picture on p. 126.

The right place at the right time

The direction of the light at certain times of the day can influence perception of a scene. As the light moves, a point of interest may undergo subtle and even dramatic changes. I started with the east-facing part of this house at 6.00 am, on a summer morning. The pond reflects the building, and the light separates planes of perspective to give depth.

At 11.00 am, the sun casts harsh shadows. I shot from shadow into highlight to capture the pattern of light and shade. The result is more dramatic than the previous picture. An hour later, the sun would have been too high to cast shadows, destroying depth, texture and form. Shot from the south-east.

As the sun moved around I moved with it to photograph the building from a fresh angle, this time the south-west side at 3.00 pm. The light is softer and the shadows are less pronounced.

Evening light at 7.00 pm was more delicate. The view is of the west side. At 6.00 in the early morning, this aspect would have been flat and dull. To exploit the possibilities fully you should consider the subject from various angles and at various times of the day. Unconventional views can often be the most effective, particularly in strong sunlight.

The Time of Day

Early morning light
Subtle effects are found during the early morning, in contrast
to the harsh sunlight of midday, because of the softness of the
light which mutes tones and colors. In this shot there is a good,
central area of color on which the eye can rest before exploring
the remaining areas subordinate to it. The use of a long lens
helped to bring the mountain background closer.
Hasselblad, long lens, 1/30 sec., f11, High-Speed Ektachrome.

Hiding the sun
Although this picture was shot at sunset, the sun was strong
enough to halate the film, and so I was careful to hide the sun
behind the tower which enabled me to get detail in the shadows.
A very powerful, direct light will always dominate a photograph
by creating dense shadows with little detail. I took an exposure
reading of both the sky and the shadows, and calculated a
combination of the two. If you expose for the shadow area, you
lose detail in the sky, and vice-versa. Remember that the light
is constantly changing as the sun sinks, so don't delay after
setting the timing and aperture.
Rolleiflex, 1/250 sec., f11, Ektachrome EX.

The Changing Weather

A summer storm is a good example of changing weather, the kind of storm that Beethoven described in his Pastoral Symphony, or that Turner was so fond of painting: a sudden flurry of last year's leaves, raindrops the size of coins, black clouds hiding the sun, distant thunder, and finally – a rainbow.

In photographs, as in paintings, landscapes should be made to appear alive, to show mood and atmosphere and movement. The most successful way of achieving this is to photograph scenes in changing weather. Much depends, of course, on your objective. A landscape in the south of France, or in California, might seem more convincing if the sky is a deep and cloudless blue. Hundreds of such pictures, pleasant but dull and repetitive, are taken every day, either as a record of a vacation, or because of our inclination to stress the obvious. Yet seemingly poor weather conditions can provide wonderful opportunities to get unusual landscape pictures, from extremes of industrial smog, to the effect of a howling snowstorm that threatens to envelop the photographer and his camera. This isn't to suggest that you should only seek the heart of a blizzard in order to shoot a successful landscape picture, but more that you should look for contrast, for exaggerated conditions, for the abnormal that conveys the very essence of landscape.

All photographers should try and include that extra quality that gives a picture its unique appeal. Landscape pictures depend so much on a variety of different influences. Some landscapes change but little from season to season, while others alter by the hour. If a certain view remains obdurately dull, you can influence the effect by using a particular camera angle, a colored filter or a special film, and by emphasizing the focal point by composition and cropping, and by the judicious use of the foreground.

By experience you will come to recognize the future potential of a certain landscape. Some photographers wait for weeks, even months, to capture an expected event that transforms a view from the mundane to the spectacular. The wait is almost always worthwhile.

Abnormal conditions – frost
Frost can transform landscapes into scenes of ethereal beauty and delicacy. To accentuate the lace-like effect of the frost on the tree above, I used a yellow filter which darkened the sky and gave good contrast. Nature provided the inspiration; all I had to do was get up early.
Rolleiflex, 1/125 sec., f8, Panatomic-X.

Shooting into the sun
Provided that the sun, or source of light, isn't too powerful, you can obtain this interesting star effect with its decorative quality. Here, I shot straight into the sun which was low on the horizon, using the smallest aperture and a fast shutter speed.
Rolleiflex, 1/500 sec., f22, Panatomic-X.

Severe conditions — snow
As I wanted to capture the effect of falling snow in the picture above, I used a slow shutter speed, and a balanced exposure between the dark tones of the building and the light tones of the snow. With snow pictures there is a danger of under- or over-exposing, particularly if you take only a highlight reading of the snow which reflects an immense amount of light. This exposure was calculated to give a balance between shadow detail and highlight detail. The viewpoint was selected to produce a sculptural effect, rather than an architectural shape.
Rolleiflex, 1/60 sec., f8, HP3.

Overcast conditions — poor light
The picture on the right was taken in overcast rainy weather when the light was poor, and when photographers are inclined to pack their cameras away to protect them from the rain. Although the conditions were saturating and oppressive, the range of tones has created an interesting, moody shot.
Hasselblad, 1/60 sec., f16, Plus-X.

Obscured conditions – fog
"Bad photography weather" –
when conditions seem most
unfavorable – can produce
very interesting pictures;
adverse weather should attract
photographers to experiment.
This shot, where foggy
conditions totally diffused the
light and made form hard to
identify, has proved
successful – the scene is
atmospheric and dramatic.
Detail in the shadow was
important, and an exposure
reading was taken of the dark
area, just below where the
men are walking.
*Leica M2, 1/125 sec., f8,
High-Speed Ektachrome.*

Aspects of the Sky

A landscape picture seldom excludes the sky; it usually takes up half the picture area, sometimes more. The sky is often the only part of a scene that is constantly changing. While trees, pastures and buildings remain static, the sky may have a profound effect in altering mood, area of interest and color.

Look through this book and notice how frequently the sky occupies an important part of the pictures. It is vital to the composition of a photograph, where it is used to emphasize and support the foreground, or the middle distance. An otherwise dull picture may be greatly enhanced by a dominant sky – stormy and dramatic, or clear, crisp and blue.

The sky can also convey information about a particular scene: a hazy, yellowish sky is the property of polluted atmospheres, of industrial areas and large cities, and can be used to stress this fact when photographing industrial landscapes.

In some parts of the world, sky conditions are infinitely variable, and can change without warning – you may have to anticipate the cloud formations and the shifting qualities of light and shade. In flat expanses of country, the sky is very prominent; in mountainous areas less so. The amount of sky you choose to include depends on the balance needed in the picture; as a general rule, try to include a certain amount of sky in a landscape, or conversely, part of the horizon in a sky picture – land and sky are naturally related. A greater degree of spaciousness can be achieved by the use of a wide-angle lens.

Preventing halation
Taking sky pictures when the sun is behind the clouds prevents halation, especially in summer when the sun is strong. Filters also help to counteract the effects of halation, and give added contrast. Opposite, I used a coastal subject where the sea and sky harmonize. Such subjects can be very rewarding, but you may need patience to get an interesting light effect.
Hasselblad, long lens, red filter, 1/250 sec., f16, Kodak Tri-X.

The sky as the focal point
Although other detail appears in this shot, it is dark and subordinate to the cloud formation. Balance is achieved by shooting into the sun and exposing for the sky, which makes a silhouette.
Leicaflex, wide-angle lens, yellow filter, 1/250 sec., f8, Kodak Tri-X.

Sky effects with filters
Filters help to give extra strength or contrast to areas of sky, also atmosphere, especially to color shots. Filters for use with black and white film correct or intensify those colors that are not accurately recorded, especially blue. The most useful filter colors for skies are yellow and red. Yellow-green filters have a further advantage in that they darken blue and lighten green, thus increasing contrast in landscapes. A common fault in black and white pictures is that the blue sky is too pale while the greens are too dark.

Without a filter
Using a normal panchromatic film, the area of sky appears weak, with no contrast.

Adding a yellow filter
The clouds appear white, and the blue is slightly darker, giving contrast.

Adding a red filter
Using a red filter in place of yellow further darkens sky, gives greater contrast.

Water & Light

As the sky changes, so does the light, altering its strength and direction. These changes are often extremely subtle, so you will need to check frequently your position and exposure readings.

When light illuminates water the intensity of the reflection can dominate the entire scene, radically affecting exposures. Watch how light strikes the surface of water to render it either jet-black, or dazzlingly bright blue, or perhaps to create a golden luminosity: light can make a lake scene pallid and dreary, or lively and exciting. Reflected light can provide a mirror effect, and is thus an extra source of illumination. Photographing across water and *against* the light, as in the example of the yacht picture below, can capture the scintillating property of an agitated surface in brilliant sunlight; shooting *with* the light produces a much calmer result.

It is important that you move around the location, particularly if you cannot spend time waiting for a break in the clouds, a ripple on the surface of the water, or conversely, a mirror-like surface. Change your angle of view, seeking the position that captures the effect or mood you wish to achieve. Very often, it is the distant patch of light reflected from a lake or river that will enhance an otherwise monotonous picture, just as light reflected from wet roofs might accentuate a view of an urban scene. Unwanted reflections or overpowering light-rays can be eliminated with a polarizing filter, while certain color filters will increase the contrast on black and white film. Remember, though, that strongly reflected light often causes flare as does shooting into the sun, so you will probably have to take exposure readings both for highlight and shadow, selecting an aperture somewhere in between.

Light diffused by mist
Later in the day this autumn scene might have provided a mere picture postcard effect, but in the early morning I was able to capture the timeless atmosphere of this stretch of the river Thames. The light diffused by mist limits the color range to cool blues and greens, creating a calm, romantic setting. The camera position was important in this shot — I wanted the rower and boat in shadow, to accentuate the ripples caused by the movement of the oars. Also, having the boat in the middle distance leads the eye around the picture, and at the same time helps to emphasize the distance. Careful exposure for the shadow gives detail in the reflections.
Pentax, wide-angle lens, 1/125 sec., f8, Ektachrome EX.

Shooting against reflected light
This picture, right, taken from the top of a cliff, shows the powerful effect of light reflected off the surface of the sea. The photograph would have had less interest and liveliness had I shot away from the sun instead of into the reflection. At sea level, the picture would have been a silhouette, but from this elevated camera position I was able to include the maximum area of water, light and texture and a tonal range.
Leicaflex, long lens, 1/250 sec., f11, High-Speed Ektachrome.

Light on agitated water — sea spray
Very careful exposure and a fast shutter speed were needed to capture the detail of light on breaking waves, while also retaining the tonal range of the sky in the photograph opposite. It is important to select a good viewpoint and camera angle, exploring the many possible positions to achieve the maximum effect of sea spray.
Leicaflex, 1/500 sec., f8, High-Speed Ektachrome.

Architecture

Most buildings serve a specific function – they were built to be lived in or worked in or worshipped in or buried in, and so on. They also reflect a style, a period in history, a particular human environment. You may choose to interpret one or more of these factors in your photographs, so you will need to examine the building from different angles and select the viewpoint which most clearly states what you want it to say.

In different parts of the world there are other considerations to be taken into account. For example, many buildings in the Middle East are light in color, with thick walls and tiny windows. They cast powerful, dark shadows, and create interesting geometric shapes and patterns in the harsh light of the sun. In Europe, the churches and cathedrals are usually tall, proud buildings with large domes, or spires that reach for the heavens. In photographing them, the value of the sky should be judged to create the right mood.

Architectural subjects need contrast. The contrast need not be excessive, but a building must relate to some additional quality, the angle of view, for instance, the light, the mood or the weather. Your first aim in photographing a building should be to consider it from a straightforward, natural aspect, then to move around the building looking for a more unusual position or dramatic effect. Whenever possible, try for an interpretive approach, shooting your picture in the rain, in mist or snow. If the weather won't come to your aid and remains obdurately sunny, take your subject in the reflection in a window, the wing mirror or a puddle, pond or river. Consider framing the building by a foreground device such as an archway, the overhanging branch of a tree, or a similarly placed shop sign; these will relate the subject to the immediate foreground, giving added depth. If the subject is in sunlight, it is helpful to have the framing device in shadow, where possible.

High buildings often pose problems where an upward tilt of the camera, made to include the whole structure, leads to a convergence of vertical lines. This can be effective if height is a feature, but it should not be too distorted, an occurrence common with small, hand-held cameras. A camera with a rising front will bring all parts of most tall subjects in focus, but there is a limit to the amount that they can manage.

As an alternative to cameras with movable fronts, place your camera at some distance from the subject, including the surrounding area, which can then be cropped in the enlarger – the use of fairly fine-grain film will enable you to blow up quite small subjects within the frame of the whole, thus avoiding close-up distortion. Furthermore, the use of a small aperture will give you greater definition and, although the exposure will therefore be longer, it will encourage you to use a tripod and cable release, so that you can position your camera with greater accuracy; a cable release is necessary because, oddly enough, it is easier to shake the camera on a tripod than when hand-held. Light is the most important and infinitely variable influence on any subject, and architecture is no exception, but you will probably find that most buildings are best photographed when the light is falling obliquely across, giving you a composite of elements – form, texture, depth and even atmosphere.

Perspective with low angle of view
I wanted to show the dominant, industrial ugliness of the architectural landscape, above. By using a wide-angle lens and a low viewpoint, the eye is led to the powerful shapes of the towers. An entirely man-made environment.
Hasselblad, 1/125 sec., f8, long lens, Kodak Tri-X.

Perspective with acute angle of view
The use of a wide-angle lens can increase extreme perspective and angles, right. Here, powerful emphasis has been given to this industrial complex of pipes and tanks. For additional atmosphere I used a yellow filter.
Linhof, 1 sec., f45, FP3.

Use of linear and aerial perspective
A photograph, above, of St Mark's Cathedral, Venice, where scale and depth are used to relate the walking figure and the geometric pattern of the stones to the architecture.
Rolleiflex, wide-angle lens, 1/125 sec., f8, Kodak Tri-X.

Perspective & Angle of View

Acute angle to show height
Additional characteristics to show height, such
as reflections of sunlight on glass, can be
included by using a certain viewpoint, in this
case an acute angle. By exposing for the
highlight I retained the reflection of clouds,
allowing the rest of the building to merge into
darkness. This helps to make a dramatic picture
from an ordinary scene.
*Leicaflex, wide-angle lens, 1/1000 sec., f16,
Ektachrome EX.*

Perspective for balance and composition
From this viewpoint, above right, the ornate
facade is balanced against the flat blue-gray of
the sky and water, a good example of the use
of both linear and aerial perspective. I took the
shot in the early morning to avoid harsh
sunlight which would have destroyed the rich
color, the intricate detail of the fabric and the
essential, watery atmosphere of Venice.
*Leicaflex, wide-angle lens, 1/250 sec., f8,
Ektachrome EX.*

Photographing small building
With experience, photog-
raphers become more selecti
in their choice of subjects.
They may ignore the
majestic architectural
showpiece to focus, instead,
on a storefront, a cottage, a
bandstand, a small hotel. Eac
has its own character. Right,
simple house with a slatted
facade, one of the oldest
houses in Australia. Top cen
another simple shape shot in
weak evening light that show
texture without overpowerin
shadows. Bottom center, a s
taken mainly in shadow, but
against the sunlight, to show
the pattern against the snow
Far right, a delicate design o
ironwork and rich color
revealed on an overcast day.

Creating Mood with Setting

The appearance of buildings changes according to the light, the weather, the time of day, the season of the year. A castle, or a ruined monastery, photographed against the background of snow or a gathering storm, might more easily evoke feelings of the medieval landscape than if photographed on a sunny summer afternoon. In snow, variations of color and tone merge into subtle gradations of black, gray and white where buildings often assume a delicate, ethereal quality. The peculiar light that grows before a storm catches stone surfaces so that they stand out in bright contrast against the dark sky. In morning or evening mist buildings are sometimes caught by the faintest hint of sunshine, while everything else remains almost the color of the mist itself. Even the effects of heavy rain can be used to good advantage, when the light reflected off rows of wet, slate roofs can make a glowing picture. Buildings seen through rain, mist or snow tend to lose their outlines, to lend an air of mystery to a landscape.

Light and shade are, of course, essential to all photographs of architecture, since shadow defines structure, and light reveals texture and detail. The best light is normally one which falls from one side, so that some surfaces are caught while others remain in shadow. Remember that the whiter the surface, the blacker the cast shadows will be, which can create abstract patterns of light and shade, especially on a bright day. It is important to be extremely careful in gauging the exposure.

As a general rule, a black, sooty building will require a 100% increase of exposure. Moderately dark surfaces need 25% more, white buildings need 25% less, and snow needs 50% less. Most modern building materials such as metal and glass, have strong, reflective qualities, and can appear uniquely beautiful at sunrise or sunset, when they become tinged with the colors of the sky. The shadows cast by a red, setting sun on a light surface are seen as blue, so that the windows near the tops of high buildings reflect red, while all else below remains in bluish shadow.

We have seen how mood and atmosphere can be introduced by the effects of light and the weather, and also by the surroundings. These elements can be combined with the point of view: a ruin photographed from some distance away might seem more isolated and eerie than if we moved into close-up.

In many such photographs it is essential that you include the setting, the building in its environment especially if it is atmosphere that you are aiming for, and not the mere record of a landscape or a scene. In one sense, *all* photographs possess a mood of some kind, but the photographer can add drama and mystery to the most mundane structure by balancing or contrasting light, weather and point of view. Sometimes a building may look uninspiring until a particular light falls on it; rooftops in silhouette can cut a jagged line across the sky, where the focal point might be a brilliant patch of reflected sunlight from a single window. The final and most important element to mood is the human one. Buildings photographed in relation to the human figure may emphasize a feeling. We can often appreciate a building more if we photograph it as a functional part of everyday life.

Light and shade to increase atmosphere
Ely Cathedral, above, was photographed through trees which frame the building and concentrate the focal point. The strong side-light reveals the delicacy of the carving and the beauty of the design. A yellow filter helped to darken the sky, and to reduce reflections.
Hasselblad, 1/125 sec., f16, Plus-X.

Use of setting for atmosphere
Very often, the setting is more important than the building in presenting mood and atmosphere. For the picture opposite, I chose a camera viewpoint so that the eye was led to the house by way of the tomb and path. The great depth of field was achieved with a wide-angle lens.
Hasselblad, 1/125 sec., f32, Kodak Tri-X.

Creating Mood with Setting

Choosing the foreground
The use of a long-focus lens (400 mm) enabled me to eliminate surrounding details, such as town roofs, in these photographs of Ely Cathedral. My aim in both shots was to try to create a mood in keeping with the structure. For the first I chose a rural foreground and took the picture at sunset to record the cathedral in the mist so often seen in eastern England. I moved to a different viewpoint, and took the second photograph in sunlight, using a bank of wild flowers to create atmosphere and give good color contrast. *Leica M2, (left) 1/100 sec., f32; (right) 1/250 sec., f32, High-Speed Ektachrome.*

Mood according to time of day
Sunlight on the beautiful, mellow bricks gives a warm feeling to this winter scene of Compton Wynyates, Warwickshire. I photographed the building by early morning light which gives crispness to the atmosphere, and creates a balance between the bright house and dark surroundings. *Hasselblad, wide-angle lens, 1/125 sec., f8, High-Speed Ektachrome.*

The composite elements of mood
The shot, opposite, was taken through the contorted shapes of weeping ash trees, using a wide-angle lens. I exposed for detail in the shadow, but also to get the castle in silhouette and capture window reflections. *Leicaflex, 1/125 sec., f5.6, High-Speed Ektachrome.*

Interiors

Photographing interiors of buildings is usually hampered by certain limitations – the quality and intensity of the light available, and the consideration of area. In other words, what to include and how to light it. Lighting, however, is only a problem where there are extremely dark areas and contrasts in light and shade. Where there is likely to be little or no movement, you can simply mount your camera on a tripod and give long exposures. There is also the method much favored by some architectural photographers, known as "painting with light," a detailed description of which is given in the caption to the diagram on p. 141.

One problem with artificial light is that it can create very dark, cast shadows, especially with directional light coming from a single source. The artificial quality can be overcome in those interiors where you can simulate firelight or candlelight, but, generally speaking, it is better to diffuse the light by bouncing it off some white area. Artificial lighting is usually needed where the photographer wishes to obtain an accurate and detailed representation of an interior, and where there is little or no natural light source. If, on the other hand, the aim is to capture the mood and atmosphere of an old building – the interior of a church, for example – a dim light can be very effective, while a sharp shaft of light cutting across the shadows from a half-opened door completes the picture. Snow, by they way, is one of the best natural sources for reflective light, particularly for photographing the interior of churches and cathedrals. Snow outside will bounce light through the windows, giving extra illumination to the dark areas of the church.

In considering the area of the interior, limitations are imposed by the camera. In the average home, for example, it is only possible to include two walls, using a wide-angle lens. It is therefore important to re-arrange furniture and wall decorations if these are vital factors to the picture. If you wish to photograph the environment exactly as it stands, then use existing light and a wide-angle lens. When taking pictures for catalogues and magazines, where the room needs to be seen as a concentrated example of its best features, select a camera angle that can be juxtaposed with a re-arrangement of objects in the room. If the camera sets limitations because of space – you cannot get back far enough to include everything – use a camera with as much flexibility as you can afford. A view camera with a movable front and bellows is essential for serious architectural photography, and its versatility and resulting quality of picture is unsurpassed.

Creating a sense of proportion
George Howard photographed in the magnificent hallway of Castle Howard, above. The side-lighting shows the intricate detail and the architectural quality of Vanbrugh's design. Included in the design was the window which allows a shaft of light to fall across the painting over the fireplace, a masterly touch in this masterpiece of English architecture. I asked George Howard to adopt a natural pose, since I was more concerned with recording the scene than with composing a picture.
MPP, wide-angle lens, 1/5 sec., f16, HP3.

Overcoming limited space
In this one-room flat in an industrial area, the home of a retired steel-worker, I used a wide-angle lens and placed the camera in the doorway to get a maximum view of the area. The center of interest was the fireplace, the illumination coming from a single window.
Hasselblad, 1/5 sec., f8, Royal-X.

The modern interior
In this photograph my aim was to convey the floating quality of these huge sections of concrete. They express tension and strength, and the manner in which they appear to hang in the air suggests depth and spaciousness.
MPP, 5 secs., f22, Ektachrome EX.

Eliminating movement

Architectural features are often obscured by people, who come between the photographer and subject. It is possible to eliminate moving figures with long exposures. Figures wearing dark clothes are less likely to record on film than those wearing light colors which appear as streaks. If the light source is very bright, use a neutral density filter so that you can increase the exposure time. In weak light conditions, you can use long exposures of several minutes. In the pictures on the right, people were moving quite quickly, so relatively short exposures were possible. Leaving a person standing still against blurred images of moving people can convey activity.

The entrance of the Natural History Museum, London, photographed with a normal exposure, 1/30 sec., f2.8.

For this shot of the same location I gave an exposure of 1/2 sec., f11. People are beginning to blur.

With the much longer exposure of 2 secs., f22, people are almost eliminated.
Hasselblad, FP4.

Lighting technique to maintain atmosphere
It was too dark in this cottage to record all the detail and pattern, so I used flash bounced off a white sheet next to a window so that all the light came from one direction and simulated sunlight. A wide-angle lens was used.
Leicaflex, 1/15 sec., f8, High-Speed Ektachrome.

Lighting technique for depth and composition
By using blinds and shutters in the richly-patterned hall shown left, I was able to place the emphasis on selected areas. The camera angle makes maximum use of linear perspective. Fully illuminated, the room may have overpowered the focal point — the girl — by its complex patterns and angles.
Hasselblad, 1/10 sec., f16, Ektachrome EX.

Use of existing conditions
The very conditions that limit space can often be used to advantage, as in the example, opposite, of reflections in an opulent Parisian restaurant. Space and size are increased and exaggerated by photographing mirrors within a mirror, to show the highly decorated interior.
Leicaflex, 1/15 sec., f8, High-Speed Ektachrome.

Isolating Details

A small area of a building, a detail such as a carved decoration or an ivy-covered wall, can often create a better impression or composition than a view of the whole, especially if the detail is framed by something in the foreground, an arch or doorway, for example.

Details of texture, pattern and form can tell us much about the basic structure of a building. In the subtle variations of texture in stone, we can see that a building is either massive and well-defended, intricately carved and gothic or machine-dressed and modern. Pattern is often evident in some basic part of the design, as in a row of evenly-spaced, identical windows or columns. It can be seen in the regular posts of a balustrade, or in an area of brickwork. Ceilings in churches frequently present intricate and beautiful patterns, as do the beams across the ceilings of old farmhouses and cottages. The bare framework of many iron or steel structures can form abstract patterns which look especially striking in silhouette.

As with pattern and texture, variations in form are determined largely by the building materials used. Concrete, for example, can be molded into thin membranes or shaped into unusual forms. Glass, on the other hand, is nearly always used as a flat rectangle, and its visual properties lie primarily in the way it responds to light. High-rise buildings are now usually faced with glass panels on thin, steel frames, creating dazzling patterns of light or clear reflections in which photographers can capture the mirror-images of other buildings.

Some of the most exquisite details of form in architecture are to be found in carved stonework. Relief work in stone gives an added dimension of depth, and in photographing relief carvings it is important to include this feeling of depth in areas of shade, by using the correct exposure and lighting. Here, the use of a tripod is essential so that the camera can be kept still for any length of time.

One system of photographing detail is to take a key picture of, say, a facade, and then take pictures of individual features, as both a record and an interpretation. Miniature cameras are perfectly suitable for getting quality in detail, provided that you use a fine grain film. Also, a variety of lenses is useful, and in particular a long-focus lens for the detail on ceilings and roof structures. The use of extension rings and bellows generally demands extra exposure time, which must be increased according to the inverse square law – for example, a triple extension will need nine times the normal exposure. Your aim in photographing any detail is to get a complete picture, so that the detail stands in its own right as a feature, yet at the same time creates the flavor of the entire structure, of which it is part.

Techniques to record detail
Here a number of lenses were used to photograph details of the building. Right: a long-focus lens telescopes a series of arches into a flat pattern, but gives an impressive view of the transept. Below: a wide-angle lens was used to photograph the repetition of columns and arches. Bottom left: the normal lens was used to photograph this doorway in natural side-light. Note the texture of the stone, and the linenfold carving. Center right: the same lens with existing side-light gives a fine, tonal quality to the silver candlesticks. Bottom right: a wide-angle lens with diffused light was used to photograph this medieval stone figure.

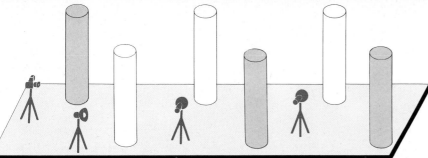

Light technique for high ceilings

To show the expanse of tracery in the Gothic lantern of Ely Cathedral I had to overcome extremes of contrast. I therefore calculated the exposure for window areas and used a small aperture. I filled in shadow areas with four bursts of flash, capping the lens after each exposure to give the flash time to recharge.

Hasselblad, wide-angle lens, total 20 secs., f22, Ektachrome EX.

Painting with light

With the technique called "painting with light," large, poorly-lit interiors can be photographed in detail. You set the camera shutter for an exposure of several minutes. Wearing dark clothes, and keeping out of the picture as much as possible, you illuminate areas of the interior with flashlight, moving around and pointing the light at each part in turn. The diagram, left, shows how one lamp can illuminate several areas.

141

Isolating Details

An eye for detail
Any environment contains
an almost inexhaustible
supply of fascinating detail.
Ideally, any detail should be
photographed as an entire
picture in its own right,
being part of the whole,
yet a separate entity.
Photographers quickly
adapt to photographing and
selecting details, and
develop an eye for balance,
harmony, contrast, color
and design — it is possible
to produce hundreds of
interesting pictures in a few
hours. By selecting a detail
the photographer can give
it greater significance than
was originally intended.
Detail and ornament were
often added to a building
by the builder or architect
as a kind of finishing touch
to the whole, or as an
intrinsic part of the design,
such as the bandstand
on the right. Usually,
details pass unnoticed by
most of us in everyday life.
If for no other reason, they
are worth photographing
as an architectural record
of our age, and also of our
preoccupations.

Photographing stained glass

This area of architectural photography can have disappointing results because of the conditions often encountered, and the technical problems involved. Many windows have wire frames to protect them from damage, and these become silhouetted on the image, especially in sunlight. Windows are frequently found in a dirty condition, or they are inaccessible, sometimes so high that they require the use of a long lens at an acute angle. For best results it is advisable to hang a white sheet behind the window to soften the light and to mask off areas with black paper to give richer intensity of color. If you are approaching the subject seriously, you will probably have to erect a scaffold frame to gain the right height. On the whole, an overcast day is best, if you want to avoid the trouble of hanging a white sheet, and masking the areas.

Using special effects

You can overcome some problems of light by using various techniques to simulate ideal conditions. The shot, left, of Ely Cathedral glass was taken from a high viewpoint, and the area masked with black paper. With the picture below, I wanted to achieve the shimmering quality of sunlight through the window, even though it was an overcast day. The effect was obtained by smearing vaseline very lightly over the lens, just where the image of the window passed through it. The impression of sunlight is further increased by the contrast of dark stone to the left, and warm stone surrounding the window.

Hasselblad, (left) long lens, 1 sec., f32; (right) 1/15 sec., f8, Ektachrome EX.

Nature

Everywhere you look you are confronted with an aspect of natural life and a wealth of photographic material. It may be found in a crevice between city paving stones, it may be in the wild and open countryside. Each picture you take will in some sense represent nature, especially in landscape photography where earth, sea and sky are the main images. But the term "nature photography" implies something more specific – the photographer of natural subjects is concerned with every detail of plant and animal life, and the camera can encourage you to develop a greater degree of awareness. Look for erosion in rocks and sand, for twisted boughs and shriveled leaves – these marks of passing time provide a great deal of nature's interest. You will not have to go far to find subjects for nature photography; even the largest city has a quota of natural life – trees, flowers, plants, birds, small animals, and of course zoological parks and gardens.

Rhythm is especially appropriate in nature photography – it can be regular, free flowing, but must have points of accent. Most plants, for instance, contain a balance of lines, planes, texture and color in the leaves and petals, although the relationship varies for each. If you are able to feel the rhythm of your subject you will have an idea of how to compose your picture – a thistle has an aggressive, sharp rhythm, the willow tree a gentle, flowing rhythm. Texture is extremely important in nature photography – think of the difference in texture between the bark of a tree and its foliage, between the fur of a cat and the scales of a fish. Always look at nature as if through the lens of your camera, remembering that one detail is often more effective than the whole.

When photographing animals, your camera technique will be largely dictated by the nature of your subject. Most animals are timid, so a fast film and shutter speed used with a long lens are often necessary; a camera with a quiet shutter will avoid frightening animals and drawing attention to yourself. Perhaps the most ideal way to photograph animals and birds is from a construction known as a "hide" which is explained in detail on pp. 148–149. Photographing wild animals requires patience and perseverance, but there are plenty of opportunities to take animal shots without the complications of a hide, long periods of waiting or arduous journeys. You will find considerable inspiration in parks, zoos and game reserves. Many people keep animals as pets, which can make excellent subjects since they are less inclined to be camera shy. Animal behavior, though, is unpredictable, and in this branch of photography failures are not infrequent, which is why the occasional outstanding success is the more satisfying.

Selective use of features
If you cannot eliminate the bars or wire in front of a cage the best plan is to make a feature of them as I did in the shot above. You will need a lot of patience to obtain a good position or expression and to get both the animal and the cage in focus. To overcome the natural caution of most animals, use a long-focus lens which will allow you to work from a suitable distance.
Leicaflex, long lens, 1/250 sec., f16, HP4.

Using focusing to advantage
This deer was in a game park protected by a wire fence. A 500 mm lens enabled me to lose the image of the wire by standing about 6 ft (1.8 m) from the fence and focusing on the animal some 60 ft (18 m) away. The fence thus became no more than a slight diffusing screen and the overall impression is of a close-up in apparently unrestricted surroundings. I selected an open aperture, to limit the depth of field. Had I stopped down to, say, f11, the wire mesh would have become visible and the background would have been in focus.
Leicaflex, extra-long lens, 1/500 sec., f5.6, HP4.

Restrictions of close-up
The problem with photographing most animals in captivity is that they are usually behind glass, wire fencing or bars. You can overcome this by pushing the camera as close as possible to the barrier as I did with the wire in front of this rabbit. This wire, however, comes into focus as it diminishes into the background. If I had taken the shot with the camera parallel to the wire and had used an open aperture, the wire would have disappeared.
Hasselblad, 1/125 sec., f8, Kodak Tri-X.

Using a small aperture
Another method of avoiding a wire fence between you and the subject is to stop right down. In this way the center of the lens can be used to capture the image through one of the openings in the wire, provided that the subject is a reasonable distance away. I used a long-focus lens and stopped down to f11 to get this shot of a Great Hornbill in a zoo.
Leicaflex, 1/60 sec., f11, FP4.

Photographing domestic pets
Unless the animal is your own, it is best to work in co-operation with the owner who will be familiar with its habits. The pose and expression change so quickly that you will have to be extremely alert, re-focusing constantly and watching for possible expressions and positions. This shot of a champion cat, left, was taken with flash, arranged to give a broad, reflective light source for even illumination.

Hasselblad, long lens, electronic flash, f8, Ektachrome EX.

Anticipating the subject
When photographing wild life you should always set the aperture and shutter speed in advance. The African lion, left, was photographed on a game reserve. It had been sleeping, and was aroused by our approach. I had previously focused on the lion, but re-focused as we got closer, and was able to get this shot the moment he rose to investigate. Although in the shade of trees, his head was lit by a shaft of light. The whole thing took only seconds.

Hasselblad, long lens, 1/500 sec., f5.6, High-Speed Ektachrome.

Photographing evasive subjects

With very timid and evasive animals, it is useful to have an experienced naturalist to assist you, as I had when photographing this tree frog. Finding the frog was a problem because it was camouflaged by its surroundings, and was difficult to separate from the background. To obtain a good image size I used a 135 mm lens at maximum extension on a Leicaflex, with the widest aperture, and a shutter speed of 1/2000 sec. This combination gave a very small depth of field, and thus separated the frog from the background. I focused by moving the camera, not the lens, holding the frog in focus and waiting for an interesting movement. This technique of isolating by eliminating the depth of field can be used for a variety of similar subjects. A fast shutter speed allowed me to arrest movement and helped to prevent camera shake — a great problem when hand holding a camera fitted with a long lens.

Using a Hide

You can obtain really excellent pictures from the refuge of a hide – close-up shots of animals and, in particular, action shots of birds; most keen ornithologists prefer a hide for bird observation and photography. On the larger nature reserves and bird sanctuaries permanent hides are often built.

If you wish to build a collapsible hide for individual purposes, you can make a simple frame covered by a stout material. Use, for example, a durable cotton or light canvas material, colored green or brown to blend with the surroundings. Make the cover with two pieces of this fabric, one measuring 16 ft (4.8 m) by 5 ft (1.5 m), the other 4 ft (1.2 m) by 5 ft (1.5 m). Sew the long side of the first to the short side of the second, leaving 8 ft (2.4 m) at one end and 4 ft (1.2 m) at the other. This will produce a box-like tent to be placed over a simple frame. Make the frame with five lengths of stout wood each 6 ft (1.8 m) long, and four lengths each 4 ft 6 ins (1.4 m) long, securing four of the long pieces in the ground to form a square with 3 ft 9 ins (1.1 m) between each corner, lashing the four, shorter

lengths across the top, the fifth long piece providing the diagonal. Build your hide as quickly and quietly as possible and at least 24 hours before use, to allow animals or birds to get accustomed to it.

Because of the long hours of waiting involved, the interior of the hide should be made reasonably comfortable, with a canvas folding stool, and supplies of food and drink. You can either cut an opening for the camera lens, or insert a zip fastener that will enable you to make a hole at any height within the hide. The hide will be fairly dark inside, and give you the feeling that the light outside is much brighter than it really is, so make frequent checks with the meter for correct exposure. All shiny surfaces and bright clothing should be avoided. A lens hood is an essential item, as is a tripod, a cable release and a camera with a quiet shutter, a quality now possessed by the majority of modern, miniature cameras. The best nature pictures are obtained by photographers who make a study of birds and animals in order to be more familiar with their habits and to anticipate their movements.

Bird photography from a permanent hide
The interior of a permanent hide, above, built in a nature reserve. The site was chosen to allow viewers close observation of many species of birds, both indigenous and migratory, at a place where rare birds are frequently recorded. Being a permanent construction, the spy apertures are larger than those of an amateur hide. Most birds tend to display regular patterns of behavior, always feeding from the same patch, or using the same post or branch when alighting, especially when near the nest. In bird photography you will need to anticipate behavioral patterns, but it is essential to be selective and to be patient. I was lucky to get this shot of a beautiful Snowy Owl, an Arctic visitor to Britain, using a Leicaflex fitted with a 500 mm lens and fast shutter speed of 1/500 sec. at f8 on HP4.

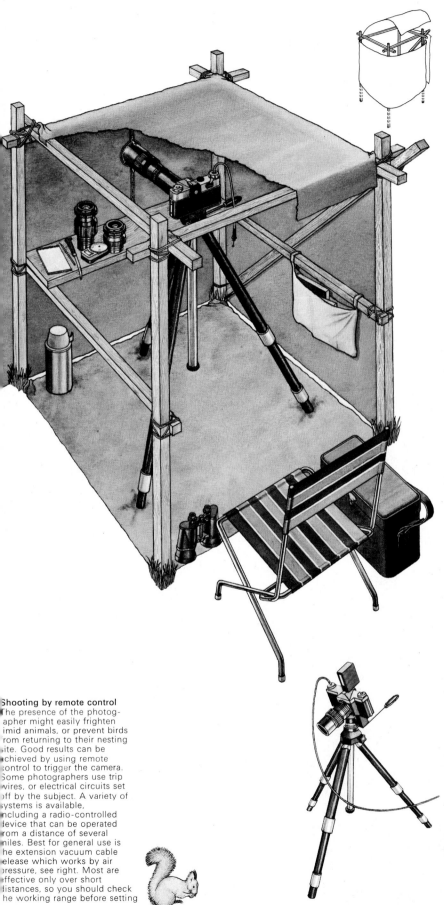

Equipping the hide

Crouching in a small, prefabricated hide can be arduous and painful if long hours are to be spent waiting for a good shot. One essential is a folding canvas stool, and preferably one with a backrest. Refreshments, while not vital, make life much easier. Remember to take the right kind of clothes, and anticipate a change in the weather. All observers of wild life carry binoculars, reference books for species identification, maps, a notebook and pencil, a bag to carry equipment, and a case for lenses, film, filters etc. Take a sharp knife in case you need to cut foliage for added camouflage though birds and animals quickly lose their fear and suspicion of a hide. One trick is to enter the hide with an assistant. When the assistant leaves, the birds usually assume that the hide is empty.

Close-ups without a hide

When I discovered this nest at the top of a hedge that had been recently trimmed, I made no attempt to photograph it because the birds had already been disturbed by the hedge cutting, and might have deserted the nest. About five days later I climbed an adjacent tree and shot with a 250 mm lens from above. The following day I placed a tripod among some bean poles, until the birds became familiar with it. I then mounted a camera with a 400 mm lens and an extension vacuum cable release. With the release I was able to conceal myself some distance from the camera and nest, and shoot each time the adult bird returned.

Hasselblad, 1/500 sec., f8, Kodak Tri-X (both pictures).

Shooting by remote control

The presence of the photographer might easily frighten timid animals, or prevent birds from returning to their nesting site. Good results can be achieved by using remote control to trigger the camera. Some photographers use trip wires, or electrical circuits set off by the subject. A variety of systems is available, including a radio-controlled device that can be operated from a distance of several miles. Best for general use is the extension vacuum cable release which works by air pressure, see right. Most are effective only over short distances, so you should check the working range before setting up your camera.

Flowers

Such is the versatility of the camera that you might easily be confused by the abundance of choice when photographing flowers – not only in the variety of flowers themselves, but in the ways of presenting them. You might, for example, choose the close-up shot, revealing the secret heart of the flower, the minute drops of moisture, so that the single bloom becomes a complete picture in itself. Photographs intended to convey strict botanical information need this description of fine detail. On the other hand, you might settle for a more pictorial type of shot in an attempt to capture the character of the flower. This can be achieved by using a wide-open aperture so that only the bloom stays sharp, while the remainder goes out of focus to make a perfect background, since too much extra detail detracts from the focal point and the subject.

The best time to photograph flowers, away from the controlled environment of the studio, is the early morning when they are freshest. Avoid photographing them at midday, or in the afternoon, if it is hot and they have become limp. Furthermore strong sunlight makes for dark shadows that might break up the perfect shape of the flower. A soft and diffused sunlight is best.

Wild flowers look more attractive in their natural environment, especially seen in profusion. Look at a patch of rough grass in the countryside and you will see how it is dotted all over with different colors – even in the dominant red of the poppy field there is a variety of yellows, blues and greens.

One of the main problems with flower photography is that of movement, especially where you are using a close-up lens and extension rings. Movement can be overcome, to a great extent, by supporting the flower on a strong but hidden wire, or by partially enclosing the plant in a three-sided box to shield it from the wind. Essential equipment includes a tripod, a cable release and, ideally, a 35 mm single-lens reflex camera.

The natural environment
Wild flowers are best seen in their normal habitat like those on the facing page. It is quite rare to find such a concentration of different wild flowers with a variety of powerful colors in the temperate climate of Britain. The dominant colors are red and green, but they are pleasingly relieved here and there by yellow, and patches of pale blue forget-me-nots. I used a 250 mm lens so that I could accentuate the feeling of texture and pattern, focusing on the middle distance.
Hasselblad, 1/250 sec., f5.6, Ektachrome EX.

Selecting the area of interest
I used a normal lens, but with a triple extension tube, which enabled me to concentrate on the stamens and style of the tulip, far left, framed by an interesting pattern of color. To prevent any movement by wind, I shielded the tulip with a plywood screen.
Hasselblad, 1 sec., f22, High-Speed Ektachrome.

With the lily, top center, I wanted to photograph the entire flower, so I placed a dark blue background immediately behind it to prevent other shapes from interfering and to achieve maximum definition. A white reflector was used to soften the shadows.
Hasselblad, long lens and extension tubes, 1/125 sec., f22, High-Speed Ektachrome.

I took the rose photograph, top left, after a shower of rain, when flowers look freshest. I chose a camera with a normal lens, with which the closest focus is 10 ins (25 cm).
Leicaflex, 1/250 sec., f8, High-Speed Ektachrome.

To concentrate many daisies in a small area, center left, I used a wide-angle lens attachment with a 150 mm lens, and selected a wide aperture for the special effect.
Hasselblad, 1/250 sec., f4, High-Speed Ektachrome.

The ornamental vase, far left, was shot through a steamed-up window to obtain a softer and more romantic picture.
Leicaflex, 1/250 sec., f5.6, Ektachrome EX.

By shooting at a 45° angle from waist-level, I was able to isolate the orange flowers, left, from a complicated background.
Leica M2, 1/250 sec., f8, Kodachrome II.

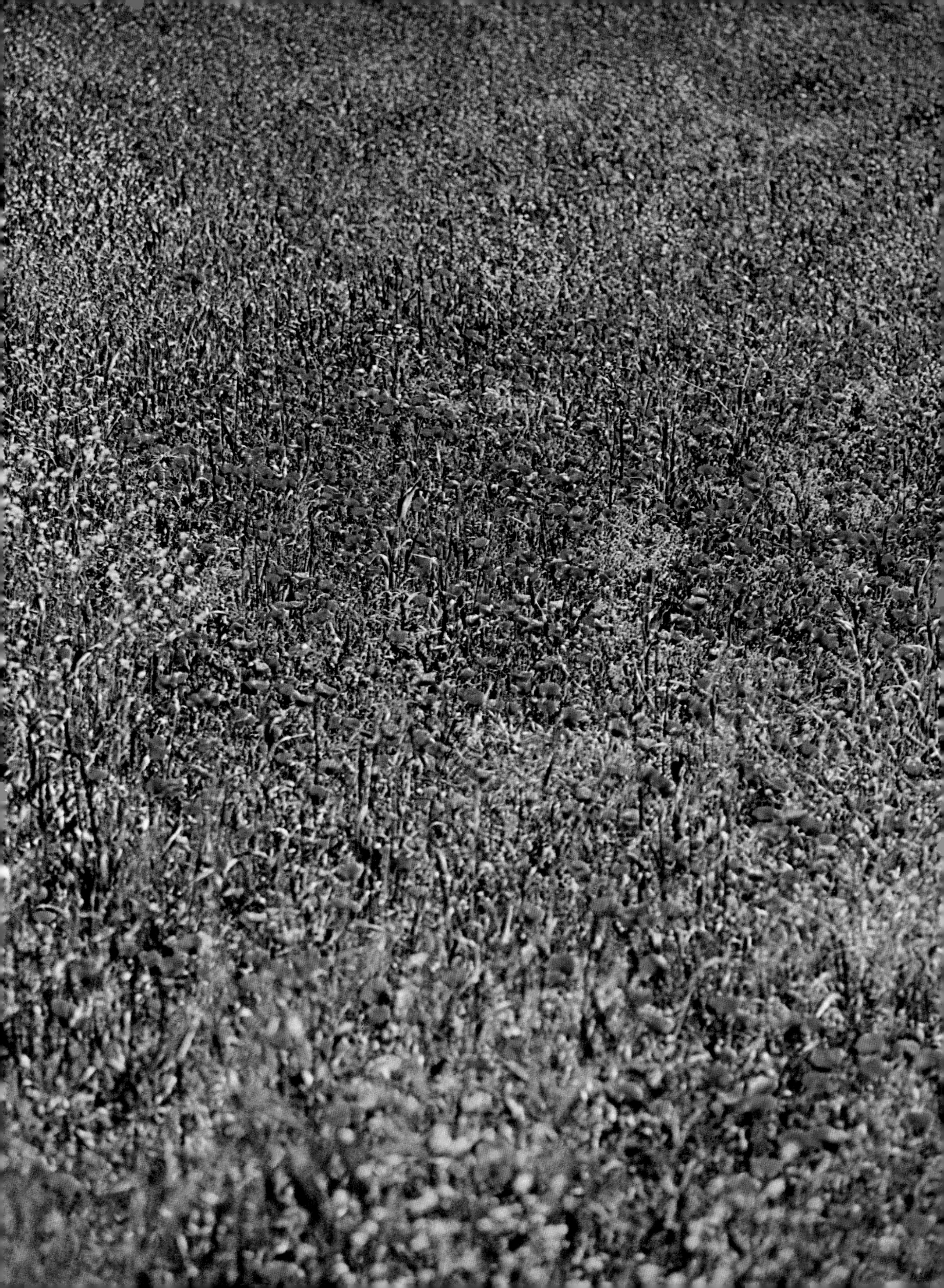

Gardens

Ideally, pictures of gardens should be composed in such a way as to capture the feeling and atmosphere as a whole. You may be tempted to photograph only the spectacular highlights – the brilliant colors of flower beds or decorative shrubs, for example, but remember that the surroundings and the layout are just as important: the paths, the trees, the lawns and garden architecture should all be considered. While the main subject might indeed be a flower bed or a statue, it must be shown as part of the entire concept.

Compose your subject to relate to the foreground, the middle distance and the background. Thoroughly explore all the possibilities and angles before deciding on a particular aspect. Gardens are usually planned with meticulous care, and the layout of the garden should help you decide your best approach. Arrange the position of your camera so that some feature of the garden leads the eye into the picture. Paths, hedges, shrubberies and fences all help to frame and concentrate the focal point.

The early morning is often the best time to photograph a garden because the light reveals the texture, and the flowers are at their freshest. If possible, choose a position where the colors blend with each other, or where one color can dominate. The direction of the light, the camera angle and the choice of lens are all important in capturing the character of a garden – a wide-angle lens can encompass an entire small garden, or give extra dimension to a landscaped garden with broad, sweeping lawns. Try low viewpoints or, alternatively, high positions where the entire plan of the garden can be seen.

In most cases, a tripod and cable release allow you to stop down for good depth of field and long exposure. Fine grain black and white film gives clarity and records subtle detail. Red and green filters can lighten foliage and assist with separation of tones and hues. A polarizing filter helps to darken the sky in color pictures, while a lens hood will help overcome flare, especially when you are shooting toward light. Don't forget that you can add your own center of interest should one be lacking, a gardener positioned in the middle distance, for example, or a familiar garden object such as a wheelbarrow.

Copying botanical specimens

For reference purposes, close-up photographs of garden specimens can be taken by placing the plant on white card or on a light box, to show the detail of the plant's structure. If you use a light box, add overhead or reflected light to give form to the specimen, and shoot from above, masking the surrounding area with black card to reduce flare. Close-up equipment may be needed with a normal lens. *Hasselblad, long lens and double extension tube, 1/15 sec., f32, Kodak Tri-X.*

Finding the obvious viewpoint
Any landscaped garden has been designed to be seen from
specific viewpoints, so search until you find them. Here the
designers deliberately included water so I made it a principal
feature of the shot.
Hasselblad, wide-angle lens, 1/60 sec., f22, FP4.

Variety in Natural Forms

If there are people who devote an entire lifetime to the study of one particular species of beetle, or type of flower – and there are such people – it seems obvious to note that the photographer has before him a vast wealth of material that he can never hope to explore fully. Photographing nature is endlessly fascinating, for it is unique at every moment in time. Ask yourself what each tree or leaf would look like from a different viewpoint or in a different light.

The photographer can enhance the beauty of nature and convey it to the viewer by his perception and selection. Consider, for instance, the varieties of texture and pattern. Striking examples can be found in high contrast shots of mushrooms and toadstools viewed from below; scale patterns in buds can be interesting, especially in close-up; corn provides textural contrast between the shiny, sculptured kernels and the flat, ribbed leaves and woody stalk.

By the seashore, erosion causes pattern in sand and rock, and lines made by the cracking of dry mud. Kelp, weeds and lichen add powerful textural contrast to rock surfaces; intricate line patterns can be seen in minerals, fossils and shells. Pebbles in water are distorted by refraction, and by their polished texture, and are highlighted where the sun catches them. For objects below the water level, rather than the reflections of things above, be sure to use a direct overhead viewpoint. Driftwood often possesses strong, sculptural forms, so do the weathered trunks of trees.

Trees have a natural grace of form whether they are young and slender or old and stately, but each has an individual character of leaf shape, bark texture and overall coloring. Winter trees seen in high contrast or in silhouette make intricate patterns, especially with a neutral sky as a background. On the other hand you can concentrate on a single aspect, such as a solitary leaf, slightly transparent where the light shines through it.

When photographing garden flowers, you should use the most perfect specimens available, but with the uncultivated aspects of nature it is often an imperfection that provides interest and reality. It is this "natural" quality found in all wild life that becomes the most important element in your pictures.

Using light techniques to record detail
A plump, healthy specimen of an uninvited guest fungus on an apple tree, above. I waited for the right angle of sunlight and placed the camera and two reflectors in the best position to record the detail.
Hasselblad, long lens and extension tube, 1/2 sec., f32, Ektachrome EX.

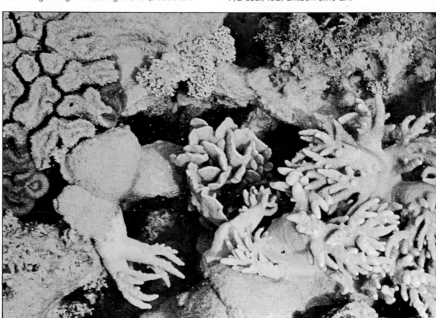

Photographing nature under water
Coral on Australia's Great Barrier Reef. Using a glass-bottomed box is the only successful method of taking underwater shots without a special camera. Surface reflections can be a problem, but they can be avoided by using a black umbrella to obliterate extraneous light.
Leicaflex, 1/30 sec., f5.6, High-Speed Ektachrome.

Abstract patterns in nature
Pattern, texture, subtle colors and strong shadows help to convey the nature of the bamboo thicket, above, and the density of its growth.
Leica M3, 1/125 sec., f16, Ektachrome EX.

Contrast of pattern and texture
Creeper-covered rocks photographed in evening light to show the random pattern and give depth to the picture, below.
Leicaflex, 1/250 sec., f8, High-Speed Ektachrome.

Environment and time of day
The autumnal, golden fleece of Epping Forest near London, shown above, photographed in the early morning when the soft, diffused light best shows the natural contortions of roots and trunks. By focusing on one gnarled tree in the foreground, I was able to suggest the age and character of the beech forest.
Leicaflex, wide-angle lens, 1/125 sec., f8, Ektachrome EX.

Selecting detail from the whole
The angle of the light, the density of the shadows and the color contrast make this red maple appear as if on fire. By concentrating the camera on a small area it enabled me to reveal the beauty of the tree in a more striking way than if I had photographed it in its entirety.
Leicaflex, 1/125 sec., f11, High-Speed Ektachrome.

155

Special Techniques

By experimenting with techniques, photographers have made considerable and quite unique contributions to science, to art, and to the way in which we see things. The eye could never fully comprehend the movements of a horse's legs until the camera "froze" the action.

Stroboscopic photography allows us to analyze movement by freezing, as it were, some of the laws of physics. Thus we are able to capture the movements of a fly to record its wing beats, to examine the structure of a falling drop of water, to see the shock waves in the wake of a speeding bullet. Photomicrography, where the camera is coupled to the microscope, enlarges an infinitesimal world for all to see.

With these special techniques, photographers have created an imaginative and individual approach to the preoccupation with novelty, the constant search for new effects and ways of presenting the traditional image. To this end, photographers have borrowed ideas from painters, scientists, movie makers, television producers, and vice versa. The film industry has only recently adopted the technique of front projection (shown on this page), one that still photographers have been using for years.

The term "special techniques" might imply both a specialist knowledge and specialist equipment, but exciting results can be obtained by very simple means, such as using a slower shutter speed than recommended, or by "using the wrong film at the right time," for example exposing artificial light film in daylight, or using high contrast document film for portraits. The use of such techniques as superimposing negatives or transparencies, photographing on infra-red film through colored filters and diffusing disks, using photomontage, or distorting images with lenses or the darkroom enlarger, have all been called "trick photography" by critics who believe that photography should be purely representational. In fact, there are no tricks in photography, only techniques that help you to express your ideas further through the medium of the camera.

While it is true that certain types of technical equipment are expensive, rental charges are usually quite reasonable, and camera clubs buy equipment for the use of their members. In the following pages we show some of the easier techniques, using a limited amount of equipment.

Projecting images
Images and patterns can be projected onto objects or people to produce unusual effects which can be photographed. The pattern can take up the shape of the object or person, but usually it destroys form, and commonplace articles then possess an ethereal and often surreal quality. While not essential, a darkened room will give you the most vivid results. Start by projecting a collection of slide onto a screen, selecting those with the strongest images and magnification. Patterns such a pictures of leaves, flowers, geometric designs in architecture, and so on work well. Quite startling effects can be achieved by projecting shots c people onto a model or portrait subject. The subject can be close to a wall or screen so that both the subject and background are covered with the same pattern. Alternatively, you can place the subject some distance from the background, projecting the pattern onto it at an oblique angle, at the same time projecting a different and independent image onto the background. In color photography you will have to use the correct type of film to re-photograph the image; usually, artificial light stock will give the best results. If color is too red, or too blue, you should correct with compensating filters. The pictures on this spread show how you can project different patterns onto a figure, arranging the pose as well as the pattern — the shape that th figure makes within the frame is just as important as the pattern itself.

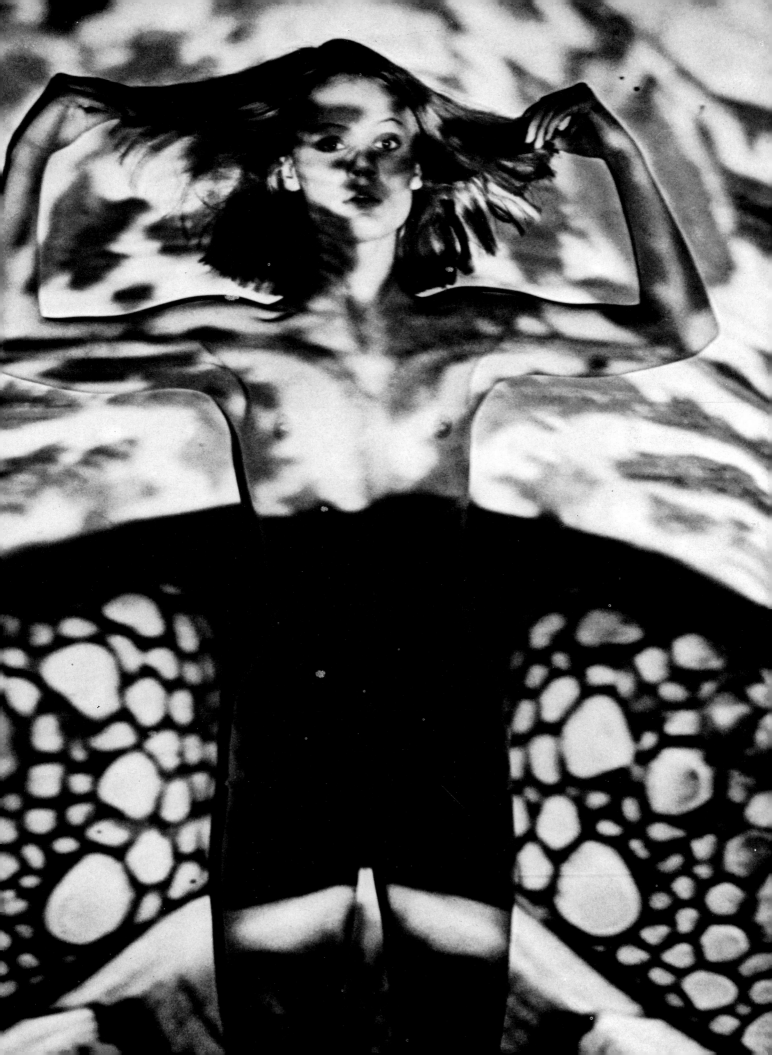

The Multiple Image

Multiple image with silhouette
The main shape is the straight-forward silhouette shot of a young boy's head, with the superimposed photograph of children playing. These two 35 mm slides were put into separate projectors. The projector lamps were matched to give accurate color. The large head was first projected onto a silvered screen, so that the intensity of the white background would obliterate any overlapping image when I projected the second slide onto the head. When the set-up was complete, as shown below, I photographed the result. This shot was taken for use on a book jacket.

Hasselblad, 1/15 sec., f5.6, Ektachrome EX.

Merging images together
In the technique used opposite the images are made to blend together. I used a shot of a window, another of a girl's head and shoulders and a third of a house and driveway. First the window was projected onto the screen but a dodger was used to leave an area blank into which the head of the girl could be projected. The bottom half of this second transparency was masked so that the house and driveway could be added, projected from the third projector. All three images were arranged for size and position on the screen, and the diagram below shows the final layout of the equipment. The image of the house was too bright for the atmosphere I wished to create, so I placed a ground glass slide between the transparency and the projector bulb, which gave me the required level of illumination. During exposure, the pictures were vignetted to avoid any obvious join of the images. A series of exposures was made, some of them through colored gelatin filters to increase the overall effect of a single image.

Leicaflex, long lens, 1/8 sec., f5.6, Ektachrome EX.

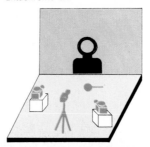

Double exposure
The artist Patrick Proctor, photographed against a black velvet background, left, so that all extraneous light was totally absorbed. I first positioned him, then marked the area he occupied on the camera screen with a pencil. After taking the shot, I re-positioned him and gave an identical exposure as for the previous shot, so that the two images were perfectly exposed on one piece of film. Although this example was made with two exposures, you can make a considerable number — I have made as many as 22 exposures on a single piece of film.

Hasselblad, electronic flash, f22, Ektachrome EX.

Negative and positive
To make the composite image above I used a negative picture of a puddle of water on a wooden floor, projected onto a silvered screen. The area surrounding the face on another transparency was painted out to give a solid black background. This was placed in a separate projector, and the appropriate sized image also projected onto the silvered screen. The whole image was then re-photographed.

Rolleiflex, 1/2 sec., f8, Ektachrome EX.

The Multiple Image

Reflected images

This picture is composed to incorporate both the image and the reflection of a girl beside a polished, plastic table. The same type of arrangement can be made using ordinary mirrors, or any highly reflective surface. The technique is used in some still life groups to give an added dimension. Bouncing all the light off a ceiling or white wall will usually give a good reflection.

Rolleiflex, wide-angle lens, 1/60 sec., f8, Kodak Tri-X.

Front projection

The technique of front projection relies on the careful placing and illumination of the subject and the image background. The picture of Venice, bottom, was projected through a two-way mirror onto a large screen with a highly reflective surface. The figure was then placed in position, about 20 ft (6–7 m) in front of the screen. I lined up the camera with the same reflective mirror, correcting the position of the subject. The background image showed up brightly on the screen, while the area of the projected image falling on the subject was not discernible; he was completely silhouetted against the background. I then illuminated him separately by using a diffused floodlight. The subject's position and the placing of the flood were so arranged that none of the light reached the front projection screen behind the subject. The final positions are shown below.

Hasselblad, 1/30 sec., f8, Plus-X.

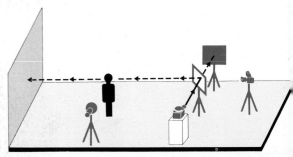

Splitting the image
To achieve the effect above I used a simple masking device made from a filmholder positioned in front of the camera lens. Two slides were necessary, one slotted into the holder from above and the other from below, so that they met in front of the center of the lens. The girl was posed on the rocks and with the top slide removed I exposed for the top half of the photograph. I then replaced the slide, moved the girl away and removed the bottom slide, as shown right. In this way the bottom half of the picture was exposed, but I made sure I used exactly the same exposure as for the top half. Sometimes a photograph of this type has either a black or white line across it. This indicates a gap between or overlap of the two slides which have been incorrectly positioned.
Hasselblad, 1/125 sec., f16 Kodak Tri-X.

Night Photography

Photographers have always been attracted by scenes at night especially when special events such as a firework display or the colors of a fairground are included. Darkness imposes considerable limitations, however, so night shots are best taken at dusk, just before darkness sets in, when the shape and form of the subject remains easily discernible. If you shoot your picture in total darkness, you end up with a picture comprised mainly of harsh highlights or burnt-out highlights with little shadow detail.

The length of exposure depends upon the amount of highlight or illumination and the area affected by reflection. In wet weather, for example, normally dark areas become much more reflective, so you will need to decrease the exposure, and make a careful balance between highlight and shadow. In most night photography, you have to experiment by exposing extra pictures one stop either side of your calculated exposure. The actual intensity of light will determine the factors, and exposures can vary from 1/30 second to about five minutes. Beyond five minutes, you often

only succeed in burning-out the highlights without any noticeable improvement in the shadows, due to reciprocity failure.

Color shots pose special problems, especially when subjects contain a mixture of daylight and artificial light such as street scenes at dusk, airports, and floodlit buildings. As day fades into night the color changes, and the artificial light dominates. Using daylight type film makes artificial light appear warmer; using artificial light film causes daylight to appear bluer. Both can be very effective. You can even simulate night by using artificial light film in daylight and under-exposing several stops or, in the case of black and white, by using neutral density or red filters.

With the very fast films now available you can photograph almost everything, even in the most obscured conditions – "if you can see it, you can photograph it." Indeed, by using the recently developed image intensifier, which employs a cathode ray tube, you can photograph images which cannot be seen by the naked eye because they appear to be in darkness.

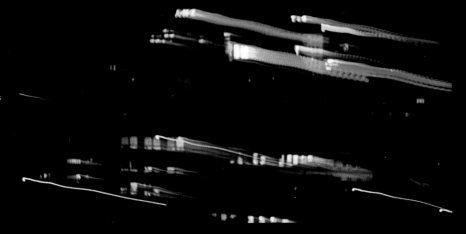

Atmosphere with movement and light
Early evening at Nottingham Goose Fair, above, a shot taken with
artificial light film and slow exposure. If I had used "correct"
exposure on daylight film it would have appeared as a dark
pattern with none of the fairground atmosphere, but by using
tungsten film in weak daylight the lights appear warmer because
of the blue-gray background. The slow exposure helped the
feeling of movement.

Hasselblad, 2 secs., f16, EHB Ektachrome.

Using daylight film at dusk
A landscape picture of the Mountains of Mourne, left, shot on
daylight film uprated to 250 ASA. For further effect I increased
development by one stop during processing. By this method I was
able to give added warmth to the light in the windows and retain
detail in the shadows without losing the impression of a night
photograph. In fact it was still quite light.

Hasselblad, 1/8 sec., f5.6, High-Speed Ektachrome.

Moving the camera for special effects
To create a more interesting effect than a straightforward
photograph, I panned the camera across the subject, right, for an
exposure of one second. This technique can often be used to add
interest when the subject is rather static, or mundane. Including
the reflections in windows or puddles is another way of making a
lively shot from a static subject.

Leicaflex, 1 sec., f8, EHB Ektachrome.

Action Photography

The technique of stopping or "freezing" a fast moving object is the unique province of photography.

The shutter speed, the position of the camera, the angle of the shot, the use of flash, the technique of panning, each describe action and movement in a particular way. The slow speed, panned shot, which can show the rhythm of the action, works most effectively in color. The panned shot, where the image is maintained in one position and the background becomes blurred, or the shot where the camera remains still and the subject image becomes blurred, each give a feeling of action. This type of photograph can be achieved with any kind of camera, from the very cheapest to the most expensive studio equipment.

Your approach to an action shot should be to decide the purpose of the action and the most interesting movement that sums up the whole picture. You will also need to anticipate the precise moment, when a swimmer will hit the water, for example, or when a horse will clear a fence. If the subjects are under your control you can plan a trial run. In panning, where the camera is moved in the same direction as the subject to keep it in the frame, you should try and shoot against a background of combined highlight and shadow, so that the highlights spread and streak over the dark area, creating an impression of movement. Obviously, a clear blue sky, or any uniform surface, is a poor background for a panned image.

The amount of picture area given to the subject is a further factor in maintaining the required impression. The balance between the moving subject and the static area must be carefully judged: you must decide whether it is better that your subject is entering the picture or just about to leave it.

The use of perspective can help to emphasize movement, so can the zoom lens, the wide-angle lens, or the simple technique of twisting the camera angle to move the image out of the vertical or horizontal plane, a device often used to give added conviction to action shots.

Illusion of speed
The aim of the shot opposite was to reproduce a realistic impression of power and speed with the train approaching the camera head on. I decided that a simple approach would give me the most effective result, and by using a wide-angle lens at ground level, I was able to heighten the perspective for greater force and impact. The camera was supported on a tripod, about 20ft (6–7 m) from the train and in between the rails. I made some experimental shots with the train coming straight towards me, jumping out of the way at the last moment. I discovered that the rapidly enlarging image of the approaching train obliterated the "speed lines" and therefore gave little impression of movement. I finally arranged for the train to be reversed at maximum speed and made an exposure of 1/15 sec. The resulting picture was used for an advertisement, and won several awards.
Hasselblad, wide-angle lens, 1/15 sec., f16, Kodak Tri-X.

Panning the camera
When panning, the camera follows the movement and direction of the object. Hold the camera at taking level, and focus at the point where you estimate the object will be when directly in front of you. As the subject moves past you follow its movement by swinging your body at the waist, pressing the shutter when the subject reaches the point focused on and continuing the movement through.

The diagram above illustrates the sequence. The shutter speed is determined by the speed of the object. For example, a walking figure could be shot at 1/15 sec. while a fast car might need 1/125 sec. Generally, the slower the speed, the greater the blur. The picture of the man on the bicycle, left, is a typical panned shot.
Rolleiflex, 1/30 sec., f16, Kodak Tri-X.

Taking an action sequence

This is relatively easy with the camera permanently focused at the point where the action is taking place. Try and choose a position that gives you an uncluttered background, use the right focal length of lens for the most convenient image size, study the action to give yourself an idea of movement and composition, and anticipate the vital moment, which in this case of a softball match was the split second before impact. In such instances of fast action pictures in sequence it is a good plan to have another loaded camera to hand. It can take valuable time to load a new film.

Action Photography

Using color to convey motion

Color can show the speed and movement of an object while creating beautiful and often exciting patterns and effects, sometimes spreading and dispersing the image. Also the impression of movement can be considerably exaggerated. I photographed this sequence of canoes from different viewpoints, panning the camera more slowly than if I had wanted to retain a defined image. For example, I would have obtained a sharp image at 1/30 sec., but at 1/2 sec. a fairly abstract pattern was recorded with a minimum of definition. The technique can be used on almost any subject at any angle, from a child coming head first toward the camera down a slide, to a person walking across the picture plane. A 35 mm camera used with slow color film is ideal.

Deliberate blur
By panning at a relatively slow speed to register a blur, although fast enough to record a fairly defined image, I was able to capture the excitement of the cycle race. The angle of the cyclist helps the illusion of speed.
Leicaflex, 1/30 sec., f11, High-Speed Ektachrome.

Arresting color in motion

This shot was taken with a telephoto lens at a shutter speed of 1/1000 sec. after I had decided the spot where the trotting horse would appear most animated. The picture captures the movement, the atmosphere and muted color, showing that it is possible to take any action picture in color, even in poor conditions. The dramatic action of this sport is further emphasized by the perspective, the concentration of the man and the horse's breath.

Leicaflex, telephoto lens, 1/1000 sec., f5.6, High-Speed Ektachrome.

Judging the essence of the action

A horse, when it jumps, approaches the fence at speed, slows its stride to judge the right angle and height, then takes off. I took a trial shot to practice the panning action, and to place the horse and rider in the best position within the frame. I chose a low viewpoint (in a ditch) where the camera was almost at ground level. To take the picture on the left I panned slightly behind the horse, following through on the movement, capturing the exact moment he was above the fence. I chose a shutter speed that made the background blur, yet retained its character. The low angle heightened the position of the horse, so that he occupied the middle of the picture frame.

Leicaflex, 1/125 sec., f11, Ektachrome EX.

Using Flash

Flash is a means of conveying a large quantity of concentrated light to locations where it is not normally available, or for use in conditions where studio lighting would cause problems. Since the introduction of magnesium powder, flash light has become a necessary item of equipment for every serious photographer.

Unfortunately, most modern cameras still have a flashgun "hot-shoe" immediately above the lens which, for the majority of photographs, is the worst possible position as it produces a hard, flat light. It is also the reason for that phenomenon common to amateur flash pictures known as "red-eye," caused by the light traveling along the lens axis to be reflected in the eyes of the people in the picture, giving the eyes an unnatural glow. This effect and also that of flat lighting is easily avoided by placing the flash source at an angle of about 45° to the camera and the subject. Better still is the technique of reflecting (or "bouncing") light off a wall or ceiling for a more diffused directional light, which will give modeling without destroying form.

Electronic flash units produce light in flashes of very short duration, and experience is needed to judge the right amount for a given subject. This is one of the few drawbacks of flash as a light source – you cannot see the results in advance. Some electronic flash units have modeling lamps attached to provide a guide to the size and position of shadow areas, but this light does not correspond in intensity. Also, the short duration of flash light can only be measured with a flash meter, or a suitable distance/f stop calculator.

The great advantage of electronic flash is that the light is consistent, whereas daylight is constantly changing in color and intensity. Flash bulbs, however, are not all matched exactly to daylight, so for accuracy you may need to use compensation filters.

Another advantage of flash over other light sources is its combination of high speed and intense illumination. The speed is much greater than that of a mechanical camera shutter, and varies from 1/300 to 1/5000 second. Special units with speeds of a millionth of a second are easy to rent. Because of the intensity of flash illumination, you can usually work with small apertures, f16 to f64, thus gaining depth of field.

Flash can be mixed with other forms of lighting, especially daylight, where it can be used to fill in shadow areas. Conversely, where the subject is lit by flash, daylight can be used to fill in shadows. Again, experience is needed to judge accurately the effect you wish to achieve. Many professional photographers take preliminary shots on instant picture film for a preview of the subject.

The most expensive type of electronic flash incorporates a photo-electric cell, and enables you to synchronize a number of separate units for illumination of large set-ups without an excess of cable, or to give a great deal of light in a very limited space.

The lightest and most portable form of light is the long-established flashbulb, of which there are several types and classes. The main types are the single bulb and the cube unit containing four quick-change bulbs. The bulbs are mostly designed for daylight and are subdivided for use with varying shutter speeds, i.e. slow, medium, medium-fast and FP (for synchronization with focal-plane shutter cameras).

Localized flash

In the shot on the left I used a small quantity of flash to highlight the face of the girl. The exposure was calculated to make the background seem much darker than it really was. Flash was bounced off a reflective umbrella.

Hasselblad, electronic flash, f16, Kodak Tri-X.

Simulating sunlight

The challenge in the picture on the right was to give the impression of sunlight, although the sky was overcast. I used a small portable generator to power the electronic flash equipment since electricity was not available. The equipment was set up as shown in the diagram above. The exposure was calculated for the shadow area, leaving the highlights to remain bright. The flash reflected through the trees has given the effect of setting sun. This effect can be achieved with any type of flash, but if you use a small power pack you must wait for weaker light conditions to achieve the right degree of balance.

Linhof, electronic flash, f16, Kodak Tri-X.

Simulating existing light

Flash was needed in this picture, left, to fulfill a number of different requirements: to give additional overall light in order to define the people; to retain the background yet give slight added light to the subject; to give the impression that light comes from the conventional source (the table lamps, for instance) and to give additional atmosphere. I used 6 studio electronic flashes, and bounced the light off the walls and ceiling of the room.

Hasselblad, electronic flash, f16, Kodak Tri-X.

Using Flash

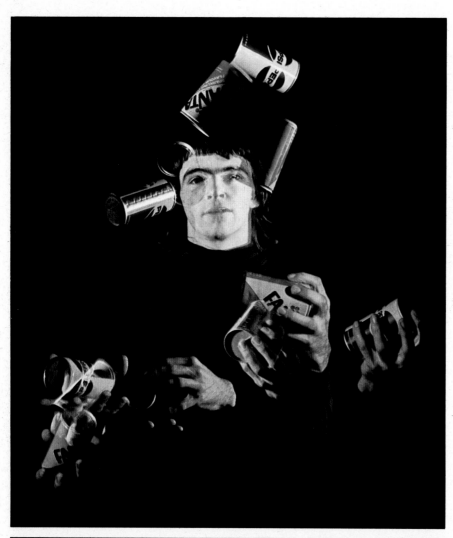

Flash and action

Without the use of flash, a camera's ability to arrest or "freeze" action depends on the speed of the shutter and, to some extent, the speed of the film. Obviously, the faster the shutter and film speed, the greater the arresting power. A camera with a shutter speed of 1/1000 sec. can usually arrest movement sufficiently for normal requirement such as a person running or cycling, a falling object, a flying tennis ball. The quality of the picture depends on available light, especially where depth of field is needed. With electronic flash the length of the light burst determines the degree by which the movement can be stopped, and so the shutter speed is immaterial. Also, the strength of the light is often considerable, allowing small apertures of f16 or less to be used. With synchronized stroboscopic flash, speeds far in excess of 1/1000 sec. are obtainable, freezing movements that are too fast for the human eye to perceive: the structure made by splashing water, the pattern of a flying bird's wings, animals running, even the image made by a speeding bullet. A stroboscopic, multi-flash unit can set off flash in an arranged sequence, so that an entire movement can be captured and studied, the sequence being determined by the subject. To take the shot of the juggler on the left, I constructed a small triggering device, a simple rotating time switch set to fire at intervals of from 1/50 sec. to 5 secs. When using strobe I usually position the lights in such a way that areas of the subject are lit separately, with the lights in an oblique position to the subject to avoid over-exposure building up from the repeated flash. It is also advisable to use a fairly dark room or background so that the background does not burn-out. The shot of wine being poured from a bottle, opposite, was captured with a single, high-speed flash. I directed the light at the background which both illuminated and froze the action at the moment of exposure.

Juggler: Hasselblad, electronic flash, f11, Ektachrome EX.
Wine: Hasselblad, long lens, electronic flash, f16, Ektachrome EX.

Using a pinhole camera

another box of identical size, I cut out one end and stretched a piece of wax paper across it to serve as a viewing screen to position the model. The very tiny aperture of the pinhole, plus the slow speed of the color film, meant that I would need a great deal of light. Accordingly, I placed 36 studio electronic flash lights in a solid bank around the pinhole camera, as shown in the diagram below, and used the viewing shoe box to compose the picture, replacing it with the pinhole camera just before making the exposure. The surprisingly clear pinhole portrait was used as a

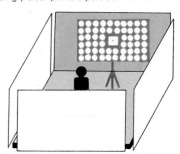

These two portraits show how definition and quality of detail are affected by the use of a lens compared with a pinhole in a camera. The picture on the left was taken with a pinhole camera, the one above with a conventional camera and lens. I constructed the pinhole camera from a shoebox, one end pierced with a minute hole. I made the camera light-proof, and taped a sheet of color film at the opposite end from the pinhole. Using

cover for a magazine, and is probably the first color shot of a model ever made with a pinhole camera. The normal shot, lit with only four lights and taken with an ordinary camera, was taken immediately after the pinhole camera shot as a comparison.

Films for Unusual Effects

An impressive variety of effects is possible with the use of special films, and by pushing the ability of normal films to an abnormal degree. Special films include extra-fast emulsions with an ASA rating of 800 and above, infra-red sensitive film, recording film and lith film, the effects of which can be further extended with special developers and the use of filters.

Extra-fast films will enable you to freeze action, and at the same time get good depth of field. You can shoot in poor light conditions, or obtain really grainy results, especially in combination with a grainy developer. Fast, high contrast films will give you good, bright results when used in overcast conditions. For example, you can shoot landscape pictures on a dull day on very contrasty film and obtain high-quality negatives by over-exposing, say, half a stop, to prevent any abrupt change of contrast.

Recording films have an emulsion that responds most to the extremes of black and white, eliminating nearly all the grays between to give negatives of great contrast; the same effect can sometimes be achieved with very hard printing papers and thin negatives.

Infra-red films record reflected infra-red waves, and block out most other colors. Pictures taken with this film in conjunction with a red filter produce eerie and unnatural pictures, as if the scene has been photographed by moonlight. This is particularly the case with landscape shots, because certain materials reflect infra-red very strongly, while others that reflect no infra-red are almost entirely blocked by the red filter. Blue is blocked, but the green chlorophyll of leaves and grass reflect infra-red and are recorded, so the blue sky appears black while the green trees appear as white. Infra-red film can be used without filters, or with a variety of different density color filters, to obtain special effects. Because the waves are invisible, you cannot judge the results with accuracy. Also infra-red waves are slightly longer than visible light waves, so you may have to alter the focus setting of your lens very slightly. The latest high quality lenses may not need this correction.

At one time there were a considerable number of special films, but today's films are more standardized, and flexibility is obtained with developing and processing techniques, and with filters and lenses. Many photographers and film manufacturers would prefer just one film to meet all demands and requirements. Perhaps some day in the future this will be achieved.

Fast film for poor light
The circus picture, above, taken in a dark green tent on a dull day was best recorded on a fast, high contrast film. The resulting image has less detail than with ordinary film used in good conditions, because of the increased contrast and low light. The exposure index is 1000 ASA, but I have often used it at 3000 ASA with adequate results. The light meter in the camera hardly responded to the light in this situation.
Leicaflex, 1/30 sec., f2.8, Kodak 2475 Recording.

Recording tone in restricted light
To achieve the degree of tonal range needed for this shot at dusk, right, I used a high speed panchromatic film. I have used the same film on dull days with slight over-exposure, when it gives contrast plus a remarkable tonal range.
Hasselblad, 1/30 sec., f5.6, Royal-X.

Techniques for high contrast
Photographs containing extremes of black and white can be achieved with recording film, or by using special paper and developer. In the example, left, I used a normal, conventional negative and increased the contrast by printing onto lith paper, and using a high contrast developer which gives rich blacks. Lith papers and hard grade bromide papers should be chosen when printing from under-developed, thin negatives.
Rolleiflex, 1/125 sec., f11, Kodak Tri-X.

The effect of infra-red
Unlike the "visible" light waves of the color spectrum that are absorbed or reflected by objects, infra-red waves are invisible and have slightly longer wavelength. They are rendered visible by the use of infra-red film combined with a red filter. Chlorophyll in green foliage is strongly reflective, while blue is blocked by the filter.
Leicaflex, 1/250 sec., f16, Infra-red.

Films for Unusual Effects

Films for combined color effects

The multi-image picture above was made with three transparencies: two infra-red and a normal photograph taken on daylight-type film. The figures were shot on infra-red film, using different color filters to obtain unusual color effects and the window picture was photographed on daylight film. The three transparencies were then superimposed using the method explained on p. 158. With special films, the range of color combinations is almost limitless. You can use normal daylight film in artificial light, or artificial light film in daylight, both combined with color filters. You can extend this range by varying the exposure. The transparencies may then be combined with color infra-red which can also be used with various filters to give vivid and exciting results.

Color by restricted light

Very soft and beautiful effects can be obtained by using fast color film in weak light, although fairly long exposures may be needed. High-speed color films give good, rich transparencies or prints but with some of the qualities associated with fast black and white film — grain, for instance. I took this picture, right, with a fast color film in weak light conditions. The result has delicate color and atmosphere, the grain giving an old-fashioned appeal.

Leicaflex, 1/60 sec., f5.6, Anscochrome 500.

The effect of chromatic aberration

Very simple and cheap lenses are unable to focus color light waves to a point, so create an unusual effect that will be recorded whether the film is color or black and white. This inability to focus color is known as chromatic aberration, and was recognized by early lens makers. In the mid-18th century it was discovered that two lenses could be combined to cancel out the other's chromatic aberration, by placing together lenses of different glass types. The failure of a lens to focus color waves is due to the fact that some waves bend at sharper angles than others, varying with the type of glass. While blue may be in focus, red is not. This is why a photograph of a red apple might record the apple with blue edges. Chromatic aberration softens colors and images, and spreads highlights, giving an impressionistic effect. I took this picture with an old camera which had a simple, one-element lens. On black and white film the picture would probably just have been slightly out of focus.

Ensign Ful-Vue (c. 1939), probably fixed at 1/25 sec., aperture set for "Dull Day", 120 Ektachrome EX.

Daylight with artificial light film
Using artificial light film with a subject illuminated by daylight gives a blue cast as shown above. After an exposure of 1 sec. the film was wound on with the shutter still open, to give an effect of streaking highlights. The picture was used upside down to defy gravity and for a more dramatic appearance. *Hasselblad, 1 sec., f8, EHB Ektachrome.*

Selecting color for atmosphere
The shot, center right, was taken at midday with daylight film, the mist provided by a bonfire covered with wet sea-weed. The burning house, right, was taken two hours later. By using artificial light film, and underexposing I simulated nightfall. The flames came from kerosene burning in an oil drum. *Hasselblad, (center right) 1/250 sec., f11, Ektachrome EX; (right) 1/25 sec., f11, EHB Ektachrome.*

Close-up Photography

When you take a close-up picture, you treat the subject with intimate scrutiny, revealing overlooked or perhaps invisible details. In portrait photography, for example, you can emphasize an aspect of a face by moving in close with the camera and concentrating the focus on that particular area.

Although the term "close-up" can imply a larger-than-life image isolated from its surroundings and presented in some detail, actual magnification is not necessarily a part of close-up photography. Take a photograph with a normal lens and blow up a small area of the negative with the darkroom enlarger. You will almost certainly create an image that brings previously unnoticed features into prominence, yet it will lack that sharp, relentless clarity achieved by close-up lenses or extension tubes.

Strictly speaking, a close-up is a photograph where the image is rendered up to natural size. Photography in which the image is slightly larger than natural size or magnified is generally called "macrophotography," while an image greatly enlarged with the aid of a microscope is called a "photomicrograph." Magnifying the image depends on the use of certain specialized lenses, or an ordinary lens used in conjunction with extension tubes or bellows, all designed for close-up work. The macro lens is designed to give a high degree of definition and detail in a close-up situation, although the definition at infinity may be less sharp than with a normal lens. It also has a smaller maximum aperture. A normal lens fitted with one or more extension tubes will enlarge the image without much distortion, but you will have to work very close to the subject. A wide-angle lens fitted with extension tubes will permit tremendous magnification but with an equal amount of distortion. For most close-up work, a medium long-focus lens with extension tubes allows you to work at a reasonable distance from your subject, gives considerable magnification and little noticeable distortion.

You will need to take one or two additional factors into account when photographing in close-up – the increase of exposure and the problem of lighting. Increasing the focal length of the lens with the necessary extra exposure required can lead to reciprocity failure, so careful calculations are needed. The other problem is that you may have to push the lens so close to the subject that you cut out much of the light. A tripod and cable release will help overcome this, but the best plan is to channel well-aimed directional light with a snoot, for instance, or even a piece of card with a hole cut in the center. If you use flash light to avoid the possibility of movement – even the faintest tremor can blur the image – make sure there are no strong shadows cast across the subject.

As we have seen, a medium long-focus lens not only allows you a good working distance, but is less liable to distort the image. Both factors are particularly helpful in portrait photography, where shorter focus lenses would distort the image and – because they must be used fairly close to the sitter – may make him more self-conscious.

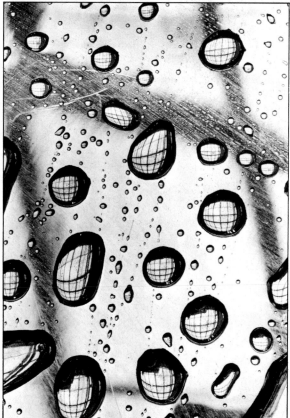

The source of light
Both the background and the butterfly are revealed with considerable clarity thanks to the low, evening light, which emphasized texture and pattern. As exposure has to be increased in relation to the extension, I calculated it as nine times above normal. *Linhof, long lens with triple extension bellows, 10 secs., f16, FP4.*

Using a long extension
I used fully extended bellows to make the raindrops, left, about 1½× greater than life size. They were further enlarged when printed. I used two tripods to overcome the vibration that occurs with long extension — one at the back of the camera and one at the front. Because of the extension I calculated exposure nine times above normal and added a second for reciprocity failure. *Linhof, extension bellows, 6 secs., f45, FP4.*

Careful use of lighting
Moving your camera close to the subject can cut out light so it is best to use a long lens with extension tubes which not only help to overcome distortion but allow you to work at a distance from the subject. In the shot opposite I used flashlight and a reflector to capture skin detail. *Pentax, long lens with extension tubes, electronic flash, f16, FP4.*

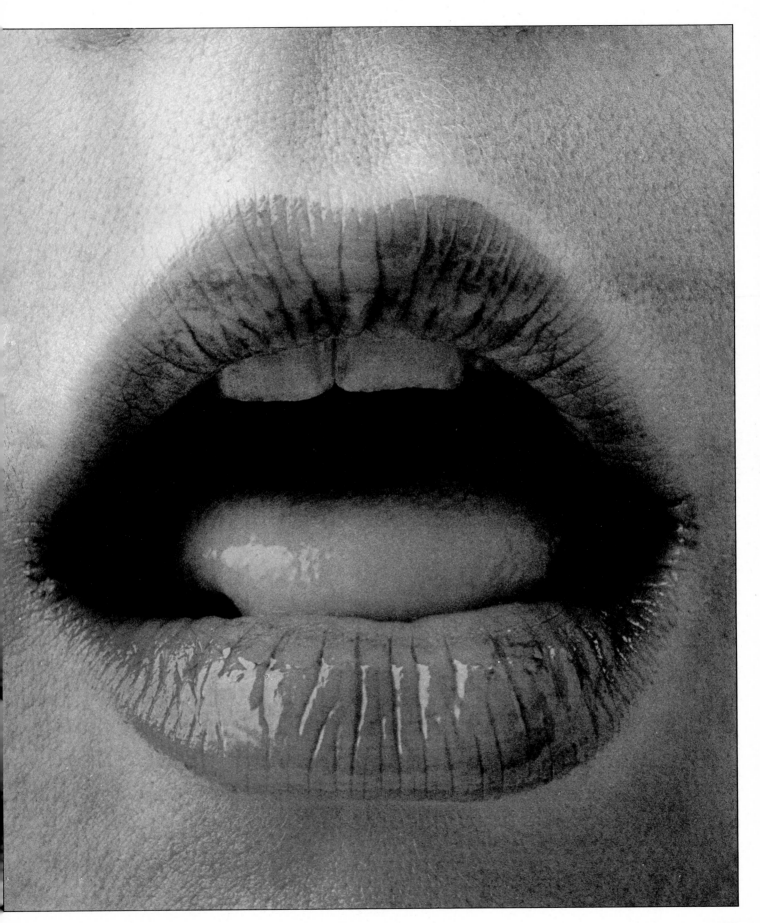

Lenses for Unusual Effects

Any serious photographer needs a camera with interchangeable lenses. While there is a considerable selection available, most photographers only use about three different lenses, unless they specialize in a branch of photography, where special lenses are often essential. Lenses differ according to the format and size of the camera; a wide-angle lens that is specified for a 35 mm camera will not suit a camera using a $2\frac{1}{4}$ in (6 cm) square format. One manufacturer might have a range of four or five wide-angle lenses, each with a different focal length and angle of view.

The main advantages of interchangeable lenses are that they allow you to alter the size of the image and manipulate perspective to bring distant objects into close-up, or to encompass a panoramic view. Although some distortion occurs with wide-angle lenses, they enable you to include a good deal of foreground while diminishing the background. These lenses are often used in still life pictures, full length portraits and photo-reportage shots; they create pictures with a feeling of immediacy, placing the viewer right in the foreground. Wide-angle lenses are necessary in confined spaces.

The perspective through a normal lens is convincing, and there is little or no image distortion – the foreground, middle distance and background all relate normally. Normal lenses usually have the widest apertures, f1.8 and f2 being average, although some cameras are fitted with f1.2, and even a lens with an aperture of f0.8 has been known. The angle of view is generally 45°–50° which means that on a 35 mm camera the image of the subject is about the same as it appears to the human eye.

The medium long-focus lens – an 80 mm to 200 mm lens on a 35 mm camera – causes little or no distortion, enables you to relate subject to background without too much exaggeration, and means you can photograph distant subjects in relative close-up. The very long-focus lens will greatly enlarge distant subjects, but with a typical flattening of perspective. Medium long-focus lenses are fairly lightweight, and can usually be hand-held, except for long exposures of 1/15 second or more. As a very rough guide, shutter speeds can be related to the focal length of the lens. For example, a 135 mm lens requires a speed of 1/125 second or thereabouts, a 500 mm lens 1/500 second in order to prevent camera-shake.

A zoom lens, once focused on a subject, remains in focus irrespective of the focal length or image size. It may not possess the same degree of definition as fixed long-focus lenses, but it is very useful for some types of sport photography where precise definition might not matter.

The long-focus lens
This was sculptor Henry Moore's first and most enduring memory of his Yorkshire home – a slag-heap adjacent to the coalfields. To capture the monumental appearance of the pyramid, and also the industrial haze, I shot the picture from two miles away with a very long-focus lens. This also enabled me to record the setting sun in exaggerated relationship. The lens has flattened the perspective and gives very little depth of field.
Pentax, 1000 mm lens, 1/500 sec., f5.6, Kodak Tri-X.

Changing the lens

These three pictures show the different results of photographing the same scene with a wide-angle, a normal, and a medium long-focus lens. The shorter the focal length the greater the depth of field. The wider the angle of view, the greater is the area encompassed by the lens. A long-focus lens gives a bigger image and a narrower field of view than a wide-angle, bringing objects closer together and compressing perspective. The picture far left was taken with a wide-angle lens; the center shot taken with a normal lens makes figures appear closer; the photograph left, taken with a long lens, enlarges the subject still further, cropping the lower half of the central figure.

Lenses for Unusual Effects

Special effect with a zoom lens

Children on a go-kart, left, photographed with a zoom lens to increase the appearance of speed and movement. I focused the fully extended lens on the children so that they filled the screen, then zoomed back to shorten the focal length at the same time pressing the shutter for an exposure of a half second.
Pentax, 1/2 sec., f16, HP3.

The fish-eye lens

Although the results are generally spectacular, the fish-eye has limited application. The lens gives an angle of view of 180°, but causes great distortion around the edges of the image opposite. No focusing is needed with the fish-eye lens, because the depth of field is so great that virtually everything is sharp.
Nikon, 1/60 sec., f8, Kodak Tri-X.

Using the close-up lens

Close-up lenses create a number of optical effects, below. Notice the limited depth of field in the detail on the face, the slight distortion of the image. I focused on the man's eyes but the tip of the nose and ears are out of focus.
Rolleiflex, 1/125 sec., f8, Kodak Tri-X.

Attachments for Unusual Effects

Special attachments for lenses further the scope of imagery. Many have been developed for technical and scientific purposes but tend to be of little real value to the average photographer. The pictures that most attachments produce rarely have much esthetic quality – the most convincing pictures are invariably made by simple and straightforward means.

Some attachments, however, can help you to overcome certain problems. Polarizing filters can block distracting reflections and reduce glare from highlights. The anamorphic lens has the property of compressing the image, and this can emphasize a particular characteristic absent from a "normal" picture, such as the width or height of a building. A prism lens will enable you to split an image and to repeat the motif several times within the same picture area. Compound lenses repeat the entire image within the frame, the images overlapping.

A right angle attachment that shoots "around corners" and fits on the end of a lens, allows you to take pictures of people without their being aware of it.

Some special effects help to increase atmosphere in pictures: the split-image prism gives landscapes a dreamlike quality, an effect sometimes used by commercial photographers and by magazines. The starburst attachment creates radiating lines from a highlight, and will enhance the quality of night shots – automobile headlights, candlelight scenes, pictures of a party, shots of a lighthouse. Cross-screen filters, soft focus lens attachments, smearing a glass in front of the lens with petroleum jelly, or covering it with a piece of colored cellophane, all distort or alter the image in a powerful or subtle way. Such effects may not necessarily produce a great photograph, but they can often improve a dull or mundane subject.

Squeezing the image with an anamorphic lens
The anamorphic lens was developed by movie cameramen to convert wide screen films to the standard picture size. It has the property of condensing an image in one direction only, without distorting other dimensions. In the pictures below, I used the attachment to demonstrate how the image can be stretched or condensed from the normal.
Hasselblad, 1/250 sec., f8, Kodak Tri-X.

Starburst attachment
This device which can be attached to the camera lens spreads the highlights of a subject into star shapes, working best with small, intense highlights. A variety of starburst attachments are available – some produce more stars than others.
Hasselblad, 1/30 sec., f8, Royal-X.

Using a polarizing filter

Reflected light, glare from polished surfaces or the sky can be reduced by using a polarizing filter. The filter has the property of passing light waves vibrating in one direction while blocking other light waves vibrating at right angles to them. The effect can be easily seen by looking through a filter at reflected light, and then rotating the filter. Polarizing filters will only block certain forms of polarized light. For example, they eliminate glare from the polished painted surface or windshield of an automobile, but cannot block the reflected light from chromium-plate. A polarizing filter is useful when photographing paintings mounted behind glass, shop windows, polished furniture and architectural subjects with large reflective areas. In the two examples, right, the first picture was taken without the filter, and has recorded distracting reflections. For the second picture the filter was attached. *Hasselblad, 1/125 sec., f6.3, Kodak Tri-X.*

Multiple images with the prism lens

The pictures below and right demonstrate the use of prism lenses to obtain a multiple image. Lenses of this type can split the image either vertically, horizontally or into a regular pattern. They can also be used in conjunction with one another. In most types the images overlap, although some transmit separate, whole images.

Special Cameras

Cameras designed to meet particular requirements have been regularly introduced since photography began. A panoramic view camera was designed as long ago as 1844, with a swiveling lens and curved plate. There have been giant cameras – one was the size of a small house – and cameras with over a dozen lenses. Cameras for work above the clouds and below the oceans have been perfected for scientific research. The resources of science have overtaken the work of photographer-pioneers to produce such astonishing inventions as holography, invented in Britain by Prof. Denis Gabor, a system using reflected laser beams that creates a perfect, three-dimensional image.

In order to photograph the front and rear of an object on one plane, the periphery camera was developed. One early example was the cyclograph of 1895, made to peri-photograph antique pottery, to obtain a 360° recording of the object's periphery. A peri-photograph is a "wrap-around" photograph, where the subject rotates on a turntable while the changing image is recorded on moving film; the turntable and speed of film movement are synchronized.

A similar result can be obtained in landscape photography with the panoramic camera, also used to photograph large groups of people. It has been known for people in the back row to appear at each end of the same picture by running along the back of the group at a slightly faster pace than the movement of the lens.

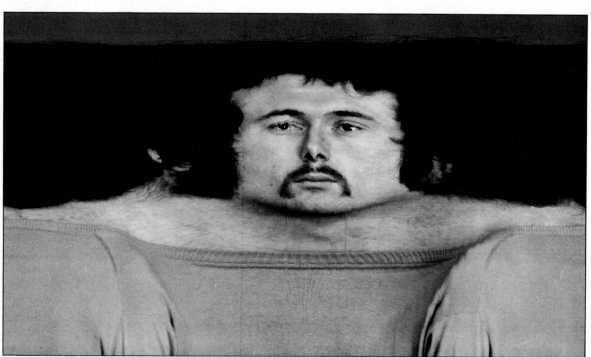

The peri-photograph
This "wrap-around" portrait, left, shows the front, back and sides of the sitter, and is a means of cheating the third dimension. The photograph was taken with a periphery camera at a scientific establishment. While a considerable degree of accuracy is possible with subjects of a regular shape, irregular objects are liable to distortion, as the peri-portrait demonstrates.

The panoramic camera
Panoramic cameras have a lens that swivels through a horizontal arc of some 120°. The image is "spread" across the negative through a slit that moves with the lens. A typical example is shown below. There is little or no distortion, and amusing results can be obtained by using the camera vertically, in portraits, for example. Panoramic cameras are relatively inexpensive to buy, but their usefulness is limited.

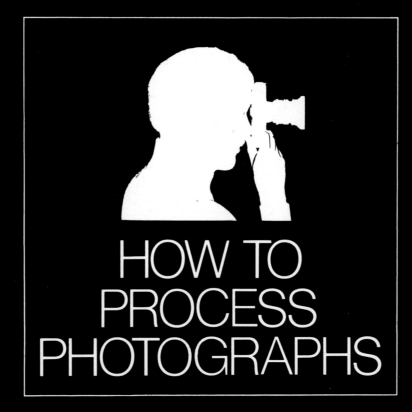

HOW TO
PROCESS
PHOTOGRAPHS

Black & White Developing

When exposed film is removed from the camera, it is still light sensitive, opaque and carries no visible image. During the developing process the film is immersed in one or more chemical baths which make the latent image visible, destroying all remaining light sensitivity and leaving a transparent based negative. Development must usually take place in complete darkness since most light affects the film. The simplest method is to place the film in a daylight developing tank which, once sealed, can be safely used in light. You load the film on to a reel, either in the darkroom or in a loading bag, and place it inside the tank where the whole of the film surface can be covered by the chemical baths. Each chemical can be poured into and out of the tank through a small light-tight opening in the top.

The first bath of the development process is the developer, a mixture of several chemicals balanced to work at a specified temperature. Usually this is 68°F (20°C). Strictly, the developing solution will affect both unexposed and exposed silver halides. Exposure increases the rate by which silver halides can be converted by the developing solution to black metallic silver, so the exposed image develops first. However, prolonged development attacks unexposed grains and any increase over manufacturer's recommended development times is inclined to give the film an additional overall gray tone, known as chemical fog.

The second stage is the stop bath. At the end of the developing time, you pour the developer out of the developing tank and replace it by the stop bath, a mildly acidic solution which halts the action of the alkaline developer. This ensures that the degree of development is accurate and prevents alkaline carry-over into the third bath containing fixer, an acid solution.

The developer and stop leave the film light-sensitive and opaque, but with a black negative image visible. The final chemical, fixer, makes the remaining light-sensitive salts on the film soluble so they can be removed by washing in running water, usually for 30 minutes. The processed film has excess water removed with a pair of rubber-lipped squeegee tongs and is then attached to weighted metal clips and hung up to dry in a dust-free room. Finally, the dry negatives are cut into strips (usually of six for 35 mm or three for 6 × 6 cm) and filed in protective envelopes.

Developing equipment
A full outfit of developing equipment is advisable to ensure absolute accuracy when developing films. Timing and temperature must be carefully controlled so a timer and thermometer are of primary importance. The daylight developing tank, once loaded in darkness can be used in normal light.

Once prepared, bottles of chemicals should be kept at a constant temperature in a tray of water at 68°F (20°C). Other useful items include a measuring jug and funnel for easy pouring of chemicals into tanks and bottles, a hose to connect the water source to the tank for washing, squeegee tongs, clips and scissors.

Stainless steel developing tank and reel

Funnel

Measuring jug

Plastic developing tank and reels

Developer

Stop

Fixer

Tray

Timer

Metal clips

Hose

Scissors

Squeegee tongs

Wetting agent

Loading a plastic reel with 35mm film

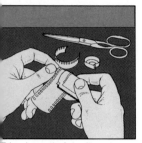

Trim the end of the film, then, in total darkness, open the cassette and remove the spool of exposed film.

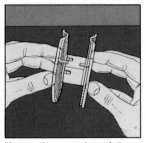

Line up the entry slots of the reel and make sure that the indentations in the sides are at the top of the reel.

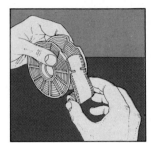

Hold the film by its edges to prevent damage and feed it into the entry slots of the reel.

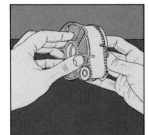

Rotate each half of the reel alternately to draw the film into the spiral grooves.

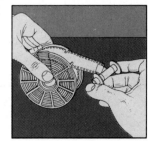

When the film is loaded, cut or tear the end of the film from the spool and put the reel in the developing tank.

Loading roll-film onto a metal reel with a loader

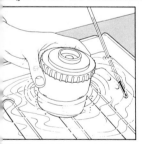

Line up the loader to receive the film and in darkness unroll the backing paper.

Feed the film into the loader and clamp the end at the center of the reel.

Wind the film into the grooves of the reel.

When the film is almost loaded, detach the backing paper from the film end and finish the loading.

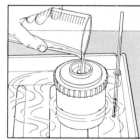

Remove the reel from the loader and put it in the daylight developing tank.

Developing the negative

When the film is in the tank and the lid secured, turn on the lights. Before beginning the developing process, check that all the necessary equipment is prepared for every stage. Follow the manufacturer's instructions for exact timing. Neither presoaking before development nor the addition of a wetting agent at the washing stage are essential, but they are useful to ensure even processing and drying.

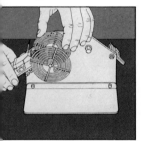

With the lights on, put the sealed tank in a water bath at 68°F (20°C) to keep its temperature constant.

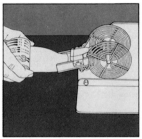

Remove the cap on the tank lid and pour developer at 68°F (20°C) quickly into the tank. Tap it to dislodge air bubbles, start the timer, replace the cap.

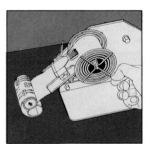

Every ½ minute during development agitate the developer by inverting the tank or with the agitation rod.

When development time is complete, pour the developer from the tank into its bottle for re-use.

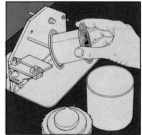

Pour the stop bath into the tank, agitate and leave it for one minute to halt development.

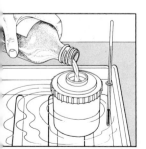

Pour out the stop and replace it with fixer. Agitate every minute during the recommended time, then return the chemical to its bottle.

Remove the tank lid and connect the water source to the tank with a hose to wash the film for the recommended length of time.

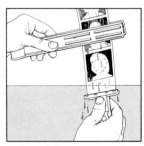

Attach clips and hang up the washed film. Squeegee surplus water from the film and leave it to dry.

Mark bottles of developer and fixer with the date of use and number of films processed. Follow manufacturer's instructions about re-use.

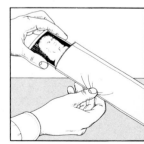

When dry, cut the negatives into convenient lengths, dust with a blower brush and file in protective envelopes.

Enlarging & Contact Printing

There are two ways of making a print. The first is to place the negative in contact with photographic printing paper and to expose it to light – to make a contact print. For the second an enlarger is used to project the negative onto the photographic paper; the resulting print, once processed, is known as a projection print or enlargement.

A contact print is the same size as the negative, and so for 35 mm and 6 × 6 cm formats it is usually only used for reference when selecting pictures for enlargement. An entire 35 mm film (36 exposures), 120 roll-film (12 exposures of 6 × 6 cm) or four 4 × 5 ins (10.2 × 12.7 cm) sheets can be "proofed" by contacting them onto a sheet of standard size photographic printing paper, 8 × 10 ins (20.3 × 25.4 cm). The simplest way of making a contact print uses a light box as the source of light. The negatives are laid on the light box and covered by photographic printing paper so that their emulsion sides are together. A sheet of glass is laid on top of the paper to ensure close contact between the paper and negatives during exposure. The exposed paper is processed as described on p. 192.

Contact prints are more commonly made by using a contact printing frame with an overhead light source such as an enlarger. Such frames are usually designed to be used with standard photographic paper sizes. Photographic printing paper is slipped under a glass sheet and covered by the negatives so that their emulsion sides are together. The glass top is clamped to the base for perfect contact between negatives and photographic paper sandwiched in between. Exposure is made when light passes through the glass and negatives to reach the printing paper.

The enlarger

Similar to a camera in many ways, the enlarger consists of a head connected by a rigid column to a baseboard. The head contains a light source, a diffusing screen or condenser lens, a negative carrier and a projection lens fitted with a removable red filter. Once a negative is in place light can be channeled through the diffuser, the negative and the lens to project an image on to the baseboard below. Image quality can be improved by a focusing control, brightness by altering the size of the lens aperture and size by moving the enlarger head up or down the column. An exposure is made by placing photographic printing paper on the baseboard and, without the red filter in place, turning on the light source for the recommended time.

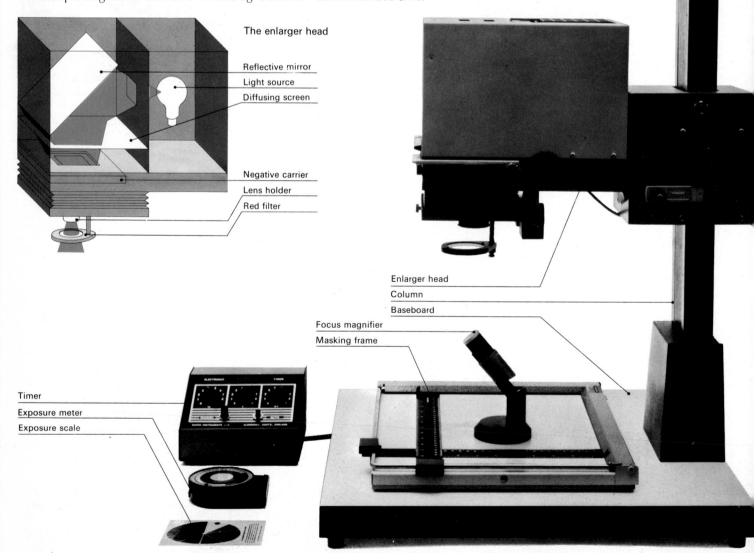

The enlarger head

Reflective mirror
Light source
Diffusing screen

Negative carrier
Lens holder
Red filter

Enlarger head
Column
Baseboard

Focus magnifier
Masking frame

Timer
Exposure meter
Exposure scale

Preparing to make a contact print

Use a proprietary cleaner or anti-static cloth to clean the contact printing frame.

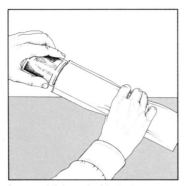

In normal light and with dry hands, remove the strip of negatives from its protective sleeve. Handle it only by the edges. Use a blower brush to remove dust.

Film curls slightly with the emulsion or dull side inwards. Decide which is the dull and which is the shiny side of the strip of negatives.

Insert each strip of film into the printer so that the shiny side touches the glass. Blower brush the strips once more.

Making a contact print

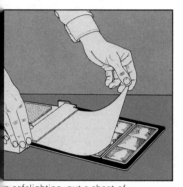

In safelighting, put a sheet of photographic printing paper into the frame so that the emulsion side comes into contact with the negative emulsion. Close the frame.

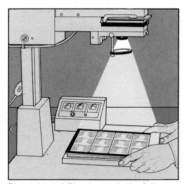

Place the red filter beneath the fully open enlarger lens and with the enlarger head high enough up the column to illuminate all the negatives, center the frame underneath the light.

Close the enlarger lens down to f8 or f11 and set the timer for about 10 secs. As you become familiar with your enlarger you will know whether to increase or decrease this time.

Remove the red filter and make the exposure. Afterwards, open the frame and remove the paper for processing but leave the negatives in position in case another print is needed.

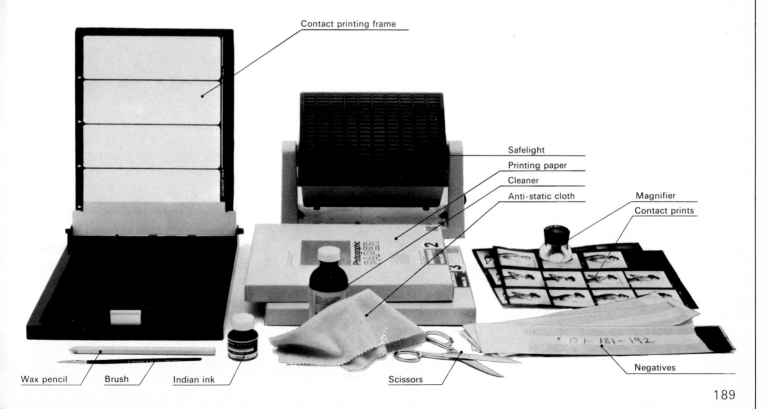

Contact printing frame

Safelight
Printing paper
Cleaner
Anti-static cloth

Magnifier
Contact prints

Wax pencil   Brush   Indian ink   Scissors   Negatives

Making a Test Strip

Although exposure meters for use, with projection printing are available, using a test strip still remains the only way of making a personal judgment of the exposure time needed to produce a print of good quality. When using unusual techniques, making large or very high quality prints, the test strip gives far more helpful information than the purely objective measurement provided by an exposure meter.

Unlike the exposure meter which only indicates an estimation of exposure time, the test strip shows a section of the final print exposed for different lengths of time. Since the same paper and chemicals are used for the test strip the finished enlargement density, contrast and image color can all be judged.

Initial experiments with your enlarger will give you some idea of the length of exposure necessary to print a particular negative on a specific grade of paper. Once the negative and paper are positioned in the enlarger, the test print can be exposed in sections.

Bands are exposed, say, for multiples of five seconds, e.g. 5, 10, 15, 20 and 25 secs., to make five bands in all. The width of each band needs to be large enough to make a visual judgment of the print quality, and the test strip must be made across an area of the image which contains a varied range of tones.

The print, when processed (see p. 192) will show five bands of density. One band will probably be correct, while the others will be too light or too dark. If you judge that correct density lies between two bands, choose an exposure halfway between these two exposure times for the final print.

If the test strip, which is usually made on normal grade paper, has too much contrast or is too soft in

The test strip

The process of selecting a negative and making trial exposures before printing the final enlargement is simple and methodical. Making accurate, clear prints depends on selecting the best negatives and printing them to the very best of your ability. This applies to any format of negative and any size of print.

Examine the contact strip with a magnifier and select the best frame to be enlarged.

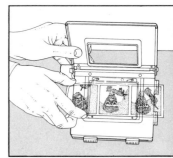

Remove the negative carrier from the enlarger and position the chosen frame inside it. The emulsion side of the negative should be downwards.

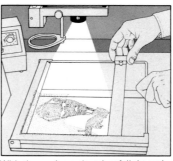

With the carrier replaced, safelight and enlarger switched on, adjust the size of the image and frame it within the masking slides.

Focus the lens until a sharp image appears on the baseboard. You may find it helpful to use a focus magnifier.

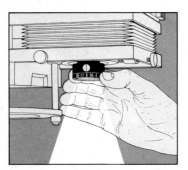

Set the f stop of the lens at about f8 or f11. Study the brightness and estimate the exposure time. If in doubt, try 10–15 secs.

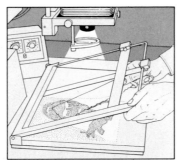

With the red filter under the lens, position a strip of printing paper across an important part of the image containing a range of negative tones.

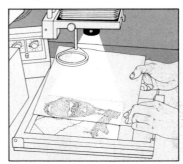

Cover all-but a fifth of the test strip with card, then move the filter from under the lens to expose the paper for 5 secs.

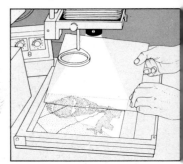

Move the card and expose (for 5 secs.) successive bands of the test strip, five times in all.

appearance a different grade can be selected for the final print. As most paper grades vary slightly in speed a further test strip should be made if contrast grade is changed. On examining your chosen negative, you may know from experience whether it will require a harder or softer grade than normal. In this case make the initial test strip on the paper you consider most suitable.

For straightforward work you can judge the right density band while the test strip is still in the fixing bath. This saves time but it is more accurate to judge the test strip in daylight after fixation and a brief wash.

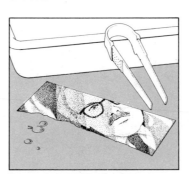

Process the test strip. Bands representing exposures of 25, 20, 15, 10, 5 secs. are clearly defined.

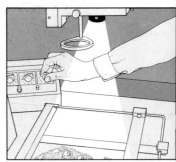

Choose the most accurate band and correctly expose a full sheet of paper to make the enlarged print.

Control Printing

Dodging and burning-in

If sharply-defined masks are used to hold back or give extra exposure to areas of the image, the final print shows outlines of these masks. Therefore, any mask or tool used for this purpose must be kept moving, and must be smaller than the area to be affected in the print. Many people use their hands as masks but proper tools can be bought or made.

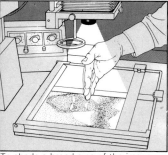

To shade a broad area of the image during exposure, interrupt the light covering the relevant area with your hand. Keep it moving.

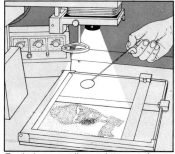

To dodge a small area, interrupt the light with a suitably shaped, moving, cardboard mask attached to wire.

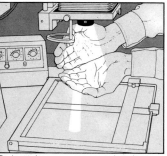

To burn-in areas, cup your hands beneath the light so that only a narrow beam reaches the image.

To burn-in areas using a mask, make a suitably sized hole in a sheet of card and hold it in the light path.

Printing for low and high contrast

For special impact photographers sometimes abandon the "true" rendering of subject tones and instead make low or high contrast prints. Low contrast, soft prints are composed mainly of gray tones, as shown above. High contrast, hard prints contain many bold and dense black tones, shown right. A normal tone rendering appears above right. Obviously some negatives are particularly suited to one or other of these special treatments, but even quite ordinary images can be enhanced by using different grades of photographic printing paper.
Papers of a low number are soft and give low contrast, whereas high numbered papers are hard and can be used to produce high contrast prints.

The exposure made using the test strip as a guide should result in a good quality print. Some negatives, however, may demand individual treatment during exposure to correct selected areas which are too dense or too light. With others, you may feel that using special effects, like gradual fading of the image into white at the edges (vignetting), or very high or low contrast, will give more meaning to the final print.

It is possible for parts of the image to receive more or less exposure by masking areas during the total or part of the exposure time. Areas which are unexposed print as white but any reduction in local exposure on a print will lighten the tone of the area and, conversely, any increase in exposure will darken it. This means that it is possible to control locally the tones in any area of a print, and although these techniques of "dodging" and "burning-in," as they are called, need practice and care, they are essential to master if you want to produce high quality prints.

There are many other ways of controlling the appearance of a final print apart from those already mentioned. You can create a soft focus image by using a diffusing material during exposure, or choose a high key effect to give prominence to light tones or a low key effect to give dark tones. It is also possible to expose the image through screens, bought or home-made.

Vignetting

Vignettes can have light or dark backgrounds although the method for making them differs slightly. To make a normal vignette cut an oval approximate in size to the image from a sheet of card. Hold this oval in the path of light throughout exposure so that the area surrounding the oval is not exposed. A reversed vignette can be made by using the oval cut from the card as a mask. Make a normal exposure, then re-expose the printing paper but use the oval mask to prevent the main image from being over-exposed.

For a normal vignette, use a mask with an oval removed from the center.

For a reversed vignette, make 2 exposures. Mask to prevent re-exposure of the image.

The vignetted image fades into a white background.

A reversed vignetted photograph fades into a black background.

Making a Print

One of the most satisfying aspects of photography is the printing process. However, it must be well organized since errors are difficult to correct once made.

Certain conditions are vital to producing successful photographic prints. A darkroom, whether purpose-built or converted from another room is essential because photographic paper should only be handled under red or orange "safelights." Working in safelight conditions is simple once your eyes have adjusted to the dimness. Electricity and water supplies are obviously necessary, although *running* water is not vital in the darkroom itself.

The solutions used to process the prints work best at 68°F (20°C). If the same room temperature can be maintained this is ideal. All liquids should be kept well away from the enlarger and unexposed printing paper.

Before beginning the printing process make sure that all the equipment and chemicals, correctly diluted, are ready for every stage. Once the first stage has begun there can be no interruption. Arrange the equipment so that it can be easily handled.

The printing process

The normal procedure is to expose a sheet of photographic paper to a negative image projected by an enlarger. As soon as it is immersed in a chemical bath, timing must begin. The print is usually left in the first bath, developer, for 2–3 mins., but the manufacturer's instructions should be followed carefully. Agitation of the chemical is important throughout this period to bring fresh solution into contact with the print. After development, the print is transferred to the water rinse or stop bath which halts the action of the developer. This stage only lasts for a few seconds, and then the print is moved to a fixing bath where it stays for up to 10 mins. Washing is the last stage of the cycle, and absolutely vital since any residue of chemical salts left on the print will cause it to deteriorate. Adding hypo clearing agent to the wash can reduce the washing time.

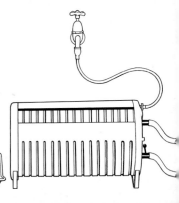

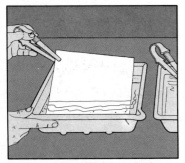
Working under safelighting, slip the exposed print quickly below the surface of the developer.

Use the tongs to agitate the chemical until the image is developed.

Remove the print with the tongs and allow the excess developer to drain from its surface.

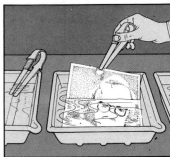
With a *clean* pair of tongs transfer the print into the stop bath.

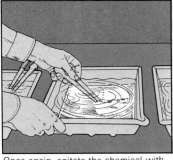
Once again, agitate the chemical with the tongs for the recommended time.

Use the tongs to remove the print and drain off excess liquid.

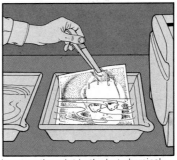
Immerse the print in the last chemical bath, the fixer.

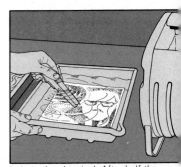
Agitate the chemical. After half the fixing time it is safe to turn on the ceiling light.

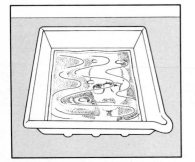
With the light on, examine the print while it is still in the fixing bath.

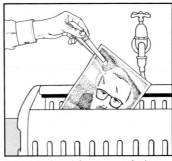
If the print is satisfactory transfer it to the washing tank or sink.

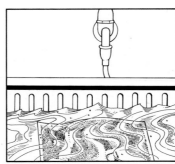
Wash the print thoroughly in fresh, running water for at least an hour.

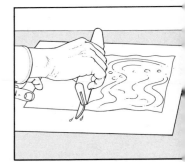
Take the print out of the washing tank and squeegee the surplus water from its surface before drying.

Drying & Finishing

Using a flatbed drier

Different models of flatbed drier can be bought to suit the size and number of prints being made. Very large prints can be dried singly, alternatively a number of small prints can be dried at the same time. A cloth canopy is laid across the prints once they have been smoothed onto the glazing plate and secured to keep them flat. Thermostatic heater elements under the glazing plate heat up to dry the prints.

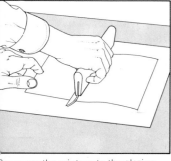

Squeegee the prints onto the glazing plate, image side down for a glazed finish, up for unglazed.

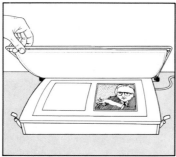

Place the glazing plate in the correct position over the heater elements.

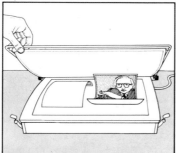

Secure the fabric canopy over the prints to keep them flat during the heating and drying processes.

Lift the canopy when dry. The glazed print will be curled over the plate and the unglazed print curled upwards.

The drum drier

The commercial rotary glazer drier has a permanent chrome or stainless glazing surface in the form of a drum which rotates slowly. It remains in contact with a taut apron of bleached canvas for two-thirds of its travel to keep the drying prints flat. A heater inside the drum begins to dry the print from its moment of entry. Prints are placed on a projecting part of the moving apron to be drawn into the drier where they come into contact with the hot surface of the drum. They remain in contact with the rotating drum for about 90 secs. and then they emerge, dry and glazed. A brush separates them from the glazing surface to make them fall into a receiving tray.

The simplest way to dry prints is to leave them on a flat surface in a warm room for several hours. For better results heat drying can be preferable.

There are two main types of photographic paper: resin-coated and fiber-based. Resin-coated paper is handled the same way as fiber-based paper during processing but requires much less time for washing. It dries rapidly in warm air with good results.

Fiber-based paper can be heat dried in either a flatbed drier or rotary glazer. The flatbed type is inexpensive and a number of prints can be dried at a time. It takes about ten minutes. The rotary type, expensive but ideal for commercial work, takes prints one by one but dries and glazes within two minutes.

To dry and glaze fiber-based glossy prints with a flatbed drier, they must be squeegeed, emulsion side down, onto the glazing plate. To make unglazed prints the emulsion faces upwards and is covered by the cloth canopy. Rapid dryers are made for resin-coated papers which dry one print every 30 seconds by blowing hot air over the surface of the paper. Resin-coated glossy paper dries with a mirror glaze without requiring a glazer.

Simple retouching

Even if you take great care, blemishes on prints cannot always be avoided. Unless they are very serious, they can be removed with a little skill and the right tools — a sharp scalpel, spotting medium and very fine sable brushes. White spots caused by dust can be removed by applying black spotting medium diluted to the correct tone. Larger white blemishes can be filled in dot-by-dot with spotting medium. On matt prints, a sharp HB pencil gives a better result. Dark spots can be gently scraped away with the scalpel to leave white spots which can then be toned.

Using a scalpel
To remove blemishes, gently scrape the emulsion from the print surface. It is possible to lighten the tone.

Spotting
With a fine brush apply spotting medium of the correct thickness and color, starting with the darkest areas.

193

The Color System

Color photography using commercially available materials has been possible since 1907. The early processes bear little resemblance to today's. They were, by comparison, unreliable and difficult to use. The turning point came in 1935 with the introduction of mass produced transparency film using the universal "tripack" system of construction. This film was easy to use, and its sharpness, stability and color quality made it a success. It was always processed by the manufacturer.

Since then, continuing research and development has led to the range of films now available. Some of these products are complete picture making systems in themselves (i.e. instant picture systems, see pp. 222–223). Most, however, are part of a multi-stage system designed to make a color print or color transparency for projection.

The variety of films available is now considerable, ranging from very fine grain types with a slow speed as low as 16 ASA to superfast films of 500 ASA. Most, however, fall into the general purpose, 50 to 100 ASA group. They are made in several forms because, unlike the human eye which adapts to changing light conditions, film can only be manufactured to give accurate color reproduction in a specific type of light.

Most are balanced for use in either daylight (5,400K) or artificial incandescent light (3,200 or 3,400K).

The extent of the color system is illustrated in the diagram below, and it shows clearly that there is more than one way of achieving a required result. Usually the fewer the stages involved, the better the quality of the end product. The exception is instant prints which tend to be inferior. However, the flexibility of the system means that if you have used, say, a negative film with the intention of making prints, it is always possible to make slides (reversal transparencies) instead. The quality of transparencies made in this way is poorer than photographing directly onto transparency film, though. This is partly because an extra optical step is involved and partly because inaccuracies in the dyes themselves tend to build up with each stage.

When deciding which products and systems to use bear in mind the limitations of the materials involved. It may seem that using transparency film and making reversal prints from them is a good system. It is but very accurate exposure is needed for good results, whereas the alternative negative/positive system can be used with much less accuracy.

Tripack color film
This film has three light sensitive layers to record the visible spectrum. The top layer is designed to record blue light, the middle layer green, and the bottom layer red. A yellow filter is placed between the blue and green sensitive layers, because although the top layer is blind to red and green light, the lower layers are partially sensitive to blue. The filter (destroyed during processing) absorbs stray blue light.

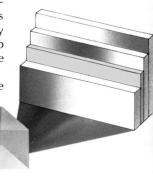

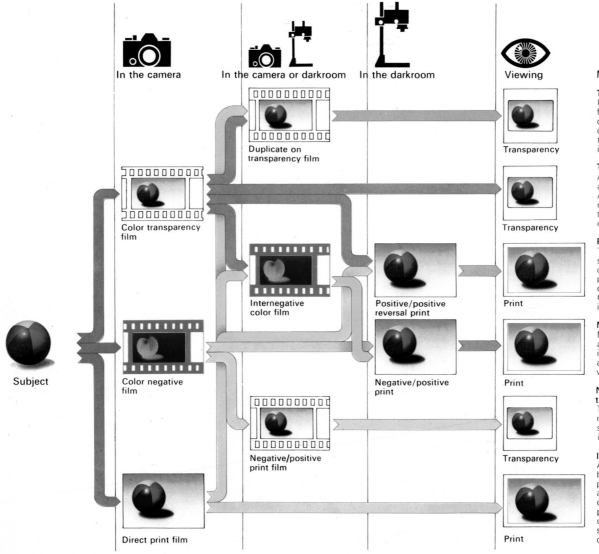

In the camera · In the camera or darkroom · In the darkroom · Viewing

Subject

Color transparency film

Duplicate on transparency film — Transparency

Transparency

Internegative color film

Positive/positive reversal print — Print

Color negative film

Negative/positive print — Print

Negative/positive print film — Transparency

Direct print film — Print

Making color photographs

Transparency duplicates
Use a low contrast fine grain film, or special purpose duplicating film. Such copies often have higher contrast than the original. Accurate exposure is required.

Transparencies
A wide range of films is available from 12 ASA to 500 ASA. Some films can be uprated during processing by two to three stops. Accurate exposure is essential.

Reversal prints
The original transparency should be accurately exposed or slightly under-exposed. Some papers require re-exposure during the printing process. Color balancing when printing is necessary for best results.

Negative/positive prints
Negative exposures + 1 stop are acceptable. Color saturation is increased by over-exposure and vice versa. Color balancing when printing is essential.

Negative/positive transparencies
The same applies as for negative/positive prints, but some increase in contrast is usual.

Instant color prints
A special camera or camera back is required. Prints are processed automatically within a few minutes, so that errors can be corrected by taking the picture again. Quality is usually poorer than with other systems. The prints can be copied and enlarged.

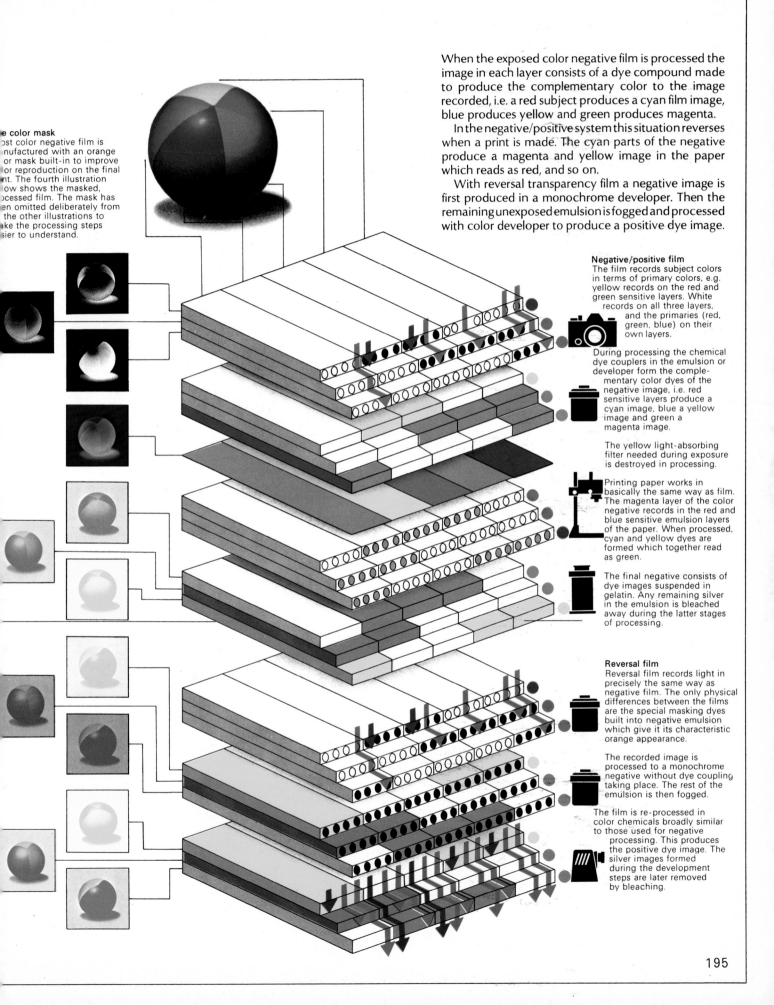

When the exposed color negative film is processed the image in each layer consists of a dye compound made to produce the complementary color to the image recorded, i.e. a red subject produces a cyan film image, blue produces yellow and green produces magenta.

In the negative/positive system this situation reverses when a print is made. The cyan parts of the negative produce a magenta and yellow image in the paper which reads as red, and so on.

With reversal transparency film a negative image is first produced in a monochrome developer. Then the remaining unexposed emulsion is fogged and processed with color developer to produce a positive dye image.

The color mask
Most color negative film is manufactured with an orange color mask built-in to improve color reproduction on the final print. The fourth illustration below shows the masked, processed film. The mask has been omitted deliberately from the other illustrations to make the processing steps easier to understand.

Negative/positive film
The film records subject colors in terms of primary colors, e.g. yellow records on the red and green sensitive layers. White records on all three layers, and the primaries (red, green, blue) on their own layers.

During processing the chemical dye couplers in the emulsion or developer form the complementary color dyes of the negative image, i.e. red sensitive layers produce a cyan image, blue a yellow image and green a magenta image.

The yellow light-absorbing filter needed during exposure is destroyed in processing.

Printing paper works in basically the same way as film. The magenta layer of the color negative records in the red and blue sensitive emulsion layers of the paper. When processed, cyan and yellow dyes are formed which together read as green.

The final negative consists of dye images suspended in gelatin. Any remaining silver in the emulsion is bleached away during the latter stages of processing.

Reversal film
Reversal film records light in precisely the same way as negative film. The only physical differences between the films are the special masking dyes built into negative emulsion which give it its characteristic orange appearance.

The recorded image is processed to a monochrome negative without dye coupling taking place. The rest of the emulsion is then fogged.

The film is re-processed in color chemicals broadly similar to those used for negative processing. This produces the positive dye image. The silver images formed during the development steps are later removed by bleaching.

The Color Darkroom

A darkroom set up for black and white processing will need extra equipment for successful color processing. The major additions are a set of additive or subtractive printing filters or a dial-in filter color head for your enlarger, a print processing drum, and a good quality enlarging lens. Other items should include an appropriate safelight screen, a daylight quality fluorescent light fitting for print color evaluation, suitable chemicals, measures and jugs, a pair of rubber gloves (for handling chemicals) and lint free cotton gloves (for handling negatives). A timer, and an accurate high temperature short range thermometer are also essential. Ventilation must be good since the chemicals produce fumes. Because much color work is done in darkness or in the very dim light of a color safelight it pays to plan the use of space and the position of equipment very carefully.

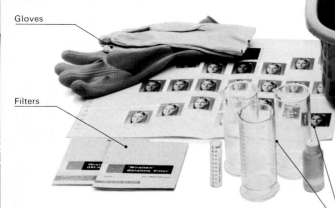

Color head
Deep water bath
Chemicals
Gloves
Filters
High temperature thermometer
Ring-around specimen prints
Measures
Print processing drum
Color analyzer

COLOR FILM PROCESSING

Color films require more complex processing procedures than monochrome films. There are many different color films and processing systems not all of which are suitable for home-processing. Those that are vary widely in the number of chemical baths, operational temperature levels and processing times they need. When you have decided which system to use read the instructions very carefully. They will specify the process accuracy requirements necessary to give acceptable results. It is important that they be understood and carefully followed.

It is likely that your process will specify a processing temperature probably within the range of 77°–104°F (25°–40°C) which is higher than for monochrome films. The temperature of certain developing baths must be controlled to within $\pm\frac{1}{4}$°C. The easiest way to meet such requirements is to use a thermal water bath to control the process temperatures. The bath needs to be big enough to hold all the chemical bottles and the developing tank.

Negative film processing usually consists of a color developing stage, a bleach bath, a wash, then a fixing bath. This is followed by another wash and finally a stabilizing rinse. Reversal films require several extra stages at the beginning of the process including a black and white developing bath. The film is fogged either by re-exposure or chemically. The remaining procedure is similar to the stages for negative films. When the process is finished the equipment should be cleaned to remove any chemical residue.

Developing a color film

Prepare the film as described on p. 187. Stand chemicals in a hot water bath to reach the correct temperature. Pour developer into the tank.

Place the tank in the water bath to keep the temperature of developer accurate. Agitate it according to the manufacturer's instructions.

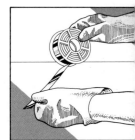

After development, re-expose reversal films if instructed. Most modern films, however, undergo chemical reversal.

Continue subsequent processes (2nd development of reversal films, bleach/fix, etc.) as specified by the manufacturer.

Wash the film with water at the correct temperature when instructed.

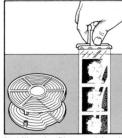

Stabilize the film emulsion if necessary. Do not wipe the film but hang it to dry natural.

Making a Color Print

Converting a black and white darkroom for color work

You will need all the equipment shown on the left to process color films in an ordinary black and white darkroom. In addition, make sure that your safelight is fitted with a suitable filter and that the lens in your enlarger will produce high quality images.

Successful color printing involves mastering two techniques – processing the paper and achieving the correct color balance and exposure. Before attempting color work, you should be thoroughly familiar with the technique of black and white printing.

There are several types of color paper and process system available, but as with color films, the chemicals designed for a specific paper should be used. Although mixing papers and processes will, in most cases, produce a recognizable print, the color quality will be poor and the print is likely to be unstable.

Some of the smaller manufacturers produce "universal process systems" which, supposedly, can be used with all papers. These produce adequate results, but they cannot match the quality obtained with the correct chemicals.

Most color print processing systems are designed for machine use, and consequently tend to work at higher than normal temperatures, around 86°–104°F (30°–40°C). For this reason, processing in trays is not recommended. A daylight processing drum is a more practical solution. This uses a pre-heating technique by which the heat needed to sustain the process temperature is provided by a pre-process hot water bath.

The variety of processing procedures, and the many different ways of achieving a successful print, means that the sequence shown below should be regarded only as a guide to the stages involved in print making.

SAFETY

Color processing chemicals are dangerous, often toxic, so follow the mixing instructions and handling recommendations with great care. Always wear rubber gloves when using the chemicals and store them safely out of reach of young children and pets.

The printing method

Carefully clean dust from the negative and carrier. Handle the negative wearing cotton gloves, and by the edges only.

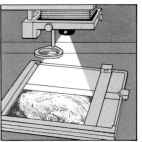

Using safelight for clarity only, mask the picture in the way described on p. 190.

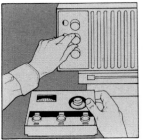

Dial the required filter values on the color head or make up the pack with filter foils and place in the filter drawer of the enlarger.

Ensure that the image is still correctly positioned. Turn off *all* lights and place the printing paper under the masking frame.

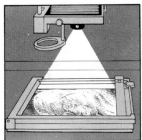

Make the exposure and dodge or burn-in areas where necessary. This is possible with subtractive but not with additive printing.

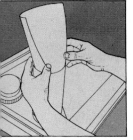

Load the exposed paper into the drum with the emulsion inwards, and then seal the drum.

In normal light measure the chemical solutions and prepare the pre-wash at the recommended temperature.

Start the processing stages. Pour the pre-wash into the drum and leave it for ½ min. Pour out and save the pre-wash for re-use.

Pour the developer quickly into the drum. Time this stage from the moment you start to roll the drum.

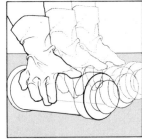

Roll the drum backward and forward continuously. Pour out solution 15 secs. before the end of the developing time.

Pour in the stop bath solution and agitate for ½ min. Pour out stop and pour in bleach/fix (½ min).

Use the pre-wash water for the washing stages of the process. 4 to 6 rinses are usually required.

When the process is finished, take the print out of the drum, wipe off excess solution and air dry the print.

Clean out the drum and chemical containers ready for the next process while the print is drying.

When dry, check in daylight that the color balance and exposure of the print are satisfactory.

Color Printing Methods

THE SUBTRACTIVE METHOD

Commonly known as white light printing, this method requires only a single printing exposure. Professionals prefer this system, since print control techniques such as burning-in and dodging can be used.

The cost of setting up your darkroom for subtractive printing is higher than for additive printing as more equipment is required. If you decide the extra cost is worthwhile you will need an enlarger fitted with either a color head, or a filter drawer which is used with a set of yellow, magenta and cyan filters.

Making a print involves using filters to adjust the relative amounts of primary color present in the enlarger light source, so that the negative and printing paper characteristics can be matched. In a color head the filter values are dialed into use, but with a filter drawer a "pack" of the required filters must be made.

Before a print can be correctly exposed a color-balanced test strip must be produced. There are several methods of doing this, including trial and error, using a matrix device, or using a color analyzer.

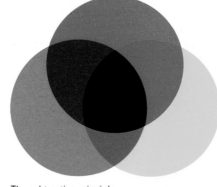

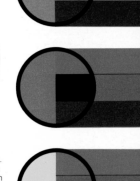

The subtractive principle
The subtractive principle involves selectively removing primary color from a white light source. For example, a cyan filter will subtract or block a percentage of the red primary but allow the green and blue light to pass through. The percentage blocked is related to the density of the filter used.

Enlargers

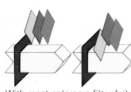

Most amateur enlargers available today are equipped with a filter drawer for subtractive color printing. The drawer is located above the negative carrier and condensers, just below the lamphousing. Subtractive yellow, magenta, and cyan filter foils are placed in the drawer to modify the color of the enlarger light source. Space is usually provided above the drawer for the heat-absorbing filter required for many processes. Some enlargers have removable condensers or provision for a diffuser screen. If diffused light is used dust and marks on the negative are less likely to be recorded on the print.

Many manufacturers make a special color head as optional or standard equipment on enlargers. These use glass filter wedges, which are dialed into use as required. A tungsten halogen lamp is used for the increased light output needed for efficient diffusion printing and the concentrated light beam required by the filter mechanism.

With most enlargers filter foils can be placed between the negative and lamphousing, top. Some enlargers use glass wedge filters which are moved into the light beam, above and below.

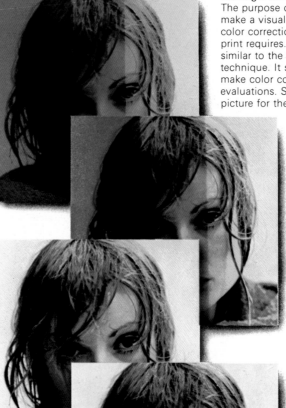

Making a test strip

The purpose of a test strip is to allow you make a visual judgment of the amount of color correction and exposure that your first print requires. The procedure for making it similar to the black and white test strip technique. It should be large enough to make color comparisons and exposure evaluations. Select a key color area of your picture for the test.

The first test, top left, should be made using the manufacturer's recommended filter pack for your film/paper combination. This information is in the data booklet supplied with the paper. A stepped exposure sequence (see p. 190 should be used. The processed test will probably have a strong color cast.

For the second test, left, the filter pack is altered by adding filters which visually match the cast in the first test. The new filter pack will make a change in exposure time necessary. Calculate this by selecting the correctly exposed band in the first test and change the time as shown in the instructions. The color balance and exposure of this test should be almost correct.

Too little filtration will produce a similar but less pronounced cast to the first test. Too much filtration will produce a complementary cast so some filter density should be removed from the filter pack. Use the same procedure as for the second test to adjust the exposure time and pack. The third test, far left, should almost certainly be correct.

If you are not absolutely sure a fourth test can be made to check if further pack and exposure adjustments bring any improvements. Always make a neutral, correctly exposed test, left, before attempting a full-size print.

USING A MATRIX DEVICE

This device is used to make a test strip which will give the information you need to produce a color-corrected and properly exposed print. It works on the principle that most pictures contain a balance of color, which if mixed produce a neutral gray tone. It consists of a matrix of translucent patches each colored to repre-

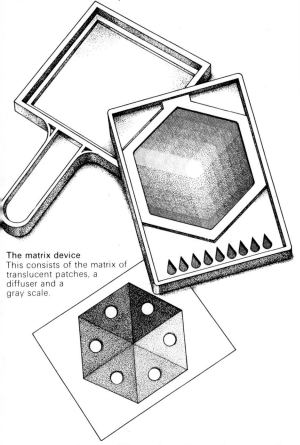

The matrix device
This consists of the matrix of translucent patches, a diffuser and a gray scale.

sent a particular set of filter values. To use it, a test strip is exposed through the matrix after the enlarger has been set up in the normal way. A diffuser is positioned under the lens to scramble the image.

When processed, one of the patches on the test should be gray. Refer to the instructions (supplied with the kit) for the filter pack to be used and how to calculate the exposure time.

USING A COLOR ANALYZER

A color analyzer is an electronic instrument which can measure the amount of primary red, blue and green light in a light source. This is used to compare the image of the negative to be printed with a "master" or "standard" negative from which a properly corrected and exposed print has been made, the results of which have been used to calibrate the instrument. The differences can be translated into the filter pack and exposure required to make a neutral print from the analyzed negative.

Amateur instruments usually read off all the negative area using a sensor unit clamped onto the enlarger lens. Expensive professional units have a probe which can select small areas from the projected image to be analyzed.

THE ADDITIVE METHOD

This is the method to use if you plan to make only a few prints. The initial outlay for equipment is less than for subtractive printing, and an enlarger without a filter drawer can be used. You need a set of "tricolor" printing filters, which are strong red, blue and green, and a frame to hold the filters beneath the lens during exposure.

Making a print involves exposing the three emulsion layers of the printing paper separately. This is done by making exposures through each of the "tricolor" filters in turn.

The three exposure times must be adjusted so that the emulsion layers are correctly exposed in relation to each other. The correct times are found by making a test strip as described below, or by using a matrix device. It is important throughout the printing sequence to maintain correct registration. Make sure that the image is not moved in relation to the paper while filter changes are being made.

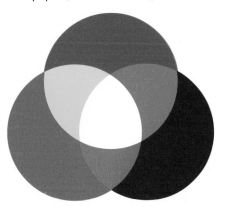

The additive principle
Blue, green and red are called primary colors because they are the primary components of white light. Primary color filters absorb two thirds of the visual spectrum and transmit the remaining one third, their own color.

10 seconds blue filter

15 seconds blue filter

20 seconds blue filter

25 seconds blue filter

Enlargers
Enlargers are built with varying degrees of sophistication for additive work.

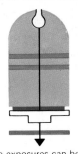

Three exposures can be made through "tricolor" filters.

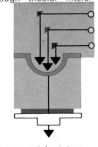

In commercial printers, separate red, blue and green light sources are used.

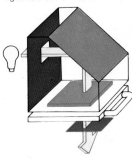

Enlargers with a color filter drawer may be used for additive printing. The filters are placed in the filter drawer instead of beneath the lens.

Making a test strip
There are 2 methods of making a test strip: by trial and error or by use of a matrix device. Trial and error tests are made as follows. With the lights off and the printing paper in place, slide the blue filter under the lens, and expose for 10 secs. This exposes the paper's yellow dye forming layer. Replace the blue filter with the green. Make a horizontally stepped exposure of 10, 15, 20 and 25 secs. Repeat this using the red filter, but step the exposures vertically. The processed test may look like the first example, top left, light and lacking yellow. To increase the yellow make tests with the same red and green exposures but with extra blue exposure time. When a satisfactory square is found, make the final print using the relevant filters for the correct times.

Making Other Prints

REVERSAL PRINTING

Color prints and copy transparencies can be made from transparencies using special reversal printing papers and copy films that are marketed by a number of manufacturers.

To make a copy transparency you need a special attachment for your camera. These come in several designs. The cheaper types will use the camera lens, but more expensive models often have a special color-corrected lens built in. If you have only occasional need for this technique, then use a slow speed, general purpose, transparency film. For large volume work one of the specially made copy films, usually sold in bulk quantities, will be cheaper and give better results.

Prints can be made on reversal print paper or on dye bleach paper – two different products. Reversal paper is similar in construction to negative/positive papers while dye bleach paper is dark in color when viewed before exposure, as it has image dyes built into the paper during manufacture. When exposed to light and processed, the exposed areas are bleached away leaving the reversed image behind.

Methods can vary a great deal, so read the instructions for your selected system.

DYE DIFFUSION PRINTING

Two new systems are now available for making color prints, both based on instant picture image transfer (or dye diffusion) principles. The first, Ektaflex PCT, can be used when printing from slides or negatives, while the second, Agfachrome Speed, can only be used when printing from slides. The advantage of dye diffusion is that prints require a simple one-bath activator for development, instead of the more usual multi-bath processing technique.

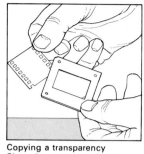
Copying a transparency
Clean the transparencies to be copied after removing the film from the mount (if necessary for your copier).

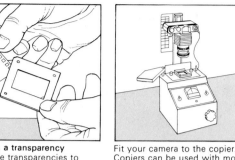
Fit your camera to the copier. Copiers can be used with most SLR cameras, and some allow selective copying.

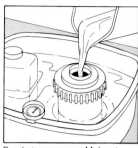
Bracket exposures. Make at least 3 different ones of the same shot. Develop the film.

Printing from a transparency
Clean the film thoroughly, and fit it into the negative carrier of the enlarger.

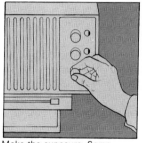
Make the exposure. Some papers require filtration to obtain a neutral print, but see the manufacturer's instructions.

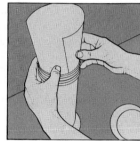
Process the print in the recommended chemicals.

Ektaflex PCT

Ektaflex uses the "peel-apart" system – you expose your slide or negative on to the correct film and then, using a special printmaking machine, soak the film in activator before laminating it on to a receiving paper. The dyes migrate from the film to the paper, leaving chemical residue and the silver image behind on the film.

After exposure, place your sheet of Ektaflex PCT film on the film ramp of the print-making machine and a sheet of PCT paper on the paper shelf.

Slide the exposed film into the activator solution contained in the base of the printmaker. Wait 20 secs.

Turn the handle on the printmaker to laminate the film and paper together. You can now turn the room light on while the "sandwich" processes itself.

After the recommended time you can peel the paper and film apart. Do not wash the finished print.

Agfachrome Speed

Agfachrome is similar in principle to Polaroid SX-70 or Kodak Trimprint film as it is a one-sheet process. You expose the paper through the back, immerse it in activator and, in un-exposed areas, dyes migrate from a transmitter layer to a receiver layer. You then view the print from the front and all chemical residue remains in the material.

Place the Agfachrome Speed material in your masking frame, dark smooth side uppermost. Set all color filtration to zero and make a test strip.

Wearing gloves, place the sheet in activator solution exposed side down. Agitate for the first 15 secs and remove after 90 secs.

Wash the film in ordinary room light. Do not wash for longer than 5 mins. Color evaluation is possible after the first 90 secs in the wash.

Assess the print. The image will darken slowly as the print dries.

Printing for Special Effects

CONTROL PRINTING

Enlarging not only allows you to make large prints; it is also a method of precisely controlling the quality of the finished photograph. Because there is room between the lens and the image on the baseboard to intercept the light being projected with the hands or masks, you can burn-in (add exposure) or dodge-out (reduce exposure) in selected areas of the print. In most cases of "local shading" it is important to keep the shading device moving during exposure to prevent sharp outlines appearing on the print (see p. 191).

COMBINATION PRINTING

Combining two separate negatives on a single print is one method of adding subject matter to a composition. Two separate negatives are necessary, for example, one of a landscape and one of clouds. A dark yellow or orange filter should be placed between the enlarger lens and baseboard so that the images can be aligned on the printing paper without exposure occurring. Once the prints are correctly positioned, you remove the filter to allow light from the enlarger to reach the photographic printing paper.

A test strip of the main subject, in this case the landscape, should be made so that a satisfactory full-size print can be processed. Another print of the landscape is then exposed, including any local shading

that may be required. This is not developed, but after exposure the edges of the horizon and the top of the picture should be marked in pencil to assist with alignment at the second exposure stage. The landscape negative is replaced by the cloud negative and the image projected onto the first rough print of the landscape. The landscape print is removed while a test strip is made of the cloud negative. When a satisfactory print of the clouds has been obtained the paper containing the second landscape exposure is carefully replaced in the easel. It is important that the easel is not moved at this stage. The clouds are exposed to

the area above the horizon while all other areas of landscape are shaded out. Complicated outlines can be shaded by using the original rough print cut to the shape of the outline as the mask.

LOCAL PRINT REDUCTION

Local reduction, or bleaching, on prints with chemicals is a useful way of lightening areas once the print has been made. It is important that the print is fixed and washed before bleaching is attempted. The bleaching solution used is Farmer's reducer (see p. 241) which should be tested on old test strips or prints. The solution is applied to the chosen areas of the print while running water passes over it to prevent uneven reduction or boundary marks. After reduction, the fixing and washing stages must be repeated.

Combined images
An example of double printing from one negative. The tree in the center of the railway line is in exactly the same position on the original negative. I simply enlarged it to confuse perspective. The first image of the railway lines and surroundings was exposed to the paper, while a dodger obliterated the area around the tree. I removed the paper, and then exposed the enlarged tree into the unexposed area left on the paper through a hole in the center of a black card.

Contrast with dodging
It is important to consider any planned darkroom technique carefully, right from the taking stage — particularly in choice of lighting, film, camera etc. In this instance, far left, I used lighting to separate the two characters. A diffused spot was directed on the girl's face, a larger diffused flood gave overall lighting. During printing the girl's face was lightened by dodging, and I gave the whole print a 50% increase over correct exposure to give a grayer background. Development was normal.

Contrast with reducer
This bromide print was made slightly darker than normal. I lightened the tone of the swans by using Farmer's reducer (see p. 241) applied locally with a brush. This reducer can be used over the whole print to "clean" any highlights.

Coloring Black & White Prints

CHEMICAL TONING

There are a wide variety of chemical toners available which can be purchased in "ready-to-use" packs. You can also make up your own by obtaining the required chemical constituents. In using toners you convert the black metallic silver image to a dye image; thus toning requires a system of bleaching and dyeing. Chemical toners only color areas where black metallic silver exists, the depth of tone depending on the density of the original prints. In clear white areas of the print little, if any, toning takes place mainly because there is no black metallic silver image to convert. The print must be adequately fixed and washed before any form of toning is attempted.

Below, two formulae and their procedures for use are described. With the first example the toner is available in a "ready-to-use" package form, the second involves the use of individual chemicals.

Sepia toning

This produces warm brown tones by a process of potassium ferricyanide bleaching followed by sulfide toning. The solutions used are:

> *Bleach*
> 50 gr. Potassium bromide
> 100 gr. Potassium ferricyanide
> Water to make up to 1 liter
> *Sulfide toner*
> 200 gr. Sodium sulfide
> Water to make up to 1 liter
> When using dilute 4 parts of these stock solutions with 20 parts water.

The procedure is:

1. Bleach prints in the first solution until the image fades to a very light brown.
2. Briefly rinse in clean water.
3. Place in the second solution, the sulfide bath, for approximately 1 minute.
4. Thoroughly wash for 30 minutes.

The stock sulfide solution has a characteristic pungent smell and should only be used in a well ventilated area. Solutions once used should be discarded, but stock solutions particularly the bleach, will keep indefinitely when stored in a dark bottle.

Copper toning

The copper process described can provide tones from warm brown to light red depending on the time the chemicals are allowed to act. In the early stages, tones are dark purple; they gradually change to brown and then to red. The solutions used are:

> *Bleach*
> 50 gr. Potassium ferricyanide
> 200 gr. Potassium citrate
> Water to make up to 1 liter
> *Copper sulfate toner*
> 200 gr. Potassium citrate
> 50 gr. Copper sulfate
> Water to make up to 1 liter

These solutions should be mixed immediately before use and discarded after the processing cycle which is the same as for sepia toner.

In all cases the contrast and density of the original print affects the end product. Density affects the depth of dye produced (degree of saturation) and contrast, particularly with sepia toner, affects the warmth or

Achieving a poster effect
You can obtain the flat color effect of a poster, above, by first making a very contrasty, hard print from a suitable negative, and then by applying flat color to selected areas, either with an air brush using a translucent ink so that the original image is not obscured, or by covering areas with transparent adhesive film.

Using a chemical toner
The wrought iron facade of this Australian house was a suitable subject for a sepia-toned print. The warm brown color is reminiscent of photographs of the same period as the house, giving the picture a nostalgic appeal. I began with a good quality black and white bromide print (i.e. fully developed) then bleached, rinsed and re-developed it in sepia toner. The result is permanent.

coldness of the tones. Generally, softer contrast prints provide warm tones and more contrasty prints give cold tones.

COLOR PAPERS AND FABRIC DYES
Bromide papers are available with a wide range of base colors, the baryta (whitening) coating normally used being replaced by color dyes. You can use fabric dyes to color black and white bromide prints. The dye colors the whole paper but the intensity of the dye depends on the color used, the temperature of the dye solution and the time it is allowed to act. A variety of effects can be achieved and, obviously, a wide range of colors. The procedure for dyeing photographic prints is the same as for fabric. It is safest and easiest to use a cold water dye which takes about five minutes to act fully. This gives a good degree of control. Use of hot water dyes may cause heat damage to the emulsion layer.

HAND COLORING
The coloring of prints by hand depends on the ability and aptitude of the individual but with practice it is possible to achieve very good results either by applying different colors to the whole of the print or by tinting specific areas. Several mediums may be used including transparent watercolor paints or dyes.

WATERCOLORS
Watercolors provide a very good medium for hand coloring. Some practice beforehand in laying down "flat" color will help you improve the final result. Matt paper is most suitable because it absorbs the color readily. Unfortunately, gelatin on glossy papers is highly absorbent so you need to judge correct depth of color at the first application since a second application is inclined to streak. With more experience you may be able to apply deeper color by cross-hatching over required areas. Good quality brushes are essential in order to avoid brush hairs adhering to the color on the print. It is advisable to use a wetting agent on the print before tinting as this helps the smooth application of color.

DYES
Color dyes can be applied easily, and they offer the additional advantage of becoming darker with repeated application. Unlike watercolors, dyes cannot be washed off. Their intensity can be reduced by soaking in a weak solution of sodium carbonate.

AIRBRUSHING
Flat colors are highly effective when applied with an airbrush. This technique is described in greater detail on p. 200.

Hand coloring
Coloring prints by hand, a recently revived technique, allows you to pick out certain areas for emphasis. You can aim for realism (as with the early ambrotypes), deliberately change tonal and color values, or limit color to one area. Begin, for example, with a light, yet detailed monochrome print, black and white, or sepia-toned, fixing it to a firm base before starting to color. Photo-tints, aniline dyes or water colors are all suitable. You apply them with a fine brush, building up density by repeated application. While working on color areas, protect other parts of the print with paper.

Creating Images in the Darkroom

BAS-RELIEF

When a negative and positive of the same size from the same subject are placed together in an enlarger but slightly displaced, a pseudo-3D effect known as *bas-relief* can be achieved. The larger the negative size (4 × 5 ins, 10.2 × 12.7 cm is ideal) the easier it is to control the print effect, but the greater the degree of displacement necessary. The density and contrast of the negative and positive must be similar for the best effect. The subject material can vary from large areas of tone to fine detail, although highly detailed subjects sometimes become difficult to recognize.

POSTERIZATION

This technique is used to make selected tonal separations from a continuous tone (normal) negative. Usually the continuous tone is reduced to three or four tonal areas and for this, tone separation negatives have to be produced. For a three tone separation, two tone-separated negatives are necessary; for a four tone separation, three tone-separation negatives are needed.

The continuous tone negative is printed onto sheets of high contrast lith film later processed in lith developer. This produces high contrast positives of the subject but on clear film. The density of the positives is determined by the exposure time used to produce them. In this way, the subject is represented by silhouettes of varying density.

The highlight separation is over-exposed making shadows and mid-tones merge to form a solid black deposit. Only bright highlights remain clear. The mid-tone separation is exposed to cause shadows and deeper mid-tones to merge to make black. Highlights and light mid-tones remain clear. The shadow separa-

tion is exposed so that only shadows form black. All mid-tones and highlights remain as clear film. Each positive is then printed in register one at a time to form a master negative on continuous tone film. The shadow separation is printed light gray (by test). When this gray has been established the other two separation negatives are printed in register for *exactly the same time*. The result is a negative of four tones (including white). Registration is critical and some form of punch register system is advisable together with a rigid and locked-focusing enlarger.

SABATTIER OR PSEUDO-SOLARIZATION

For this effect an exposed negative, partially developed, is briefly re-exposed to white light. Development is then continued for the manufacturer's recommended time. The effect is partial or total reversal of tones in some areas of the image, giving a mixed negative/positive on the resulting processed film.

This form of solarization is a matter of trial and error but there are general guidelines to provide a starting point. You can try interrupting the developing cycle two-thirds of the way through and exposing medium speed film to a 25 watt bulb for 20 seconds. This is only a guide and variations will be necessary to achieve good results depending on your darkroom set-up. If the solarization effect is weak, interrupt development earlier. True solarization only occurs with gross over-exposure and is very difficult to achieve in practice.

A similar pseudo-solarization can be used on prints to produce dark results. The procedure is the same, interrupting print development approximately half way through the recommended time and then fogging to white light for approximately ten seconds. Print development then continues.

Adding atmosphere
You can add certain atmospheric effects to a picture in the darkroom. The landscape shot opposite was made on a dull day, when the required atmosphere was impossible to achieve with a straightforward photograph. I accordingly placed transparent tape across the middle of the lens hood, thus softening the central area. The rest was done during the printing process. Towards the end of development I exposed the print to the darkroom light for a partially solarized effect. I continued the development by applying developer with a cotton swab soaked in the chemical and in this way I achieved the patchy effect.

Exaggerated detail
This etched effect of *bas-relief* has changed the familiar photographic image into a simplified, apparently three-dimensional form. Any picture with images having well-defined edges is suitable. The amount of *bas-relief* can be varied and in this example it has been kept to a minimum. I contact printed the original negative on to a piece of continuous tone film, to give a positive similar in contrast but slightly lighter than the negative. I then sandwiched the positive and negative together, slightly off-register, and made a conventional print.

Flattening areas of tone
Posterization is a technique which turns a normal photograph into flat areas of tone: black, light gray, dark gray and white, see right. The original negative is printed onto three separate sheets of high-contrast lith film. One is under-exposed, the second correctly exposed, the third over-exposed. These positives are then printed in turn onto one sheet of continuous tone film. You give the same exposure time for each, making sure the images are in exact register, and then print the master negative on normal grade paper.

Eliminating tone
With this technique you can convert an ordinary photograph into a powerful graphic image, as shown far right, by increasing the contrast so that half-tones disappear. I enlarged this negative on to high-contrast lith paper, using a high-contrast developer. If you cannot get the right degree of contrast, re-photograph the print with line film, then make a print from the negative.

205

Creating Images in the Darkroom

COLOR SOLARIZATION

Print solarization in color need not be considered impractical, although certain types of subject produce more acceptable results than others. Prints with large areas of light tone show the effect most readily. Similar and, indeed, more controllable results can be obtained by producing black and white solarizations as described previously and then printing them through colored filters onto color printing paper. The printing stage obviously offers a greater means of control over the final result and removes much of the frustration that is associated with solarizing directly onto color print material.

If the solarized effect is to be attempted in color either through a color negative or a black and white negative, the lighting of the subject and the negatives produced need to be of high contrast – certainly, in the case of a color negative, much higher contrast than would be the case for normal color printing.

Using black and white negatives as the "original" allows control over contrast because of the variety of film stocks available in monochrome. To produce primary color effects (red, blue, green) from a black and white solarized negative with color filters, you will need to print through primary filters of red, blue and green. Remember that as you alter filtration, you will also need to vary printing exposure.

Processing of the print is by the normal color print processing cycle no matter what coloring technique is employed.

Solarization can be achieved on color transparencies with care. After exposure and approximately midway through the first developing stage, expose the material to a colored light (red or blue work very well) then continue the processing cycle to the end. With patience and practice it is possible to narrow the degree of error in deciding where to interrupt the first development, and to determine the required duration and strength of exposure.

BAS-RELIEF IN COLOR

This is best produced with black and white negative and positive originals printed through one or a number of colored filters onto color printing paper. For more unusual effects try "local shading" through a colored filter but remember the effect on exposure. A color negative and color positive placed together slightly out of register can work, although in both cases they need to be light in density and harsh in contrast. Further, such a pack can lead to rather prolonged exposure times on color print materials.

COLOR POSTERIZATION

This is an extension of black and white tone separation, where the original can be a positive or a negative, monochrome or color. The original will need to be copied onto a high contrast lith film as described on pp. 204–205. You may need to produce a number of negatives and positives to achieve the ideal master negative with tone separation as required. Blacking-out with opaque liquid may be necessary to tidy up detail. The procedure for this stage is the same as described for black and white posterization. You finish with a master negative containing separated tonal areas or a set of tone-separated negatives.

A color posterization print is produced by printing

the separate negatives through blue, green or red filters for different periods of time. The variations are endless especially when you consider that solarization negatives or bas-relief masters could be incorporated at the same time. Again, registration is of prime importance, and where more than one negative is used in printing, a registration punch system on the printing paper linked to spacers on the enlarging easel is essential, because no safelighting can be used with these color print materials.

DIFFUSION TECHNIQUES

The original can be black and white or color, negative or positive. Any number of filters or diffusing materials can be used to vary the optical quality and color rendering of the original. Patterned glass, colored linens and colored celluloid are all worth experimenting with to create variations from the straight shot. You can try using diffusers that themselves have varying density and color content, but remember they can and should be kept in motion between the enlarger light source and baseboard during print exposure. The most important point to remember is that they must not be completely opaque.

Increasing color with filters
Color filters were used at the enlarging stage to increase the contrast and give additional warmth to the picture above. Altering the image in this manner can increase the atmosphere, and you have greater opportunity to express yourself, manipulating colors and tones to suit the scene. Here, the contrast between the window and the room is strengthened by the extreme difference in color.

Color printing from black and white
Abstract color prints like those opposite can be made from black and white negatives. First print your negative on three or more sheets of "equadensity" black and white film, giving different exposure levels in each case. Contact print the processed positives on to reversal color film, using a strong color filter over the light source. Use different filters for each separation. Process the color films, sandwich them together in register, and enlarge them on color printing paper.

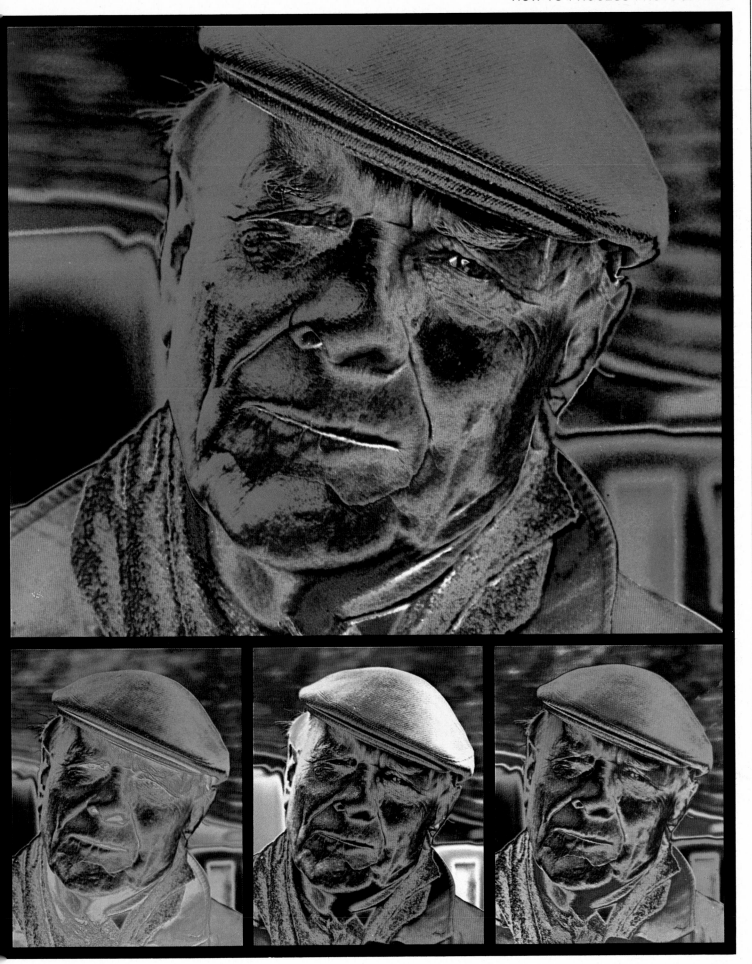

Creating Images in the Darkroom

RETICULATION

Reticulation produces a fine, regular, crazing pattern over a negative. It occurred as a common fault on early film and glass-based negative emulsions, but the problem of it happening accidentally has now been overcome by manufacturers' improvements in the stability of the materials used to make film. Because of this, reticulation is difficult to produce as an effect with modern film but with perseverance it can be achieved by greatly varying the temperature of working solutions (e.g. fixer to wash) and by making extreme changes in alkalinity (e.g. developer to rinse). Obviously the reticulation becomes more apparent when both methods are used.

LITH PAPER

This is a very high contrast paper which will reduce continuous tone negatives to two tones, black and white. It must be handled in deep red safelighting and processed in special lith developer.

For good blacks, processing chemicals must be used at the recommended temperature of 68°F (20°C) and continuously agitated. Underdevelopment of this material will produce light brown images.

MONTAGE

A montage, sometimes called a composite, is produced by selecting and cutting out parts of a number of prints and mounting them together side-by-side or overlapping. If you are trying to create an illusion, remember to take care with the relative scale of prints and to remove any white edges where prints join. When a montage has been finished, a copy negative can be made so that further prints can be produced.

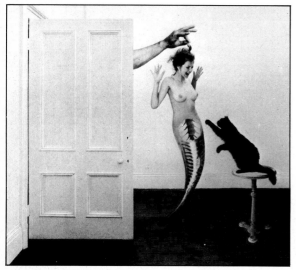

Photo-montage
This picture, reproduced in the Introduction, is a combination of six photographs: the empty room with the open door; the man's arm and hand; the upper part of the girl; the fishbone; the fish tail and the cat on the stool (which was actually being tempted with a piece of liver in order to make it reach out with its paw). The various images were projected on to a piece of tracing paper through the enlarger to establish the correct size, and then printed. The images were carefully cut out, the edges chamfered and blackened with marking ink before being pasted into position. I finally photo-copied the finished montage, and made some minor improvements by retouching the print.

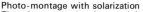

Photo-montage with solarization
The mirror was taken in a straightforward manner, and the image of the girl was solarized. I contact printed the negative of the girl on to line film: Two-thirds of the way through development I switched on the darkroom light very briefly to solarize the negative. The development was continued until no further change occurred. I then fixed the (very dark) film, washed and dried it, and printed through the enlarger, giving a long exposure. You can contact print the solarized film on to another sheet of film to obtain a less dense image, even solarizing this film to double the effect.

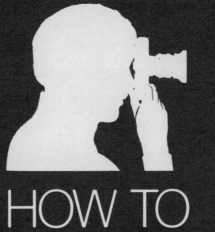

HOW TO
CHOOSE & USE
EQUIPMENT

Selecting a Camera

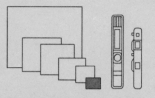

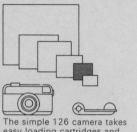

The smallest cameras available, the 110 and the subminiature, use 16 mm film in cartridges.

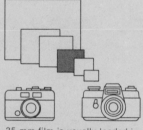

The simple 126 camera takes easy loading cartridges and produces square negatives on film the same width as 35 mm.

35 mm film is usually loaded in cassettes for 35 mm viewfinder cameras and SLRs.

2¼ ins (6 cm) square format film is needed by TLRs and some large format SLRs.

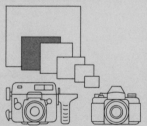

"Ideal format" is the 6×7 cm roll-film suitable for some small technical cameras and large format SLRs.

First decide on your priorities. Are you going to take pictures for pleasure, profit, or both? Do you want a camera which is complete in itself, light and compact to carry, or one to which you will gradually be able to add different lenses and attachments? Do you hope to specialize in say, sports photography, or close-ups? If so, what size and shape of print or transparency do you want?

Film size

The smallest camera in use is the pocket-size 110, which uses 16 mm film in cartridges. It produces good quality but small prints, and a special projector is needed. The disc series of cameras also uses cartridges designed as a wheel of 15 frames 8×10 mm in size. The film, available as color negative type VR only, is rated at 200 ASA (24 DIN) and has to be processed with special photo-finishing equipment using process C-41A.

The advantage of cartridge-loading cameras is the simplicity of changing the film. The drawback is the lack of accuracy in focusing, because there is no proper pressure plate to hold the film in exactly the right place. Also the choice of film is very limited. The most popular film size, and the one you would be wise to choose (unless you have a very good reason for seeking a different format), is 35 mm, which gives 24 × 36 mm negatives. This film size means you will have both a wide price range of cameras and an excellent variety of film types to choose from, and you will be able to get large prints of good quality.

Most roll-film cameras take pictures in the 2¼ × 2¼ in (6 × 6 cm) size. As film quality has improved th trend has been toward smaller formats. Many pr fessional photographers still use roll-film cameras rath than 35 mm, however, especially when large prints, sa 16 × 20 ins (40.6 × 50.8 cm) are required from col negative film. Roll-film also allows 6 × 7 cm pictures be made. Known as "ideal format," it provides rectang lar prints with less wastage of the negative area. Som cameras take 6 × 9 cm size pictures on roll-film an although this is growing increasingly rare, it is still use in the roll-film backs used on some sheet film camera Use a roll-film camera if you are very quality consciou or if you require large prints or wish to sell trans parencies easily.

The smallest sheet film size in common use is 4 × 5 in (10.2 × 12.7 cm), though smaller formats exist. Larg sizes include 5 × 7 ins (12.7 × 17.8 cm) and 8 × 10 in (20.3 × 25.4 cm). With a few exceptions, only pr fessional photographers working in studios or on loca tion use such cameras. A few press photographers st use 4 × 5 ins (10.2 × 12.7 cm) cameras.

If cost is a consideration, 110 and 126 films are mo expensive per shot than 35 mm. Otherwise comparabl 110 cameras tend to cost more than 126. Roll-fil cameras cost more than 35 mm cameras.

Focusing methods

The simplest cameras have lenses permanently focuse at a certain distance – often 12 ft (3.7 m) – which mean

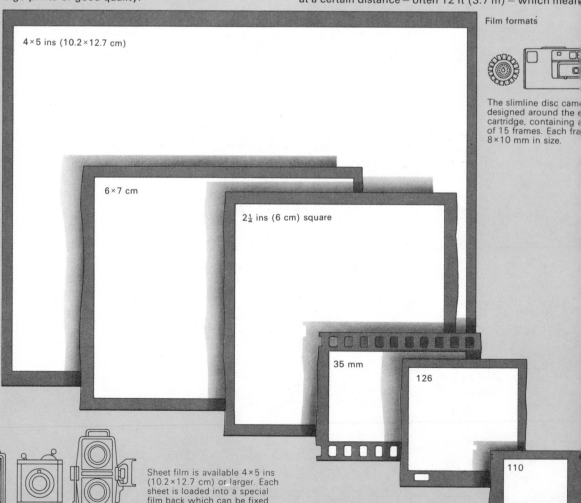

Film formats

4×5 ins (10.2×12.7 cm)

6×7 cm

2¼ ins (6 cm) square

The slimline disc came designed around the cartridge, containing of 15 frames. Each fra 8×10 mm in size.

35 mm

126

110

Sheet film is available 4×5 ins (10.2×12.7 cm) or larger. Each sheet is loaded into a special film back which can be fixed onto most studio cameras.

that small prints are acceptably sharp from about 6 ft (1.8 m) to infinity. Any camera can be used in this way, but focusing on the most important distance gives better results, and with lenses of wide aperture, becomes essential. The simplest means of focusing is with a scale on the lens, using figures or zones marked suitable for portraits, groups and landscapes etc. A rangefinder (see p. 35) is more accurate than guesswork and now almost all rangefinders are coupled directly to the lens.

Reflex cameras, whether single-lens (SLR) or twin-lens (TLR), focus on a screen and usually have a rangefinder or microprism spot in the center. There are many variations. Try out different models to see which suit your eyes best.

If you want a compact camera to carry constantly, and don't intend to use extra lenses, bellows, or extension tubes, then a camera with a focusing scale or rangefinder is a good choice. The greater size and cost of an SLR is largely wasted unless you want interchangeable lenses.

The twin-lens reflex appears, on first consideration, to have few virtues apart from a big, bright viewing screen which makes focusing easy. It is bulky and less versatile than the SLR, suffers from parallax error and has a laterally-reversed image. However, it is reliable because there are fewer moving parts to go wrong, it produces generally good results and if a roll-film size is required, it is considerably cheaper than the SLR. Unless other lenses are needed, many photographers use the twin-lens reflex for all work except extreme close-ups. There is only one model at present that can be fitted with interchangeable lenses.

Lenses

Maximum aperture and focal length are specified on lenses; degree of sharpness is not. In general a high price is paid for a fast lens with a wide aperture. An f1.4 lens is not usually as efficient as the same manufacturer's f1.8 or f2 lenses, even when both are stopped down to f5.6. The lens with the wider aperture is heavier and more expensive, so don't choose it as your standard unless you are planning a great deal of photography under poor light conditions.

In the SLR camera the lens also influences the brightness of the screen image and the accuracy of focusing, so there is more reason for using a wide aperture, but avoid buying a model with a lens aperture wider than you need. Interchangeable lenses have either screw or bayonet mounts. In general, bayonet mounts will fit only one camera design while screw mounts will fit many.

Instant picture cameras

The two popular sizes of instant picture cameras produce prints 3¼ × 4¼ ins (8.3 × 10.7 cm) and 3¼ × 3⅜ ins (8.3 × 8.6 cm). The smaller size is cheaper per

Many cameras do not have a built-in light meter so the most accurate way of deciding on a suitable exposure is with a separate meter.

A few cameras are built with "close-coupled" exposure meters where the meter is attached to the camera but works as a separate piece of equipment.

Most single-lens reflex cameras have through-the-lens metering. The built-in exposure meter reacts to the amount of light passing through the camera lens.

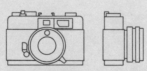

Some expensive cameras have automatic exposure control. This type is called "shutter-preferred." Once the photographer has chosen the shutter speed, the meter cell in the camera automatically sets the aperture size for the correct exposure.

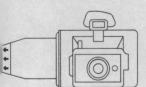

The simplest instant picture cameras are loaded with film packs which also contain processing chemicals. After the photograph has been taken the film is pulled out of the camera for development to take place.

Some instant picture cameras are fully automatic. They need special film packs but the photographer does nothing more than press the shutter release to achieve a fully developed, permanent photograph. The process takes about 10 mins.

Other automatic cameras work in reverse to "shutter-preferred" types. The aperture is set by the photographer while the shutter speed is controlled electronically. This system is known as "aperture-preferred."

print. The folding types with bellows are flatter than the non-folding plastic models, but all are fairly bulky. Most have automatic shutter control for exposure, and lens aperture is altered for color or black and white film, but there is also a manual model. A feature on some cameras is a timer to assist processing, and there are various types of rangefinder. Remember that cost per print is high regardless of the camera's price or size.

Some models use film which does not need timed processing. These are folding single-lens reflex cameras with an automatic print-ejection system but without interchangeable lenses. Size folded is about 7 × 4 × 1 ins (17.8 × 10.2 × 2.5 cm). With all of these cameras flash can be used to supplement dim light.

Metering systems

The cheapest and simplest cameras are suitable only for use with negative film in good natural light or with flash.

When making transparencies more careful control of exposure is necessary, lenses with adjustable irises and multispeed shutters are really required and, although exposure can be calculated from tables, an exposure meter — separate, or built-in — is better. Of separate meters (see pp. 46–47), the cross-linked type is quicker and easier to use than one in which the figures must be read and transferred to the lens and shutter. Meters built into cameras can work independently of the camera or they may be an integral part of it. Most single-lens reflex (SLR) cameras have through-the-lens (TTL) metering which allows you to use different lenses and attachments.

Meter cells can be placed in several positions on the camera, using different systems of calculating exposures. Provided you understand it, it makes little difference what system you use.

Automatic exposure control

Automatic exposure control is a feature of some expensive cameras. There are several degrees of automation. A simple method is to let the film speed control the shutter speed, while the meter cell adjusts the lens aperture. More sophisticated is the programmed shutter which provides a series of shutter speed/aperture combinations over a range wider than could be obtained by altering aperture alone.

Perhaps the most common system is *shutter-preferred*, which means that the photographer can set the shutter speed while the aperture is determined by the cell. Cameras with electronic shutters often work in a different way. The photographer chooses the aperture and the metering system sets the shutter speed. This *aperture-preferred* method is becoming increasingly popular. Speeds can be changed gradually instead of in jumps from 1/60 to 1/125 to 1/250 second and so on. Often the range extends to speeds as long as 10 seconds. It is helpful to know the settings selected by an automatic mechanism, and thus able to override the automation for taking pictures in unusual conditions.

Lenses

Changing the lens

Using a 6 mm lens

Using an 18 mm lens

Using a 35 mm lens

Using a 50 mm lens

Using an 85 mm lens

Using a 200 mm lens

Using an 800 mm lens

The photographs in the series above show how you can keep the same viewpoint but change the degree of magnification in a scene by using different lenses on a camera body.

Focal length

Photographic lenses are of three basic types: "normal" focal length, wide-angle, and long-focus, the description of a particular focal length being dictated by the format (negative size) of a camera.

A "normal" lens is one with the focal length approximately *equal* to the diagonal measurement of the camera format. For example, the diagonal of a $2\frac{1}{4}$ ins (6 cm) square negative is approximately 80 mm, so the normal focal length lens would be 80 mm. Anything less than 80 mm is, for this size of negative, a wide-angle; anything in excess of it, a long lens.

As the format changes, say to 35 mm (24 × 36 mm), an 80 mm lens is considered a long lens, and the "normal" focal length would be 50–55 mm (diagonal of negative size). A wide-angle in this case would be of even shorter focal length, i.e. approximately 28–35 mm. In a 4 × 5 ins (10.2 × 12.7 cm) camera, 150 mm is the normal lens while the 80 mm would be a wide-angle. A long lens in this case would be in the region of 200–250 mm.

Angle of view

A second factor in this relationship between normal,

wide-angle and long-focus, is the angle of view of the lens (see p. 42). A true wide-angle lens, whatever the format in use, would be expected to have an angle of view exceeding 70°, whereas a normal lens has an angle of view between 45°–55°. A long-focus varies but rarely exceeds 35°.

Wide-angle lenses

A wide-angle lens usually has a small maximum aperture compared with the other two lenses. It tends to distort cylindrical objects at the edges of the field, so take care when using a wide-angle lens for portraiture unless distortion is the effect you want. To use a short focal length lens is to become closely involved with the subject. A large depth of field is almost inevitable especially with small negative formats (e.g. 35 mm) because of the short focal lengths involved. Obviously, the wide-angle is ideal when such a large subject area must be included and the shooting conditions in terms of physical space are limited. But it can be used with equal success in a large landscape, adding mass to the foreground and breadth to the whole scene.

The fish-eye lens

The fish-eye is an extreme wide-angle lens which reproduces the center of the picture on the scale expected from the quoted focal length, but distorts the image shape more and more as the scale diminishes towards the edges. A photograph taken with a fish-eye

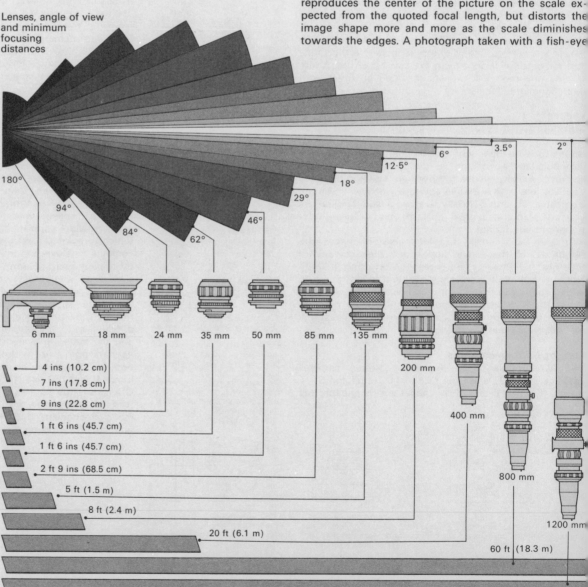

Lenses, angle of view and minimum focusing distances

180° | 94° | 84° | 62° | 46° | 29° | 18° | 12·5° | 6° | 3.5° | 2°

6 mm | 18 mm | 24 mm | 35 mm | 50 mm | 85 mm | 135 mm | 200 mm | 400 mm | 800 mm | 1200 mm

4 ins (10.2 cm)
7 ins (17.8 cm)
9 ins (22.8 cm)
1 ft 6 ins (45.7 cm)
1 ft 6 ins (45.7 cm)
2 ft 9 ins (68.5 cm)
5 ft (1.5 m)
8 ft (2.4 m)
20 ft (6.1 m)
60 ft (18.3 m)
140 ft (42.7

lens resembles a reflection in a globe. With the exception of the center lines, all horizontal and vertical lines are curved. The result is a highly distorted image.

Long-focus lenses

At the opposite end of the scale the long-focus lens offers observation from a distance and close-up detail without close involvement with the subject. It is used extensively by the press for portraiture, and in the photography of wildlife and sport. Its limited angle of view demands distant viewpoints and is inclined to flatten perspective. Long-focus lenses have comparatively limited depth of field.

The telephoto lens

The telephoto lens is a particular type of long-focus lens using two groups of lens elements which enable the lens designer to achieve long focal lengths without extreme lens-to-focal plane distance.

The normal lens

The "normal" lens (or standard) supplied with most camera systems is a compromise between the two extremes. It is convenient for most subjects, but convenience seldom produces the most interesting photographs and this lens should be used with care, particularly with regard to framing. It is sometimes useful to have a normal lens slightly longer than the diagonal of the camera format. For example, an 80 mm lens on 35 mm instead of a 55 mm lens. This helps to avoid the "general view" type of photograph, by making more of a close-up with the framing.

Focusing distance

The longer the focal length of the lens, the longer the minimum focusing distance will tend to be. This situation is, to some extent, self-correcting, as the image scale increases with focal length. It follows that with long-focus lenses, you do not need to be so close to the subject. With wide-angle lenses you can come closer.

Depth of field

Depth of field also varies according to focal length. The greater the focal length, the shallower the depth of field and the more careful you must be with focusing. A long focal length is a drawback if you want the whole of the subject to be sharp, but an advantage if you want to use selective focusing.

Shift lens

A shift or perspective lens is basically a wide-angle design capable of covering a larger negative than that employed in the camera, which is usually 35 mm. The lens can be moved off the normal axis to provide a result similar to that from a rising front on a view camera (see p. 220).
It is used mainly for photographing tall buildings without tilting the camera, because it allows the uprights to remain parallel instead of converging. Movement of the lens downward gives the equivalent of a drop front, and turning the camera provides sideways movement.

Zoom lens

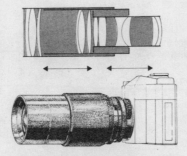

To have to keep changing lenses to obtain different focal lengths is a nuisance. You may also want to alter focal length gradually, between limits, while keeping images acceptably sharp. A zoom lens takes the place of several separate lenses, thereby eliminating a lot of time and trouble, and helps you to fit the picture exactly into the frame. Its drawbacks are its weight and cost. In some cases, too, particularly in older equipment, the optical quality resulting from the complicated construction does not always match that from lenses of fixed focal length. The most up to date designs, however, cope with this problem more effectively.

Mirror lens

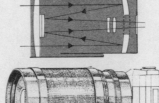

Because it has such a small angle of view a long-focus lens does not need to be complicated. Complexities only arise out of design attempts to make long-focus lenses more compact. Much has been done with telephoto construction which reduces the distance between lens and film to considerably less than the focal length. The mirror lens reduces the size still further by "folding" the light path into three, so making an extremely compact long-focus lens, usually of 500 mm or 1000 mm or longer focal length. The disadvantage of these otherwise useful, lightweight and compact mirror lenses is that the size of the aperture is fixed.

Depth of field

The diagram on the right shows how depth of field alters when lenses from the same manufacturer's range are interchanged on a camera. The depth of field was measured, in every case, with the lens focused on 100 ft (30.4 m) and the aperture set at f5.6. Notice how depth of field increases as the focal length of the lens decreases.

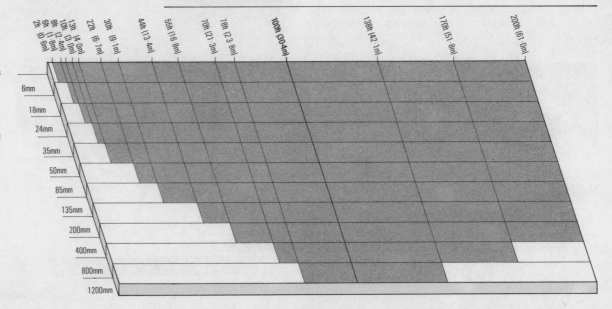

Equipment for Close-up

Close-up photography is the method of photographing subjects when they are too close to the camera to be brought into focus by the normal lens or camera mechanisms. It is often further categorized according to the degree of magnification of the image. The term "close-up photography" generally refers to the recording of subjects between one tenth of life-size and life-size (0.1–1.0×). "Macrophotography" involves photographing subjects between life-size and magnified up to about ten times (1.0×–10×) and "photomicrography" photographing subjects as greater than ten times life-size.

There are a number of ways in which close-up photographs can be taken: by using a special macro lens; adding extension tubes or rings, bellows or a close-up attachment to a normal lens or even photographing through a microscope. Choosing such equipment depends on the degree of magnification you want to achieve and the type of camera you have – not all close-up equipment can be used with all cameras. It is also worth remembering that magnification in the camera is only part of close-up photography since photographs can be further enlarged in the darkroom or with a slide projector.

Depth of field is extremely limited when focusing on close subjects. By stopping the lens right down the whole subject can be made sharp, but this may mean using a very slow shutter speed which increases the risk of camera shake if the camera is hand held. For this reason, it is always wise to use a tripod and cable release when taking close-up shots. Subject movement can also be a problem, so a wind shield to protect outdoor subjects such as flowers can be helpful.

Image scale increases as the lens is moved further from the film and this always requires an increase in exposure. Imagine light being spread and becoming dimmer as the image expands. It is best to look up exposure factors in suitable tables when using any close-up equipment if exposure is to be accurate. Although the single-lens reflex with through-the-lens metering is well suited to close-up work because it is easy to handle and can usually be fitted with the necessary attachments, the light reaching the meter once the attachments have been added may be too dim for it to work properly.

With all cameras except single-lens reflexes and studio models parallax is a great problem when taking close-ups – the closer the camera to the subject the greater the parallax error. Many cameras have some method of compensation, some have guide lines in the viewfinder window, others have special framing devices.

Macro lenses

Most standard lenses for single-lens reflex cameras focus on subjects as close as 18 ins (45.7 cm). Some special models known as macro lenses are designed to allow the focusing movement to be continued through several more revolutions for focusing on subjects at even closer distances. The reproduction ratio (image size compared with subject size) is usually shown on the lens, the maximum value being around 0.5×, although with some designs it can be as great as 1.0×. When using a macro lens stop down to achieve maximum sharpness.

Extension tubes or rings

These are tubes or rings of various depths which fit between the camera body and the lens of single-lens reflexes and some 35 mm interchangeable lens viewfinder cameras. They are usually sold in sets and can be used singly or in combination, with different lenses, to magnify the size of the image as shown in the tables. The longer the tube, the larger the image. The drawback to using extension tubes is that it takes time to unscrew and exchange them to alter the scale of the image, and also, depth of focus is extremely limited which means that focusing must be very accurate. Again, it is best to use a small aperture to ensure sharpness.

Macro lens
The macro lens (above) differs from the normal (top), in that it is designed to give high quality images under close-up conditions. Its mount extends to allow closer focusing than a normal lens.

Extension tubes
These tubes, usually bought in sets, can be fitted singly or together between the camera lens and body. The longer the tube the greater the magnification of the image.

Close-up lens
The close-up lens can be screwed onto the end of a suitable camera lens to allow closer focusing than the lens would normally achieve. Many versions are made for different degrees of magnification.

Extension tubes used with a 35 mm lens focused at 1.5 ft (45.7 cm)
Tube 1 = 0.35 ins (9.5 mm) Tube 2 = 0.75 ins (19.0 mm) Tube 3 = 1.1 ins (28.5 mm)

Extension tube combination	Subject size		Film-to-subject distance		Magnification	Exposure factor
	cm	ins	cm	ins		
Not used	36.3 × 24.1	14.3 × 9.5	45.2	17.8	0.1	×1.2
1	9.9 × 6.6	3.9 × 2.6	20.1	7.9	0.35	×1.6
2	5.8 × 3.8	2.3 × 1.5	17.0	6.7	0.6	×2.1
3	4.1 × 2.8	1.6 × 1.1	16.3	6.4	0.9	×2.7
1+3	3.0 × 2.0	1.2 × 0.8	16.3	6.4	1.15	×3.4
2+3	2.5 × 1.8	1.0 × 0.7	16.5	6.5	1.45	×4.1
1+2+3	2.0 × 1.5	0.8 × 0.6	17.3	6.8	1.7	×4.9

Seed heads

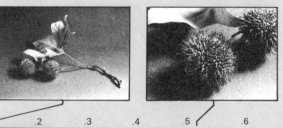

The magnification scale
By using any one or a combination of the close-up attachments mentioned above, different degrees of image magnification can be achieved. The diagram below shows the range.

Match heads

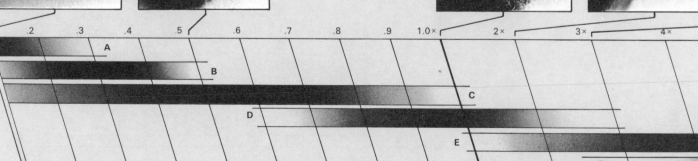

A Close-up lens   B Macro lens   C Normal lens and extension tubes   D Normal lens and bellows   E Macro lens and bellows   F Normal lens and microscope

Extension tubes used with a 55 mm lens focused at 1.5 ft (45.7 cm)

Extension tube combination	Subject size		Film-to-subject distance		Magnification	Exposure factor
	cm	ins	cm	ins		
Not used	21.3×14.2	8.4×5.6	45.0	17.7	0.15	×1.4
1	10.7×7.1	4.2×2.8	29.5	11.6	0.35	×1.7
2	7.1×4.8	2.8×1.9	24.6	9.7	0.5	×2.2
3	5.3×3.6	2.1×1.4	22.9	9.0	0.65	×2.7
1+3	4.3×2.8	1.7×1.1	22.1	8.7	0.85	×3.2
2+3	3.6×2.5	1.4×1.0	21.8	8.6	1.0	×3.8
1+2+3	3.0×1.5	1.2×0.8	22.1	8.7	1.15	×4.5

Extension tubes used with a 135 mm lens focused at 5 ft (1.5 m)

Extension tube combination	Subject size		Film-to-subject distance		Magnification	Exposure factor
	cm	ins	cm	ins		
Not used	45.5×30.0	17.9×11.8	200.2	78.8	0.1	×1.3
1	24.1×16.0	9.5×6.3	120.7	47.5	0.15	×1.6
2	16.5×10.9	6.5×4.3	92.7	36.5	0.2	×1.9
3	12.4×8.4	4.9×3.3	78.7	31.0	0.3	×2.2
1+3	9.9×6.6	3.9×2.6	70.4	27.7	0.35	×2.5
2+3	8.4×5.6	3.3×2.2	65.3	25.7	0.4	×2.9
1+2+3	7.1×4.8	2.8×1.9	62.0	24.4	0.5	×3.3

The illumination of subjects to be photographed in close-up can be a problem as equipment so near the subject can block out much of the light. For this reason, some photographers use extension tubes on long-focus lenses, rather than special short-focus lenses. This allows them to shoot from further away and still achieve large-scale images. In general, however, short-focus lenses specifically designed for close-up work give the best results.

Close-up lenses

Close-up lenses are simple, positive lens attachments which fit onto the camera lens like a filter to allow close focusing. Normally they are only used on cameras where the lens is fixed and cannot be used with extension tubes or bellows.

The strength of a close-up lens is measured in diopters: the greater its power in diopters, the larger the image it will produce. A three-diopter lens is the strongest that can be used without affecting the definition of the image. Close-up lenses, like extension tubes, can be used in combination for greater magnification of an image — for example a one-diopter and a two-diopter lens can be used together to make a three-diopter lens. The diopter strength of a lens is related to its focal length i.e. a one-diopter close-up lens has a focal length of 40 ins (1.0 m).

Bellows attachments

Bellows attachments fit the camera in much the same way as extension tubes. Different extensions are easily achieved by extending the bellows along a monorail. The advantage of using bellows rather than extension tubes is that variations in magnification can be made easily and quickly as shown in the table below. Their bulkiness, however, can be a disadvantage.

Extension bellows used with different lenses
Minimum extension=1.5 ins (38 mm) Maximum extension=7 ins (17.8 cm)

Bellows extension	Subject size		Film-to-subject distance		Magnification	Exposure factor
	cm	ins	cm	ins		
35 mm						
Minimum	2.5×3.8	1.0×1.5	14.6	5.8	1.0	×4.0
Maximum	0.4×0.6	0.2×0.3	26.7	10.5	5.2	×38.0
55 mm						
Minimum	3.8×5.8	1.5×2.3	22.9	9.0	0.7	×2.7
Maximum	0.9×1.2	0.4×0.5	30.5	12.0	3.2	×17.5
135 mm						
Minimum	8.9×14.0	3.5×5.5	81.3	32.0	0.3	×1.5
Maximum	1.9×2.5	0.8×1.0	58.4	22.0	1.3	×5.5

Photomicrography

For great magnification, 10× life-size or more, a camera can be used to photograph an image through a microscope. A special adapter can be bought to mount the camera body onto the microscope. Lighting should be as bright and as constant as possible so that a reasonably fast shutter speed can be used. Exposure, however, is a matter of trial and error, so records should be kept for future reference.

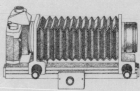

Bellows attachments
Bellows can be fitted between the camera body and lens. They work in a similar way to extension tubes but may allow greater magnification.

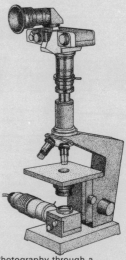

Photography through a microscope
By using a special adapter the camera can be used to photograph images through a microscope. Magnifications of 10× life-size or more can be recorded.

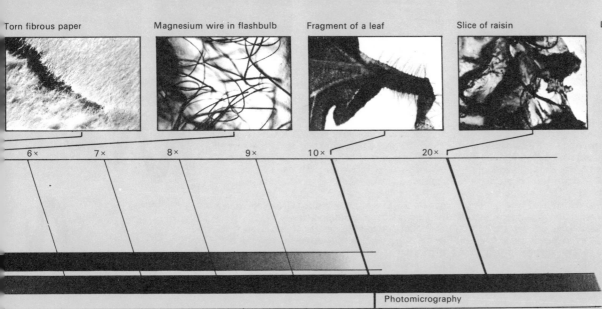

Torn fibrous paper   Magnesium wire in flashbulb   Fragment of a leaf   Slice of raisin

6×   7×   8×   9×   10×   20×

Photomicrography

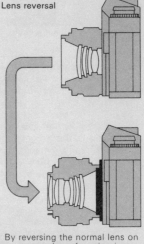

Lens reversal

By reversing the normal lens on a camera, closer focusing is allowed. Some manufacturers make an adapter to fit the camera to enable the lens to be mounted back-to-front

Filters

Photographic filters are pieces of colored transparent material which absorb a portion of the light passing through them. Most filters are glass but special plastics are also used. Foil or gelatin squares are cheap but very easily scratched. Filters are usually placed in front of the lens and influence the picture by absorbing certain wavelengths or bands of the color spectrum.

There is a difference in the ways in which photographic film and the human eye respond to light of different colors. For example, in strong light the eye sees yellow as the brightest color while film reacts that way

to blue. Filters can alter the response of film to color.

For black and white work, with panchromatic film, results can be predicted by the rule that there are three main colors, red, green and blue, and that any one of these absorbs the other two. The basic theory is that filters lighten objects of their own and similar colors and darken others. For example, a red filter transmits red light and absorbs green and blue. It follows that, with a red filter, reddish objects will be reproduced in a lighter tone while green and blue record as darker. Orange and yellow can be thought of as lighter forms of red.

Filters and their effects
The human eye and photographic film respond to light of different colors in different ways. For example, the eye accepts yellow as the brightest color, but film sees blue as brighter. By adding filters to a camera lens, the response of the film can be altered as shown in the diagram below.

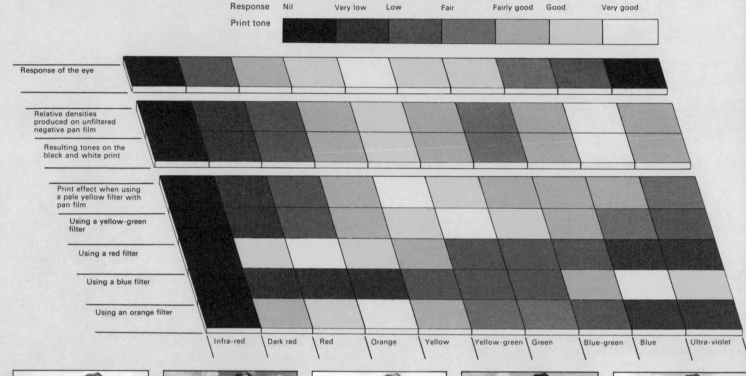

Response — Nil · Very low · Low · Fair · Fairly good · Good · Very good
Print tone

- Response of the eye
- Relative densities produced on unfiltered negative pan film
- Resulting tones on the black and white print
- Print effect when using a pale yellow filter with pan film
- Using a yellow-green filter
- Using a red filter
- Using a blue filter
- Using an orange filter

Infra-red · Dark red · Red · Orange · Yellow · Yellow-green · Green · Blue-green · Blue · Ultra-violet

Photographing without a filter

Using a red filter

Using a blue filter

Using an orange filter

Using a yellow-green filter

Filter factors

Filters vary in strength as well as color. Extra exposure is required to compensate for light absorbed by the filter. A filter factor tells you how much exposure must be increased and also indicates the relative strength of the filter. A 2× filter needs the normal exposure multiplied by 2. Remember that each stop lower on the camera doubles the exposure given by the previous stop. Thus if the exposure in normal light is f 8, the exposure with a 2× filter should be f 5.6. If a 4× filter is used in the same instance, the exposure should be f 4. (Multiplying the exposure by 4 means moving up two stops, since each stop doubles the exposure.) A reduction in shutter speed can equally well compensate for the use of a filter. Filter factors are not constant, they vary with the light. A 4× orange filter may only need 2× exposure in reddish sunset light. TTL metering may not give correct meter readings when filters are used on the lens. This is because cadmium sulfide cells are over-sensitive to red. Take a reading without the filter, then correct the controls.

Polarizing filter

Ordinary light has waves which vibrate in all directions, up and down, from side to side and at all angles between. Polarized light vibrates in one direction only. A polarizing filter allows light to pass which vibrates in one direction (see top right), but stops light vibrating at right angles to that direction (see below right). By rotating a polarizing filter different effects can be obtained. Light from a blue north sky is polarized, so a polarizing filter (which is a neutral gray in color) can be used with color film to deepen the blue without affecting anything else.
Reflections from non-metallic surfaces, such as glass or water, are polarized so they can be decreased or rendered normally just by turning the filter. The effect is greater at oblique angles of reflection.

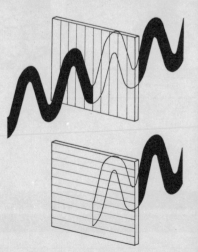

Probably the most popular filter is yellow, which darkens a blue sky, and so shows white clouds better. It also reduces haze to the amount actually seen by the eye. Orange is used for a stronger, more dramatic effect. Red is still stronger, for deliberate drama. Blue is the reverse, strengthening the mist.

Camera filters for color photography

The strong filters used in black and white photography are not suitable for color work, in which paler and more subtle filters are employed. A huge range of filters is available but it is arguable how many are required for ordinary photography.

Daylight color slide film is balanced for a color temperature of about 5400K, corresponding to noon sunlight. When natural lighting varies in color, as at dawn and sunset, the mind tends to alter the signals from the eye so that the change is not greatly noticed and, for example, a piece of white paper still looks white. When a slide is projected the mind does not apply the same correction so that pictures taken in colored lighting are seen to have an overall tint. Some photographers think that the charm of a sunset, for example, lies in the mellow lighting and that full correction to an approximation of noon sunlight is a perversion of technique. Others prefer to apply some correction, perhaps half the theoretical amount. This applies only to daylight pictures taken on daylight film. Full correction is required when a film balanced for use in artificial light is used in daylight. It is usually acceptable for an entire sequence of slides to have the same color bias but a change from, say, a warm reddish slide to a bluish one is too startling for comfort. If such mixtures are likely to occur when slides are projected in sequence, filtration is more necessary than if slides are viewed singly.

Color temperature

When a black metal is heated it first glows a dull red, then as it grows hotter, the light it emits passes through yellow and the rest of the spectrum to blue and beyond. Colors of light can be expressed in terms of the temperature of the imaginary substance which would give out such light. The temperature is quoted in Kelvins. A problem is that a filter giving a shift of, say 100K at 2800K has a shift of 130K at 3200K and 300K at 5000K. To make it easier to pick the right filter for each situation the mired system is used, as explained below. If there is any doubt about the color temperature of the light, a special meter can be used which compares the relative amounts of blue and green light to give a direct reading in Kelvins.

Using filters with film to alter color balance

Daylight films are also correctly balanced for flash, electronic or bulb. If this film is used in artificial light a blue filter is needed, but because of the drop in effective speed this procedure is not recommended. If the same film must be used in both kinds of lighting it is better to employ a type A film (balanced for 3400K) or type B (3200K), with an orange conversion filter in daylight. Usually the artificial light film is faster, and the filter simply reduces the speed to that of daylight film.

Haze filters

A haze filter can be left on the camera all the time to protect the lens. It is a colorless filter and absorbs some ultra-violet. A slightly tinted filter, very pale yellow or pink, absorbs more ultra-violet and a little blue, which is worthwhile. Always use a haze filter at high altitudes and when there is a blue haze in the distance.

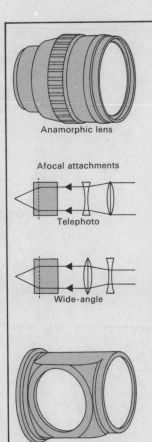

Anamorphic lens

Afocal attachments

Telephoto

Wide-angle

Right-angle attachment

Lens attachments

There are a number of attachments, apart from filters, that can be fitted to the front of a lens: some change the focal length of the lens, others alter the appearance of the image. Many manufacturers make attachments but it is best to use those recommended for a particular lens type to keep the quality of the image as high as possible. There is nearly always some loss of quality when attachments are used. The *anamorphic lens*, see top left, can be used with standard width film to take extra-wide angle views. The view is compressed by the lens so that the recorded image is vertically elongated. By fitting a special rectifying lens onto a projector, the image can be projected as normal. There are two types of *afocal attachment*, a wide-angle and a telephoto. Their purpose is to alter the effective focal length of a lens, as shown in the diagrams, middle left. They are particularly useful attachments for cameras without interchangeable lenses. When in use, the lens must be focused on infinity. A *right-angle attachment* can be fitted to most single-lens reflex cameras. It is used to take candid photographs of subjects at right-angles to the scene in front of the camera. The system uses a surface-silvered mirror to reflect light rays from the subject through 90° and onto the film. *Prism attachments* can be used on still and movie cameras to create a series of split or overlapping images of the subject on a single frame. They are screwed to the front of the lens like a filter and can be bought to create many different optical effects. *Starburst attachments* fit in a similar way. The surface is engraved with triangles which cause star-shaped flares wherever highlights appear in the subject. The *center focus attachment* reproduces the center of the image as sharp when the lens is correctly focused but diffuses the surrounding picture area. The *soft focus attachment* softens the overall definition of the picture.

Filters at the printing stage

With negative films slight variations in lighting color temperature can be corrected when printing, as can some other variations. Some photographers like to cut down printing correction by using camera filters to correct big variations; consult the instruction sheet with the film.

Printing filters are thin foils easily marked by the fingers. Subtractive types, used above the condenser are cyan, magenta and yellow. Additive ones, used below the lens, are red, green and blue.

Conversion from Kelvins to mireds

Mireds are microreciprocal degrees. To find the mired value of a light source, divide 1,000,000 by its color temperature. The higher the Kelvins the lower the mired figure. A blue filter has a negative mired effect, a pinkish one a positive value. A filter always gives the same mired shift value with all colors of light. Some manufacturers quote filters in decamireds (1 decamired = 10 mireds). The eye can detect changes of about 10 mireds or more.

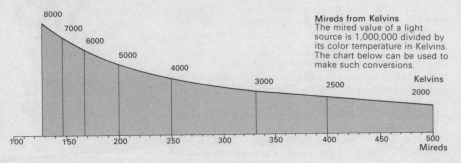

Mireds from Kelvins
The mired value of a light source is 1,000,000 divided by its color temperature in Kelvins. The chart below can be used to make such conversions.

Camera Supports

Supporting the camera

The longer the exposure time of a shot the greater the risk of camera-shake. Much depends on the way the camera is held, but a general rule is that 1/30 sec. is the longest exposure which is reasonably safe if a camera support is not used.

Long-focus lenses produce more shake because they are longer and heavier. So, to avoid shake, the longer the lens, the faster the shutter speed must be. If big enlargements are to be made, it is even more vital to avoid blurring the photograph through shake. A camera support is the best answer, the most popular type being a tripod.

Tripods

The steadiest tripods are too heavy to carry easily and are therefore only used in studio work. At the other end of the scale the smallest and lightest tripods are too wobbly for serious use. A good compromise is a three-section tripod made of light but strong aluminum alloy; you can use the center column to adjust height without having to alter the legs. Some columns are elevated by a crank handle, but a simple friction lock is more usual. The column can often be reversed, so that to shoot subjects on the ground, the camera can be held upside down between the tripod legs.

Tripod heights vary (to use the tallest ones on the market, you need a ladder!) but for general purposes a maximum 4 to 5 ft (1 to 1.5 m) is sufficient. When not using your tripod at its fullest extension, keep the lowest legs, i.e. the thinnest ones, retracted. Some tripod legs terminate in spikes for outdoor use, with screw-down collars for indoor use. Legs which end in all-purpose plastic studs however, are a simple compromise. When using a tripod, be careful to have the central leg pointing forwards, under the lens; use a cable release and do not touch the camera during exposure.

Tripod heads

Most tripods are fitted with an adjustable head which tilts the camera in different directions. The ball and socket type of head is compact and inexpensive, and allows the camera to move freely. The pan and tilt type, though heavier and costing more, gives separate control of vertical and horizontal movements. It is more convenient for still work and essential for motion pictures.

Other camera supports

If you intend to concentrate on, say, action or close-up photography, it is probably worth buying one of the camera supports designed specially for that kind of work.

A monopod is like a single tripod leg; although it reduces shake under some conditions, it is not so effective as a tripod and is seldom used. Clamps are most useful for dimly-lit interiors such as churches. They have padding on the jaws to avoid damaging woodwork. Table tripods have very short legs and are useful not only for table-top work but also for subjects close to ground level. A small table tripod or clamp can be carried in a gadget bag when a full-size tripod would be a nuisance. A shoulderpad, rather like a rifle butt, for pressing against the shoulder, is sometimes used as an aid to steadiness with long-focus lenses, especially for sports subjects.

Steadying the camera without a support

If you do not have a camera support try bracing yourself against a convenient wall or tree, resting the end of a very long-focus lens on the shoulder of a friend or, especially for interiors, holding the camera with its back firmly pressed against a wall. As a last resort, the camera strap can help to hold the camera steady; twist it round your hands or pull it tight around the back of your neck.

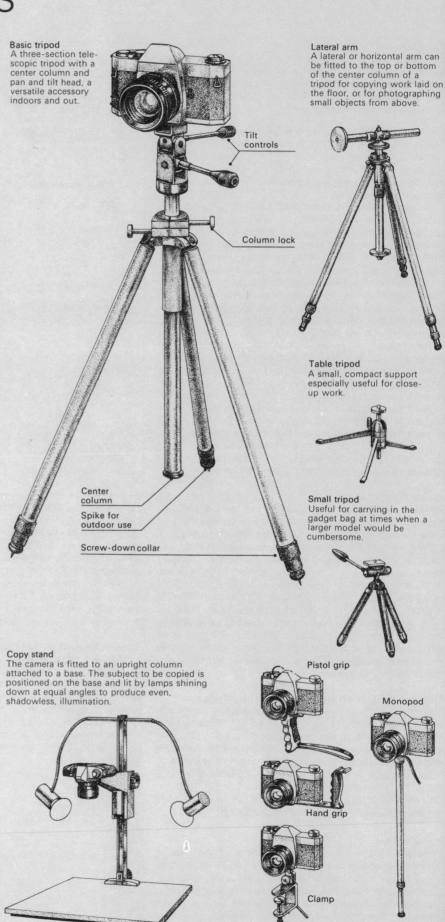

Basic tripod
A three-section telescopic tripod with a center column and pan and tilt head, a versatile accessory indoors and out.

Lateral arm
A lateral or horizontal arm can be fitted to the top or bottom of the center column of a tripod for copying work laid on the floor, or for photographing small objects from above.

Tilt controls

Column lock

Table tripod
A small, compact support especially useful for close-up work.

Small tripod
Useful for carrying in the gadget bag at times when a larger model would be cumbersome.

Center column

Spike for outdoor use

Screw-down collar

Copy stand
The camera is fitted to an upright column attached to a base. The subject to be copied is positioned on the base and lit by lamps shining down at equal angles to produce even, shadowless illumination.

Pistol grip

Monopod

Hand grip

Clamp

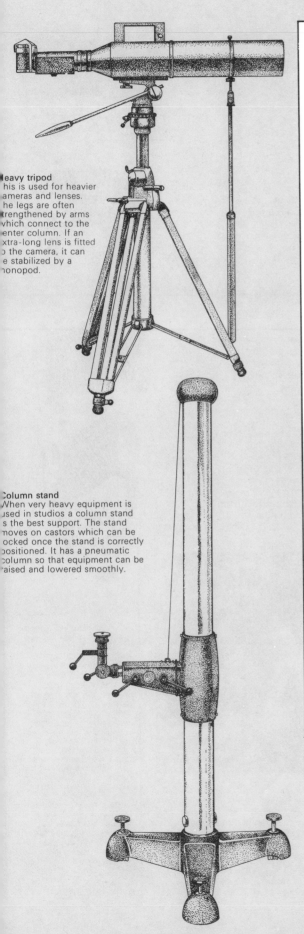

Heavy tripod
This is used for heavier cameras and lenses. The legs are often strengthened by arms which connect to the center column. If an extra-long lens is fitted to the camera, it can be stabilized by a monopod.

Column stand
When very heavy equipment is used in studios a column stand is the best support. The stand moves on castors which can be locked once the stand is correctly positioned. It has a pneumatic column so that equipment can be raised and lowered smoothly.

Holding the camera

Normal horizontal
Tuck in elbows and turn your head to rest the camera against your cheek.

Vertical, elbows in
Use your forehead as a platform. Make sure your fingers do not cover the exposure meter window.

Vertical, one elbow out
Use your left hand to support the camera, but keep your arm tucked in. The right hand is free to operate the shutter.

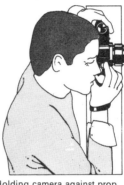

Resting against prop
Rest the top of your camera against a support to prevent yourself from swaying.

Holding camera against prop
Press the base of the camera against a rigid support. Even long exposures are possible with careful use of this method.

Kneeling position
Kneel down on one leg and rest the soft part of your upper arm, *not* your elbow, on the other knee.

Lying position
Lie flat on your stomach but support the upper part of your body with your elbows.

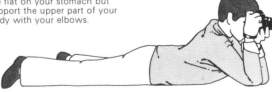

Holding a large format camera

Waist-level **Eye-level** **"Sports" finder** **Overhead**

Twin-lens reflex, and some roll-film single-lens reflex cameras are normally held differently. When used at waist-level, pulling down on the strap gives more stability. Press the back of the camera against your body. To use the screen magnifier the camera is held at eye level. For panning, prefocus and use the "sports" finder, moving your body from the waist and continuing after shutter release. In crowds the camera can be held high and inverted, but some shake is likely.

219

The View Camera

The usual position of the lens in the "view" or "studio" camera is directly centered with and parallel to the film, so that a central ray of light passing through the lens reaches the center of the film. The lens panel and back panel containing the film are usually at right angles to the optical axis. These positions can be considered normal or neutral, and they can be used to take many subjects. However, using the movements on a view camera can help you to control the final images of some subjects — particularly architecture and still life.

Camera movements

Camera movements are controlled, independent movements of the lens panel or back panel which enable a more useful image to be formed. They can produce a greater and more effective depth of field, control the image shape, sharpen the focus, and bring into the picture area parts of the subject which would otherwise be excluded.

A camera with a wide variety of movements tends to be large and most models use large film sizes. Because of their weight they are nearly always used on a tripod.

In a camera with full movements the lens panel and the back panel can pivot both horizontally or vertically, and also slide up, down or sideways.

Obviously a vertical movement with the camera in the usual position becomes a horizontal one when the camera is on its side, an intermediate one when it is at an inclined tilt. However, the main movements are:

Swing Where the camera panels are swiveled around their vertical axes;

Tilt Where the panels are tilted either backward or forward on their horizontal axes;

Shift Where the panels slide to the left or the right;

Rise and fall Where the panels slide up or down.

If the lens panel or back panel is moved in any direction, the image seen on the ground-glass screen changes. It follows that the image field must be larger than the film size for such movement to be effective. Often a combination of several movements is needed.

Swing

This movement distorts shapes and affects focus because as the camera panel is moved, some parts of the subject become closer to the panel than others, and this distorts their size. Swinging the back panel has most effect on shape, while swinging the lens panel greatly alters focus. Swing can be used with other movements to prevent image cut-off, to focus subjects at an angle to the camera, to affect perspective, and so on.

Tilt

Like swing, this movement affects image shape and focus. The further away the back panel is from the subject, the larger the image becomes. Because tilt makes parts of the back panel move closer to the subject, the image will become distorted, larger in some areas than in others.

Shift

This movement shifts the image position to one side and alters effective coverage by moving the lens axis away from the center of the film. It allows subjects to the side of the normal field of view to be included without the camera being inclined and so shapes being distorted.

Rise and fall

This has a similar effect to shift but alters the image's position vertically. It is particularly useful for including the tops of tall buildings without tilting the camera upwards, which makes the verticals converge. With rise, fall and cross movements watch for image fall-off at the corners.

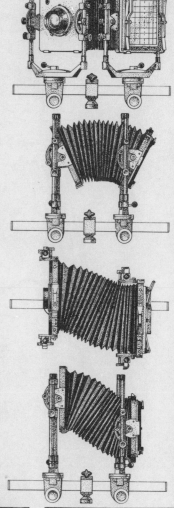

Elimination of unwanted detail
The main factor influencing the photograph is the placing of the camera. Movements are secondary factors. Here the camera, using no movements, was placed squarely in front of the subject so that the window was in the center of the image. Some interesting detail was hidden, however, by the large flower urn in the foreground.

By moving the camera to the right, the urn was completely eliminated, but the window was no longer centered in the image. By using the left shift movement on the lens panel and the right shift movement on the back panel the window was re-centered in the image and all the surrounding objects included in the frame.

The Scheimpflug Principle
Named after the Austrian surveyor who discovered it the Scheimpflug Principle sounds imposing but is actually quite simple. If imaginary lines drawn through the subject plane, lens plane and image plane meet at the same point, then image sharpness is uniformly spread over the image plane. In other words, this is the condition giving the greatest depth of field, although objects nearest the lens may suffer from distortion. If the subject plane is at an angle to the film, overall sharpness can be restored by tilting the lens so that all three planes intersect at the same point.

Camera movements and their effects

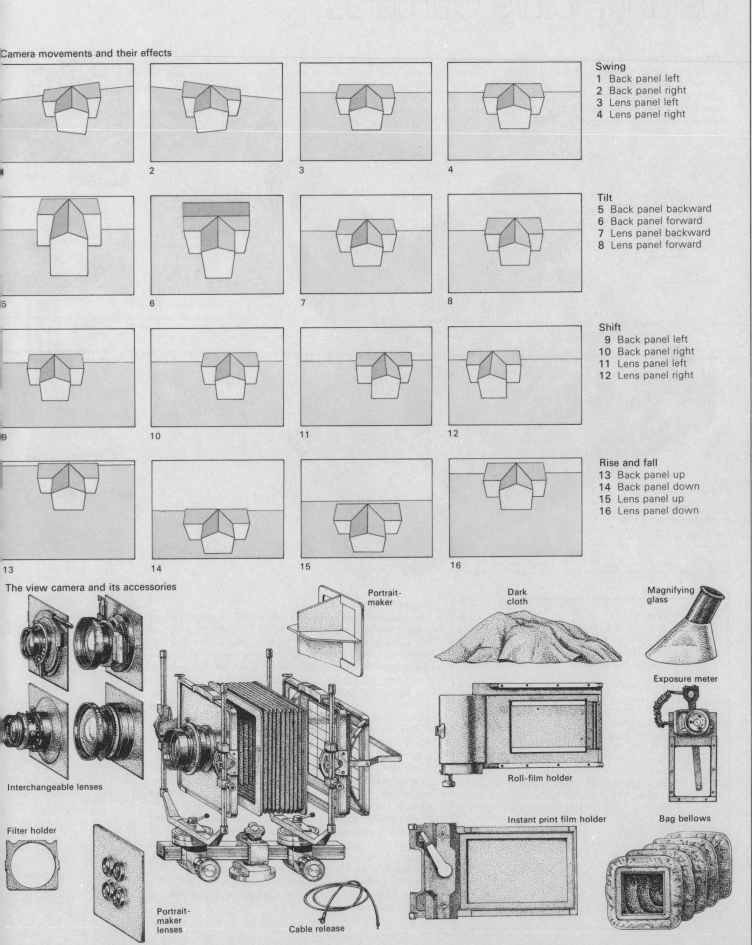

Swing
1 Back panel left
2 Back panel right
3 Lens panel left
4 Lens panel right

Tilt
5 Back panel backward
6 Back panel forward
7 Lens panel backward
8 Lens panel forward

Shift
9 Back panel left
10 Back panel right
11 Lens panel left
12 Lens panel right

Rise and fall
13 Back panel up
14 Back panel down
15 Lens panel up
16 Lens panel down

The view camera and its accessories

Portrait-maker

Dark cloth

Magnifying glass

Exposure meter

Roll-film holder

Interchangeable lenses

Instant print film holder

Bag bellows

Filter holder

Portrait-maker lenses

Cable release

Instant Picture Cameras

Instant picture cameras have virtually eliminated the time lag between taking and viewing. If a photograph is a failure, another can be taken. With one exception, IP cameras produce only a simple print with no negative; but prints can be copied. The cameras tend to be bulky, but they do, after all, include a remarkably compact darkroom. In most models exposure control is automatic, lenses are autofocus or fixed focus and the cameras are easy to operate. Flashbars are normally used for dim light work. Low temperatures can cause problems with the peel-off type of film; one answer is to hold it while processing in a metal holder in an inside pocket. This keeps the temperature constant.

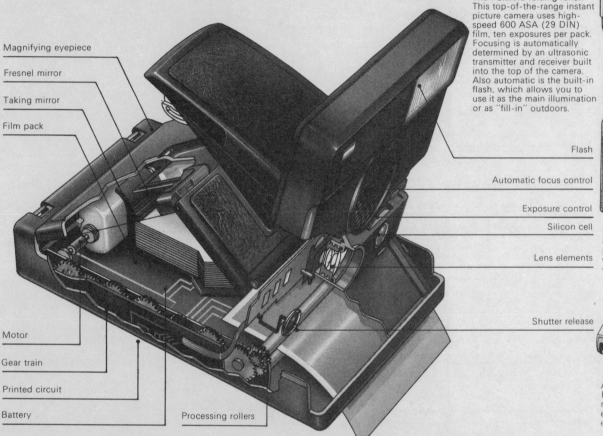

Magnifying eyepiece

Fresnel mirror

Taking mirror

Film pack

Motor

Gear train

Printed circuit

Battery

Processing rollers

Flash

Automatic focus control

Exposure control

Silicon cell

Lens elements

Shutter release

The Polaroid folding reflex
This top-of-the-range instant picture camera uses high-speed 600 ASA (29 DIN) film, ten exposures per pack. Focusing is automatically determined by an ultrasonic transmitter and receiver built into the top of the camera. Also automatic is the built-in flash, which allows you to use it as the main illumination or as "fill-in" outdoors.

At the lower end of the range this model from Kodak, the "Champ", offers automatic exposure control and a fixed-focus lens.

Model 940 from Kodak incorporates all basic features plus built-in electronic flash, which fires automatically when needed.

At the top of the range is Kodak's 980L, featuring manual override of automatic exposure as well as an extended flash range.

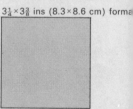

$3\frac{1}{4} \times 3\frac{3}{8}$ ins (8.3 × 8.6 cm) format

$3\frac{1}{4} \times 4\frac{1}{4}$ ins (8.3 × 10.7 cm) format

$3\frac{1}{8} \times 3\frac{1}{8}$ ins (8 × 8 cm) format

Exposing the film pack

This type of single-lens reflex is highly complex and electronically powered by a battery in each film pack. Before exposure (below left) light reflected from the subject enters the camera through the lens and is reflected by mirrors into the viewfinder area where more mirrors transmit the image to the magnifying eyepiece. The image is upright and the correct way round. When the shutter release is pressed (below right) the mirrors change their positions so that the image is reflected downward onto the film. Simultaneously a silicon photocell measures the intensity of incoming light and controls the electronic shutter to give the correct exposure. A motor inside the camera then drives the film through rollers to burst and spread the contents of the pod of developer over the film. A framed but blank photograph emerges from the camera.

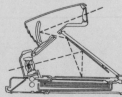 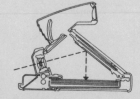

Camera formats

The almost-square pictures produced in 'some instant picture cameras are $3\frac{1}{4} \times 3\frac{3}{8}$ ins (8.3 × 8.6 cm) and they are usually in 8-exposure packs. This is the lowest-priced size for instant picture material, and the cameras themselves in this range also tend to be inexpensive. The cheapest are for black and white film only. Others are solely for color, while the more versatile are programmed for both black and white and color. Exposure control is automatic and flashcubes can be used.

The widest variety of models are made to take the $3\frac{1}{4} \times 4\frac{1}{4}$ ins (8.3 × 10.7 cm) rectangular size. All film packs contain exposures in ASA 75 color or ASA 3000 black and white. As well as the range of automatic models which correspond to that for square pictures, there are manually controlled models with more complex lenses and a wide range of accessories.

The smaller square pictures are $3\frac{1}{8} \times 3\frac{1}{8}$ ins (8 × 8 cm) and are only produced by the folding reflex type of camera. The pack holds 10 exposures and contains an integral battery (other cameras have separate batteries). An electric motor immediately ejects exposed prints from the camera and the image appears within seconds. There is no waste paper to discard and the print is resistant to damage.

Film types

The older type of instant picture material is pulled out of the camera in sandwich form, with the negative and positive material adhering face to face. After a timed 60 seconds, the print is peeled off and the rest discarded.

The negative/positive black and white material gives a re-usable negative as well as an instant print. The

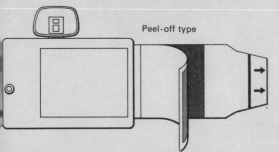

Peel-off type

processing time is 30 seconds (at 70°F or 21°C), after which the paper print is peeled from the film negative which must be cleared in 12% sulfite solution and washed before it is allowed to dry. A specially designed tank is available for use during this clearing process.

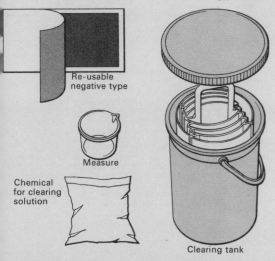

Re-usable negative type

Measure

Chemical for clearing solution

Clearing tank

The plastic-based color print material used in the folding reflex integral processing camera is not a peel-apart type. Development is automatic, needing no timing and starting as the print emerges, extruded at the bottom of the camera by an electric motor. The sensitive surface is protected from light during development by an opaque layer of pigment through which the image gradually begins to appear.

The plastic-based color print
Once the blank film, turquoise in color, has emerged from the front of the instant picture reflex camera, the image begins to appear. It increases in intensity over the next few minutes.

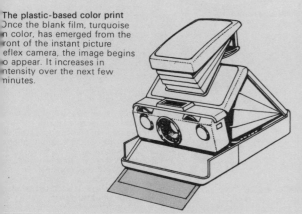

How the film pack works

Negative and positive materials are folded separately inside a container which fits into the back of the camera. The developer is contained in pods which are sandwiched between a negative and a positive layer. The pod bursts as the material is drawn out between rollers, and the developer is spread out.

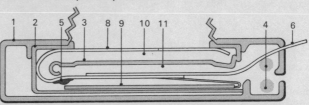

1	Camera
2	Film pack
3	Pressure plate
4	Rollers
5	Developer
6	First tab
7	Second tab
8	Negative in use
9	Positive in use
10	Spare negatives
11	Spare positives

A stack of 8 negatives is held in position by a pressure plate. Behind this plate is a similar stack of 8 positives. Each negative is covered by black paper which must be pulled out of the camera to allow exposure.

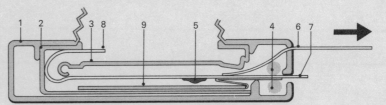

After exposing the negative, the first tab is pulled. This moves the exposed negative to a new position behind the pressure plate where it faces the positive material. It also pushes out the second tab. The film can be left indefinitely in this position until the photographer is ready for the next step.

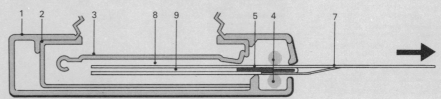

When the second tab is pulled, the negative and positive materials are fed, face to face, through the rollers or bars. The developer is squeezed out of the pod and forms a jelly-like layer between the materials. The entire sandwich is removed from the camera and the processing timed. Within seconds a negative image is formed. Unused silver salts migrate into the positive material where a positive image forms. The negative is peeled away to reveal the final photograph.

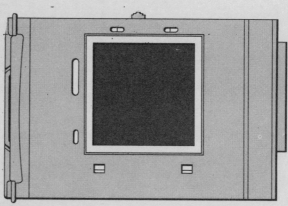

The instant picture film back
To use instant picture material on view cameras a special back is available, which fits into the place where the normal dark slide goes, or else replaces the usual filmback. This is particularly useful for examining an image before taking a conventional picture. Instant picture backs are also used with negative/positive monochrome material.

223

Special Purpose Equipment

Many devices are made which allow photographs to be taken under special circumstances. Others produce unusual pictures. Carefully consider your need for such specialized equipment and make sure that any accessory you plan to buy will fit your camera and will work in conjunction with other equipment you already have. Many systems are not interchangeable with those of other manufacturers.

Motor drives are generally made for a specific model of camera, usually the more expensive single-lens reflexes using 35 mm or roll-film. They advance the film automatically so they can be used in a number of ways: to take pictures by remote control; to shoot at regular predetermined intervals; to photograph automatically when triggered by something other than the photographer, or to take a more rapid sequence of pictures than is possible with ordinary cameras. The motor drive can be used in nature photography, for surveillance and crime detection, for sport and fashion photography and so on.

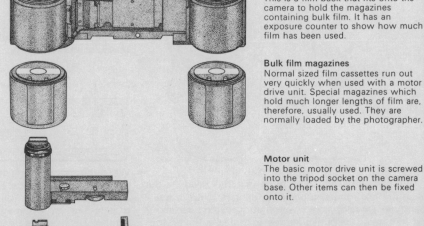

The motor drive system
Different grips, magazines and control mechanisms can be used in conjunction with a basic motor drive unit. This means that a system can be built up to meet any specific need, that it can be as sophisticated or specialized as the photographer wants it to be. A typical system shown left consists of the parts below.

Simple motor drive
The camera must have a suitable fitting, usually on the base plate, to take the motor drive. Batteries to power the electric motor fit inside the handle and can be expendable or rechargeable. One set of batteries lasts for about 1500 to 2000 exposures. The motor drive can be made to work by a switch on the handle or by remote control and can be set to take a single shot or repeated ones automatically. At a shutter speed of 1/1000 sec. the motor drive will shoot about 2.5 to 3 frames per sec. Usually the motor stops when the film has been used up.

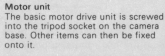

Magazine carrier
This is a film back that fits onto the camera to hold the magazines containing bulk film. It has an exposure counter to show how much film has been used.

Bulk film magazines
Normal sized film cassettes run out very quickly when used with a motor drive unit. Special magazines which hold much longer lengths of film are, therefore, usually used. They are normally loaded by the photographer.

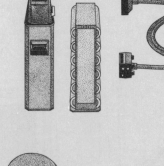

Motor unit
The basic motor drive unit is screwed into the tripod socket on the camera base. Other items can then be fixed onto it.

Battery holder and grip
The battery holder contains either expendable or rechargeable batteries. It fits into a control grip and can be attached to the motor unit or be remotely controlled with a relay cord. Settings on the control grip can be for single or repeated shots. A safety device prevents the film winding on while the shutter is open and stops the film when it is finished.

Bulk film loader
The bulk film loader is used in the darkroom to load bulk film into the special 250-exposure magazines needed to take fullest advantage of motor drive systems. The loader usually stops automatically when the magazine is full.

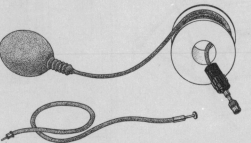

Remote control
An ordinary cable release will not work if it is much longer than about 3 ft (1 m). A pneumatic release, worked by air pressure, can be used from further away, often as far as 33 ft (10 m). With some, separate sections can be joined to make even longer cables. More sophisticated electro-magnetic releases or electrically operated relay leads can be bought in many different lengths.

The large format SLR motor drive system

Most large format single-lens reflexes must have a motor drive unit built into the camera body, unlike the smaller cameras which can often have the device added. The basic motor driven camera is fitted with a normal film back to take 12 exposures and the battery driven motor unit simply advances the film and cocks the shutter automatically. However, many interchangeable pieces of equipment can be fitted to a basic model to make it more versatile. A larger magazine holding film in cassettes can replace the normal film back to take 70 exposures. An even larger and more complicated bulk film magazine can be attached to the camera when a great many shots need to be taken in quick succession. This magazine has its own battery and motor which allow several photographs to be taken each second.

The motor drive can be operated in different ways; it can be triggered from the camera or by remote control. Several types of remote control unit can be used. One will trigger the camera shutter at regular intervals, another will fire up to four cameras at once. There is even a radio device where a battery powered transmitter sends impulses to a receiver attached to the camera as far as 1000 ft (304 m) away.

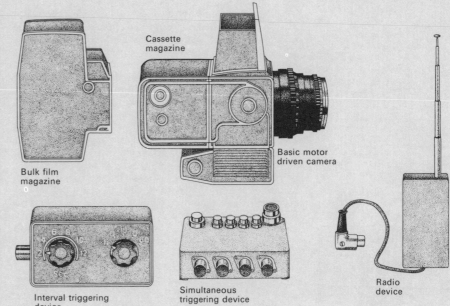

Cassette magazine

Bulk film magazine

Basic motor driven camera

Interval triggering device

Simultaneous triggering device

Radio device

Underwater equipment

As underwater swimming is becoming more popular it is not surprising that underwater photography is too. Any camera can be put in a waterproof case but some cameras are more suitable than others. Salt water immediately ruins a camera, so it is wise to invest in good protection. Rigid cases made of welded perspex withstand considerable pressure, metal housings are strong but you cannot read the scales on the camera lens. For really deep diving, pressurized housings fed with gas are necessary but these are very expensive. Manufacturers often design cases to fit their own cameras. When taking underwater photographs it is best to use a wide-angle lens as the refractive effect of water reduces angle of view. Also it allows the camera to be used as close to the subject as possible. This is important because the further away the camera is from the subject, the more the light can be scattered by water particles in between and the more cloudy the water appears. A wide aperture is usually necessary because of the low light intensity underwater. Focusing is difficult so a dependable scale is vital as well as a large, clear viewfinder.

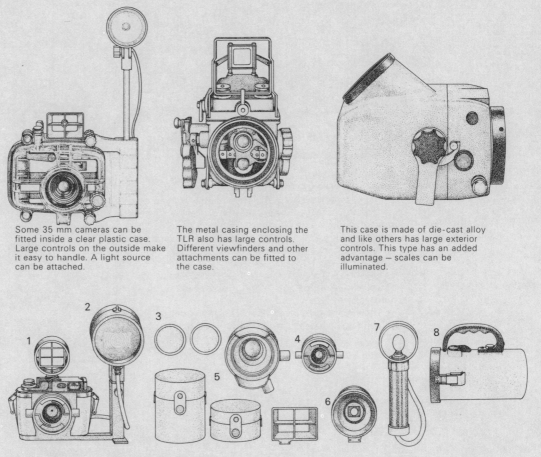

Some 35 mm cameras can be fitted inside a clear plastic case. Large controls on the outside make it easy to handle. A light source can be attached.

The metal casing enclosing the TLR also has large controls. Different viewfinders and other attachments can be fitted to the case.

This case is made of die-cast alloy and like others has large exterior controls. This type has an added advantage — scales can be illuminated.

This type of system consists of a camera in an integral sealed case and a large number of interchangeable accessories which allow the system to be used in different ways. The basic equipment and some of the attachments are shown above. 1 Camera with frame finder. 2 Light source. 3 Filters for color correction or special effects. 4 Interchangeable lenses with large controls. 5 Lens cases. 6 Interchangeable frame finders for use with different lenses. 7 Underwater flash unit. 8 Hand light.

Special Purpose Equipment

The panoramic camera

This type of camera is commonly used to take large groups of people, landscapes and interiors. It usually takes 35 mm film but produces a picture $2\frac{1}{4}$ ins (6 cm) long so that a roll-film size enlarger is needed. The film is curved over a drum in a semi-circle and the lens pivots during exposure so that the image covers a very wide angle horizontally, something like 140°. Since the lens has a reasonably long focal length, probably about 26 mm, it causes little distortion. Also it is easier to design and cheaper to make than a very wide-angle lens.

The camera must be kept level as any tilt produces strange effects. There is usually a spirit level attached to help with this, though not all designs allow it to be seen in the viewfinder. A tripod should be used for formal pictures, especially of buildings. And great care must be taken with moving objects. The image is likely to be stretched out when the object moves with the rotating lens, and compressed when it moves against it.

Extra wide-angle camera
A panoramic camera, showing the lens which moves in a semi-circle to take wide-angle panoramas. The resulting panoramic photograph is shown below. Notice how the camera causes much less distortion of shapes than an equivalent extreme wide-angle lens.

Stereo equipment

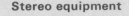

Stereo viewer
The mounted slide, consisting of a pair of pictures, is viewed through 2 lenses set side by side in the viewer. The simple model shown right is held up to the light.

Stereo adapter
The stereo adapter fits on the lens of most good quality 35 mm cameras, above left. It has two sets of mirrors, side by side, with a space in between like human eyes. Light entering the adapter is reflected from the mirrors and through the camera lens as shown in the diagram, left, so that two images taken from fractionally different viewpoints are recorded side by side on the emulsion. A typical result can be seen below.

The spot meter

Spot meters are used to get accurate exposure readings of small parts of a subject. They use a special optical system to measure light over very narrow angles. A typical spot meter's viewfinder will show 21°, but the reading will apply only to the area in a central circle, probably 3°, but sometimes even less than 1°. Scales cover wide ranges: such as from 4 minutes to 1/4000 second; ASA 6 to 6400 (DIN 9 to 39); f/1 to f/128. The scales are illuminated so that measurements can be read in dim light.

The advantage of the system is that exposure readings of very small areas can be made with great precision.

A selective exposure meter
A spot meter, below, showing its very narrow angle of coverage compared with its angle of view. Extremely accurate light readings of very small areas of a subject can be taken but it is a technique requiring skill.

The difficulty lies in relating such measurements to an overall exposure. Measurements of the luminance range of the subject can be made by comparing readings from extreme highlight and shadow areas. Distracting areas, which would upset an ordinary meter reading, can be completely avoided.

Photographs for viewing in three dimensions

A stereo camera is fitted with two lenses, spaced apart like human eyes, to produce two pictures which can subsequently be combined to give an impression of depth. Special viewing or projection equipment is usually necessary for the full effect to be appreciated. However a cheaper and less complex piece of equipment, a stereo adapter, can be fitted to the front of the normal lens of most 35 mm cameras for similar results. Two images are recorded on one frame, side by side, but they are slightly different because they are taken from two viewpoints. By viewing the pair through a stereo viewer, the three dimensional effect can be seen.

Protection for your equipment

If you have a camera with, say, two lenses it is easiest to keep the different items in separate cases, held together on a single shoulder strap. But if you have a lot of equipment, a fitted case or gadget bag is probably the best way to keep everything together and in order. Gadget bags are soft and easy to carry and are ideal for fairly small outfits. Cases are often filled with sponge rubber into which holes are cut to hold specific items. Sometimes the catches on cases weaken with wear so fit a strap round the case for safety.

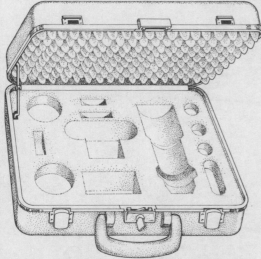

Foam rubber lined case
Cases lined with foam rubber protect equipment from vibration and impact. Such cases have a tight seal when shut to guard against dampness.

A versatile case
Many equipment cases have moveable internal partitions. Small items can be held in the lid by elastic straps or loops.

The gadget bag
Use the pockets on a gadget bag to carry films and items needed quickly. Straps usually have an anti-slip pad for the shoulder and can be shortened for hand-carrying. Sometimes there are loops on the base to hold a tripod.

Protecting filters and lenses
Transparent plastic cases allow filters or lenses to be identified instantly, without the need for labels. Lenses can be carried in and protected by purse-type holders or rigid cases.

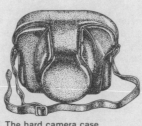

The hard camera case
A hard or rigid camera case gives useful protection from knocks as well as the weather. It is usually purpose-made for a particular camera model.

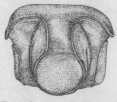

The soft camera case
Soft leather cases wear well and need not be tailored exactly to the camera dimensions.

Protecting a camera and long lens
Cases with especially long noses are made so that a long-focus lens may be left on a camera ready for instant use.

Lens caps
Keep front and back caps on lenses not in use. A haze filter is best kept on the camera lens to protect it against scratches and dust.

Lens hoods
A lens hood not only prevents direct light from striking the front lens surface, it also protects the front of the lens.

Lens hoods are made in different shapes and sizes and should always be used on lenses for which they have been designed.

Cleaning your camera

The outside of the camera requires very little attention. A soft, fluffless cloth can restore luster. On the inside, dust and tiny pieces of film leader or paper backing can be removed with a brush, but be sure no hairs break off as these can cause more trouble than the dust. Avoid touching the shutter blinds. If the camera is held with the open side downward dust can fall out when loosened by the brush. Blower brushes and aerosols are also available.

It is better to keep lenses dust-free than to clean them continually. A filter over the lens provides excellent protection against dust and dirt — an ultra-violet or haze filter does not affect exposure and can be left in place permanently. If it is scratched by careless cleaning it is cheap to replace, whereas having a lens repolished is expensive. Be especially careful at the seaside. Salt spray corrodes and sand is abrasive. Hot sun can also cause damage so keep the camera covered.

Cleaning lenses
A good way to clean lenses is with an impregnated cloth intended for optical glass, or tissue, the strong kind which leaves no loose fibers. First remove loose grit or dust as this will scratch the surface. Roll the tissue into a tube about the size of a cigarette and tear it in two crossways. Place the ragged edges together and use them to clean the surface, working from the outside toward the center. (If you work from the center outward dirt builds up inside the rim.) Avoid impregnated tissues unless they can be safely used on coated lenses.

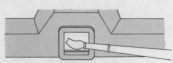

The problem of dust
To remove dust turn the lens upside down so particles fall off when loosened by the brush or tissue. If absolutely necessary a lens cleaning fluid can be used, in which case inverting the lens stops liquid running into the mount.

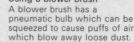

Reaching difficult places
Small, awkward areas such as the rectangular rear window of the viewfinder can be cleaned with a small, soft brush or cotton swab.

Using a blower brush
A blower brush has a pneumatic bulb which can be squeezed to cause puffs of air which blow away loose dust.

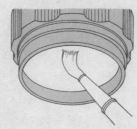

Fitting out a Studio

The studio

The main requirement for a good studio is plenty of space. Commercial studios are often large enough to accommodate well-spaced groups and large objects like cars. Amateur studios can be less ambitious but there is a minimum size for good results. To take full-length photographs of people, or portraits with long-focus lenses with a reasonable distance between subject and background, at least 15 ft (4.5 m) is required, and more space is desirable. A width of at least half the length is necessary and plenty of height is helpful. At least one wall, preferably two, should be plain to act as background and have no projections so that backdrops may be hung flat.

Shiny surfaces on walls can cause troublesome reflections. A matt washable white is the most universally accepted surface, though sometimes one wall may be tinted to serve as background for color pictures. Ceilings should not be colored and as large an area as possible should be left clear to reflect light.

Floors are best left plain. Well-sealed wood or a special composition surface is ideal, the aim being a dust-free non-slip floor which will not mark. If linoleum is used it is better not to polish it. Skirting boards are a nuisance if walls are to be used as a background.

Windows and skylights should be fitted with blinds, or at least opaque curtains, which do not let light in at the edges. Some photographers like to have a choice of white or black.

There can hardly be too many electrical outlets. Check to see whether existing wiring is adequate. Do not forget heating and ventilation; a fan heater can help.

1   Dressing table
2   Mirror
3   Extension lead
4   Folding screen
5   Stand
6   Studio flash unit
7   Floodlight
8   Snoot
9   Quartz iodine light
10 Refrigerator

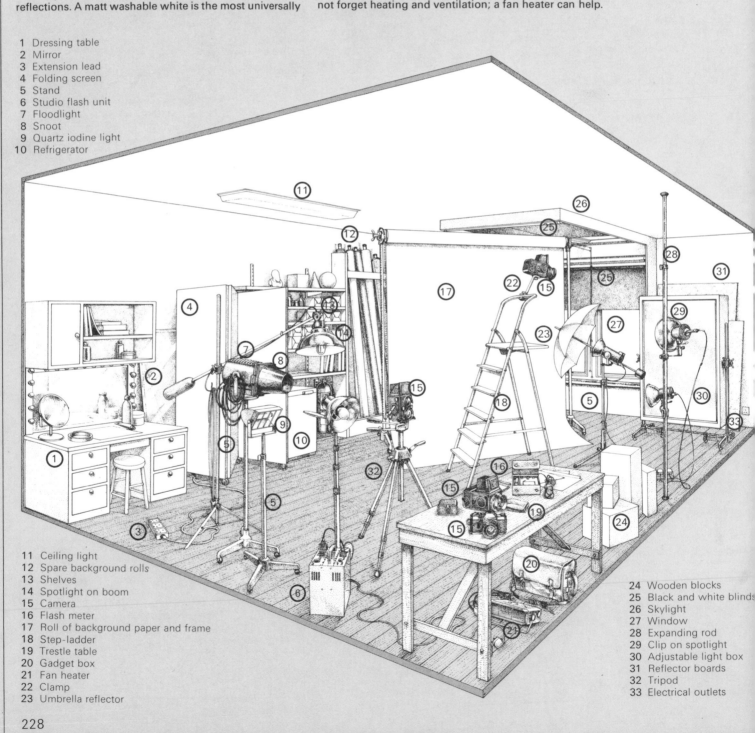

11 Ceiling light
12 Spare background rolls
13 Shelves
14 Spotlight on boom
15 Camera
16 Flash meter
17 Roll of background paper and frame
18 Step-ladder
19 Trestle table
20 Gadget box
21 Fan heater
22 Clamp
23 Umbrella reflector

24 Wooden blocks
25 Black and white blinds
26 Skylight
27 Window
28 Expanding rod
29 Clip on spotlight
30 Adjustable light box
31 Reflector boards
32 Tripod
33 Electrical outlets

If a room cannot be reserved exclusively as a studio, much can still be accomplished by improvisation. Simple equipment can produce good results when correctly used. If the room is too small, try shooting through an open door to increase the camera-to-subject distance.

Studio equipment
The ideal studio will have a make-up mirror, stool and dressing table for the model, a folding screen (which can be plain white to serve as a reflector) and a refrigerator for storing film and perishable props. Useful items are a trestle table, which can be folded away for extra space when not needed, and a strong step-ladder for high viewpoints and adjusting equipment. Shelves and furniture should be confined to as few walls as possible, leaving the rest free for backgrounds.

A few wooden blocks or strong boxes are ideal for supporting props, and for standing on, particularly when using twin-lens reflex cameras on tripods. If there are not enough electrical outlets use a multiple socket on an extension cord; this also helps to reduce the number of trailing wires.

Changing backgrounds
Backgrounds are extremely important. The most useful is plain white since this can be made any shade from white to black according to the amount of light which reaches it. Various colors can be produced by using colored foils in front of the lights directed onto the background. A very popular background is a roll of paper suspended above head height. The paper can be unrolled down onto the floor and the subject placed on it, a gentle curve in the paper taking the place of the otherwise awkward join between wall and floor. When the paper becomes creased or dirty a further section can be pulled down to replace the part discarded. The roll is often placed in a holder at the top of a wall but greater freedom of positioning is achieved with a moveable paper stand. While white is the most popular a whole range of shades and colors is available. A mid-gray can be useful for portraiture and black for trick photography. A well-equipped studio will have several rolls of background paper in stock since this is a simple way to achieve different effects.

If a room cannot be kept permanently as a studio, it is easy to create a temporary one by pinning the free end of a roll of background paper to a picture rail, leaving the roll on the floor. This makes a workable studio of any sizeable room. In such circumstances do not choose too wide a roll. A 9 ft (2.7 m) roll can be heavy and difficult to store.

Projectors can be used to throw light patterns on the background. Slides can also be projected — remember to match the subject lighting to the lighting in the background if a natural effect is required. Front projection units for projecting an image from the camera viewpoint which shows on the background but not on the subject itself are rarely found in amateur studios.

Reflectors and stands
It is handy to have some reflector boards. The folding screen mentioned previously can be used as a reflector but polystyrene sheets are more popular. They are light and portable. Lighting stands are usually telescopic, the heavier ones often have a pneumatic column. In small studios it is worth saving floor space by using clamps to fix lamps onto picture rails or other projections. Another method is to use expanding rods which are braced against the floor and ceiling, forming a rigid

Filament lamps

Tungsten-halogen with mushroom reflector

Spotlight

Floodlight

Tungsten-halogen floodlight

Tungsten-halogen spotlight

column without a base. Lamps can then be clamped to the column.

Studio lights
A selection of different lights is valuable in a studio. Ordinary domestic fittings can be used but be sure not to couple them with bulbs of excessive wattage. Special bulbs provide more light and are definitely more suitable for color photography. They come in several types and sizes; generally the more light they give out, the less time they last.

Photofloods
The most common bulb is the ordinary photoflood. These range from 150–500W and their working life is between three and ten hours. Nothing over 150W should be used in a domestic light fitting. Most larger photofloods have a screw base intended for photographic light fittings.

Photopearl type bulbs are less over-run, lasting for about 100 hours, and forming a compromise between the ordinary household bulb and the short-lived photoflood. With modern fast films and wide-aperture lenses the need for high light intensity has diminished and the 100-hour bulb is becoming increasingly popular.

Bulbs with built-in reflectors are also available. These can be used in very simple fittings but more elaborate housings are available if required. All bulbs are made in clear glass, pearl and opal, and often with a metallic crown to prevent direct light escaping. The most widely used is pearl.

Tungsten-halogen lamps
Ordinary bulbs, both photographic and domestic, grow dimmer with age as tungsten from the filament migrates to the glass bulb. The light also becomes redder, which causes difficulties with color photography. Tungsten-halogen bulbs — formerly called quartz-iodine or QI — incorporate a halogen — originally iodine — which combines with the gaseous tungsten. Provided the transparent envelope is sufficiently hot, the bulb stays clean and tungsten is redeposited on the element upon cooling. Quartz was used because ordinary glass would melt. These bulbs have a longer life and the output stays constant. They cost more initially, but longer life and convenience make them well worthwhile. Tungsten-halogen strip lamps are long, thin tubes used for general lighting in reflectors.

Incandescent lights
Incandescent lamps are used in a wide variety of fittings to control the angle and distribution of emitted light. The most common form is the floodlamp, which spreads light evenly over a fairly wide angle. A 60° cone is average among a number of different reflectors. The shallower the reflector the wider the angle, the deeper the more concentrated the light.

A fill-in lamp will have a wide, shallow reflector and a cap to prevent direct light leaving the bulb. All the light which reaches the subject is bounced off the reflector and this provides an even lighting with very soft shadows. Indeed, the diffused light is almost shadowless.

A spotlamp uses a special bulb with a clear glass envelope. A reflector behind the bulb helps to concentrate the light and the spotlamp lens casts a tight, narrow beam of intensive illumination. A fresnel lens is often used with a spotlamp. The focusing control allows the diameter of the beam to be altered, say from 6 inches (15.2 cm) to several feet. The smaller the diameter the harder and more sharp-edged the shadows.

Lighting Equipment

Reflectors and attachments

Reflecting surfaces in lamps may be smooth, bright metal, but often there are dimples or ripples, or the surface is intentionally roughened, to scatter the light and produce even distribution without hot spots.

Diffusing light with a light box

Light boxes are sometimes used to produce soft diffused lighting. These are of varying sizes and are made of diffusing plastic with fluorescent strip lights inside, and can be mounted on wheeled stands for ease of mobility. They are especially useful for taking silhouettes, with the subject's head posed in front of the box with no other lighting. Sometimes light boxes can be used to photograph small items, when a white shadowless background is required.

Making use of umbrella reflectors

Umbrella reflectors are very popular. The lamp is pointed away from the subject into an umbrella producing a very soft, diffused light. Umbrellas are often used with studio electronic flash. Although lighting intensity is much less than when the same source is used to light the subject directly, this method is remarkably simple and is especially suitable for color photography. Umbrellas are usually white, but can be silvered for less diffusion, or painted gold for a warmer tone. If very bright, reflected light is needed, several lamps may be used directed into one giant umbrella.

Adding attachments for more control

Many attachments can be fitted to lamps to create particular effects. A shade of flat opaque material can be clipped on the rim of a floodlight to prevent light reaching part of the picture.

More elaborate is a set of "barn doors," whose four flaps can be hinged down to block off light. This is especially useful in cases where direct light would otherwise be shining into the camera lens. Avoid leaving all four barn doors folded down for long periods, as the lamp will overheat.

A "snoot" is a cone whose larger end fits on the lamp while the smaller opens toward the subject. It directs a narrow circle of light, somewhat like a spotlamp but less versatile. Snoots are sometimes used on studio flash equipment.

Optical "noses" act like lenses on a projector. They can be fitted to a spotlight to increase brightness. Metal or cardboard masks can be slotted into the noses and can be used to cast patterns on the background and occasionally on the subject. Shapes can be cut in thin metal or cardboard for special effects. A slide projector can be used in the same way, with similar results.

Bouncing light

Reflectors, made of white polystyrene or cardboard, can take the place of a fill-in lamp. A wall, preferably light-colored, acts as a good reflector bouncing light back into the shadows and lowering the contrast. A white matt surface is usually the best. Employ a washable paint and keep the surface clean. Silvered reflectors made with aluminum paint or foil (unless crinkled), provide a slightly hard reflection and are therefore less popular. Mirrors give hard and directional reflections which are very difficult to use. Colored surfaces give slightly tinted reflections, which are hard to deal with unless you are an expert. White ceilings are good natural reflectors, and a strong light, such as that from a high-wattage tungsten-halogen lamp, can be bounced from a ceiling to spread a soft light evenly over the entire floor space. It helps to have a light-colored floor.

Large and small light boxes
Light boxes contain several lamps behind translucent panels. They provide soft lighting, and are particularly useful for lighting full-length figures evenly. Fluorescent tubes are suitable for black-and-white work, but electronic flashes are preferable for color photography.

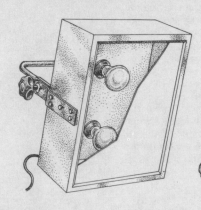
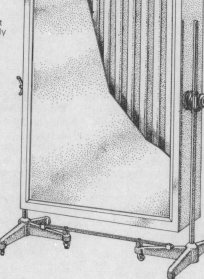

Umbrella reflectors
Reflectors which fold down like umbrellas can be used in lighting set-ups. They may be white, silver or gold according to the quality and color of light required.

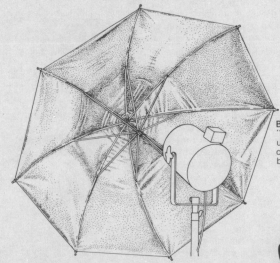

Barn door reflectors
"Barn doors" are metal flaps, usually black, hinged so they can be folded into the light beam as desired.

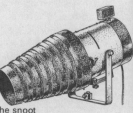

The snoot
A "snoot" channels light into a narrow beam. It is less expensive than a spotlight but can be used in a similar way.

Light tent
Objects which have shiny, highly polished surfaces are hard to photograph because reflections of the photographer, camera and other equipment spoil the picture. If the surfaces are curved such reflections are hard to avoid. The problem can be solved by making a tent out of white muslin or similar material. The lights are directed on the outside of the tent while the camera peeps in through a hole.

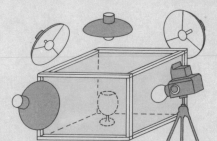

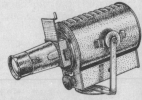

Optical attachments
An optical "nose" to increase brightness can be fitted in place of the fresnel lens on a spotlight. Screened or decorative masks can be slotted into the nose for special light effects.

Light sources and their color temperatures

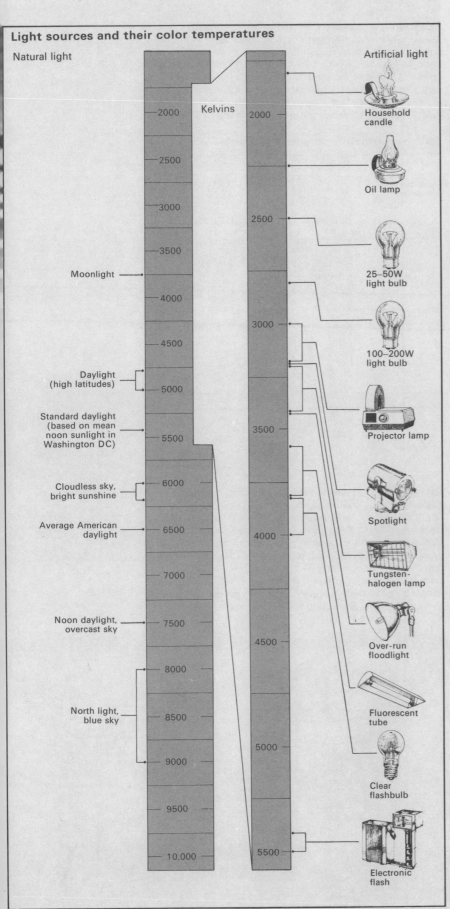

Natural light

Kelvins

Artificial light

- Household candle
- Oil lamp
- 25–50W light bulb
- 100–200W light bulb
- Projector lamp
- Spotlight
- Tungsten-halogen lamp
- Over-run floodlight
- Fluorescent tube
- Clear flashbulb
- Electronic flash

Moonlight

Daylight (high latitudes)

Standard daylight (based on mean noon sunlight in Washington DC)

Cloudless sky, bright sunshine

Average American daylight

Noon daylight, overcast sky

North light, blue sky

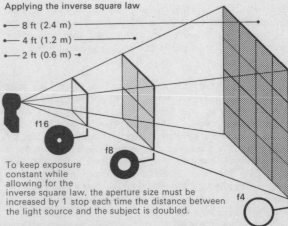

Applying the inverse square law

- 8 ft (2.4 m)
- 4 ft (1.2 m)
- 2 ft (0.6 m)

f16   f8   f4

To keep exposure constant while allowing for the inverse square law, the aperture size must be increased by 1 stop each time the distance between the light source and the subject is doubled.

Inverse square law

The farther an object is from a lamp the dimmer the light falling on it. Illumination is inversely proportional to the square of the distance between a point source and the surface being lit. If an object at 2 ft (0.6 m) receives a given quantity of light, the same amount of light will be spread over four times the area at 4 ft (1.2 m), and over sixteen times the area at 8 ft (2.4 m). In other words, at twice a given distance the intensity of light from a single source is reduced four times; at three times the distance the intensity is reduced nine times and so on.

The rule does not apply with absolute accuracy in a studio because light sources are fairly large, and light is reflected from walls and ceilings, but the rule is good enough for most purposes. If, for example, a fill-in light is required at a quarter the strength of a main light, and both lamps are the same, the fill-in should be placed twice as far from the subject as the key light.

The more scattered and diffused the light, the less exact is the application of the inverse square law. Thus the placing of an umbrella reflector need not be as precise as the placing of a direct light.

Color temperature

A convenient way to describe the color of light is by color temperature in Kelvins (K). If a selected metal substance is heated to incandescence, it emits light of all wavelengths, the relative proportion of short and long wavelengths depending on the temperature. As the substance heats up it glows first a dull red, then orange, and so on through the spectrum until it becomes blue-white, after which the rays emitted move into the invisible ultra-violet range. The table shows the color temperature values of many kinds of lighting.

Color temperature and film

Black and white films can be used with light of any color temperature. Color negative films can sometimes be corrected while printing (check with the manufacturer's instructions).

Color transparency, or slide films must suit the color temperature or be corrected by filters (see pp. 216–217). Most slide films are made for daylight, between 5,000 and 6,000K, and give yellowish pictures with incandescent lamps having a lower color temperature than daylight, unless a blue filter is used. Type A films are balanced for about 3,400K and type B for 3,200K but the difference is only important to an expert. If pictures are taken in both daylight and incandescent light with the same film, use a type A or B film with an amber filter in daylight, because this helps to keep loss of film speed to a minimum.

Flash Lighting

Most modern cameras have provision for flash, and several different types are available. All the small bulbs and cubes are now colored blue, so that the color temperature of the light is correct for daylight films.

Bulb flash

Most cheaper cameras use flashcubes, which are four flashbulbs mounted in reflectors and assembled into a cube which plugs into the camera as a single unit. After one bulb has been fired the cube is turned so a fresh one points toward the subject. Some flashcubes are fired by a battery. Others are fired mechanically and have no need of a battery. These two types have different bases so you must pick the type that fits your camera. If the lens aperture cannot be altered, flash pictures can only be taken over a narrow range of distances, usually from 6 to 10 ft (1.8 to 3 m).

Flashbulbs come in several sizes. The small ones, without a metal base, are the most popular and the cheapest. Large flashbulbs, about the size of a domestic incandescent lamp, provide huge amounts of light, and are commonly used by professional photographers. Special long-burning flashbulbs are made for cameras with focal plane shutters to be used when fast flash exposures are required, but these are seldom seen today.

Flashbulbs fit into a holder with a reflector, and a battery is needed to fire the bulb. Also available are magazines of small bulbs which plug into cameras so that bulbs need not be changed each time one is fired.

All flashbulbs are made in much the same way. A filament glows red when current is passed through it. This ignites a priming paste which in turn sets fire to foil or wire of magnesium/aluminum alloy or zirconium. Oxygen is contained in the glass bulb which is itself coated with protective plastic as a safety precaution.

Electronic flash

The duration of light from an electronic flash unit is very short, so there is no danger of camera shake or subject movement unless ambient lighting is bright. Small flash units usually fit on top of the camera. Large ones go on brackets fitted to the camera. Connection to the shutter for synchronization may be through a coaxial cable, or direct through a shoe fitting on the camera. If many flash photographs are to be taken the cost per flash is cheaper with an electronic unit than with expendable flashbulbs.

Automatic exposure control with flashguns

Some electronic flashguns have automatic exposure control. Light from the gun is reflected from the subject back to a sensing cell. When sufficient light has been reflected the cell cuts off the current and the light is switched off – all this happens very quickly, sometimes in 1/30,000 second. This avoids the necessity for calculations and helps to get more flashes out of a battery.

Flash synchronization with the shutter

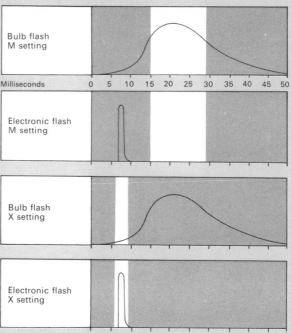

Cheaper cameras are synchronized with flashbulbs or cubes at low speeds (around 1/25 second). More sophisticated cameras have several speed settings to be used with flash; X for use with electronic flash; M for use with flashbulbs and F (now uncommon) for use with long burning bulbs. It is important that you use the correct setting because different types of flash reach their brightness peak in different lengths of time. Bulbs take longer to peak than electronic flash which peaks almost instantaneously. By setting the correct speed, you make

Portable flash units

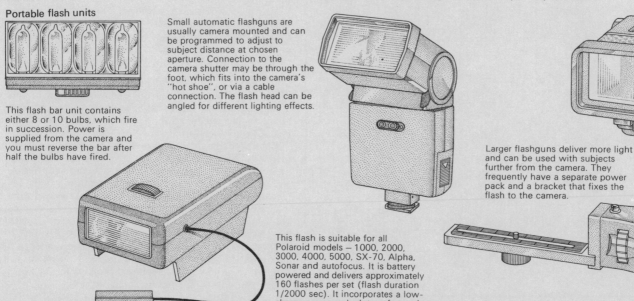

This flash bar unit contains either 8 or 10 bulbs, which fire in succession. Power is supplied from the camera and you must reverse the bar after half the bulbs have fired.

Small automatic flashguns are usually camera mounted and can be programmed to adjust to subject distance at chosen aperture. Connection to the camera shutter may be through the foot, which fits into the camera's "hot shoe", or via a cable connection. The flash head can be angled for different lighting effects.

This flash is suitable for all Polaroid models – 1000, 2000, 3000, 4000, 5000, SX-70, Alpha, Sonar and autofocus. It is battery powered and delivers approximately 160 flashes per set (flash duration 1/2000 sec). It incorporates a low-charge exposure lock to safeguard against underexposure.

Larger flashguns deliver more light and can be used with subjects further from the camera. They frequently have a separate power pack and a bracket that fixes the flash to the camera.

sure that the shutter is fully open when the flash is peaking. With the wrong setting you are unlikely to record an image. Look at the diagram (opposite). If you use the M setting with bulb flash, the shutter is fully open when the flash peaks. If the M setting is used with electronic flash, the peak is over before the shutter opens. Conversely, with the shutter speed set at X bulb flash peaks after the shutter has closed. Electronic flash, however, peaks when the shutter is open.

Guide numbers

Light from a flashgun follows the inverse square law (see p. 231) quite closely. Exposure can be estimated by using a guide number. Every flashbulb or electronic flash has a particular flash factor or guide number, when used with film of a certain speed. Using this number lens apertures can be swiftly calculated according to the distance between flashgun and subject. Suppose the factor is 160, then at 10 ft (3 m) the lens would be set at f/16, at 20 ft (6 m) f/8, and so on. The guide number is simply divided by the distance. If using flash outdoors or in a large dark hall, allow extra exposure (about half a stop) as factors are usually calculated to allow for the reflections in a normal room.

Studio flash

Flash is ideal lighting for studios. An ordinary lamp allows modeling to be viewed and the flash takes the picture. There are no problems with color temperature. It is possible to obtain flashing electronic spotlamps, but more often flash is bounced from umbrella reflectors or shone directly from floodlight-type reflectors.

Having several lights is a huge advantage in a studio, but the lighting scheme for each subject must be built up from simple principles, one light at a time. Bear in mind that most photographs are taken with one light only – the sun.

Place the main light first since this controls the atmosphere of the picture and the overall effect. Remember that if the subject is taken away from the background the shadows will be softer and may not appear in the picture area. A second, or fill-in, light softens shadows on the subject. Another light shining on the background only will dilute any unwanted shadows there.

Build up lighting, one lamp at a time and avoid multiple shadows.

Specialized studio equipment

Slave flash units will fire other flashguns, without wire connections, when activated by the first flash. Similar photocells are often fitted to studio electronic flash units and are valuable in avoiding a tangle of wires.

Lighting arrangements

Using flash

The most simple lighting is with flash on the camera. Avoid reflective surfaces behind the subject which can bounce direct light back at the lens. If people appear with pink eyes — due to direct reflection of light from the retina — move the flashgun away from the camera, possibly with a flash extender.

Bounce flash

Bouncing flash from a ceiling — ideally a white one — provides a soft light without hard, black shadows on the background. It works best with light colored carpets or floors but needs 2 or 3 stops extra exposure. It is especially useful if areas of the subject are at different distances from the camera.

Diffused flash

Direct flash may be diffused by putting material over the bulb, making sure it does not obscure the lens or, with automatic electronic flash, the sensing cell. A handkerchief is often used, preferably a white one, and this usually absorbs about half the light. Lighting is softer, but more directional than bounced flash.

Adding reflectors

If the walls of a studio do not provide enough reflection, a separate reflector may help to add light to over-dark shadows. Remember that light reflects from a surface at the same angle as it strikes it and this helps in judging where to place reflectors relative to the main light.

Using a second light

A second light produces a stronger fill-in than a reflector. If the main light is near the camera, the second lamp is usually placed at the side often directed at the background to drown the shadows cast by the first light. Do not have both lamps casting equal amounts of light on the subject.

Making use of three lights

Two movable lamps provide a flexible system when used to supplement the basic light source. A good plan is to have the main lamp shining on the subject at 45°, horizontally and vertically. Less intense lights can be placed at the other side of the subject and near the camera to soften shadows and create highlights.

Multiple studio flash units may be controlled by a console, into which the lamp leads are plugged. Six or more outlets for separate flashheads are provided. Usually such consoles are on wheels for easy movement in the studio.

Ring flash units are for close-up work. The subject is lit from all sides and shadows do not have sharp edges. If the tube moves with the lens, exposure remains constant over a range of magnifications. The lens functions through the center of the tube.

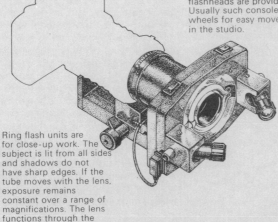

Exposures for electronic flash can be measured with flashmeters. Some small models are battery operated, others need a cable connection to the flashgun. All types indicate incident light readings when a trial flash is made.

Studio electronic lighting units may have a separate powerpack or be of the unit type with lamphouse and power pack combined in the same housing as illustrated right.

Darkroom Materials

Setting up a darkroom

A permanent darkroom means you can work at any time, and the room is geared entirely to the needs of the photographer. Too few amateur photographers have such facilities. Most borrow a room for a few hours that must then be converted back to domestic purposes. Circumstances dictate which room is chosen – a spare bedroom, an attic, a loft or even the cupboard under the stairs can be used, for although space is cramped, much can be done in a small area.

It is not essential to have running water in the darkroom; fixed prints or films can be washed elsewhere. When the fixation period is complete, transfer prints into water prior to washing. Carry them in a plastic pail as this is less likely to spill than a shallow pan.

Ventilation and heating for cold weather make working easier. A fan heater assists with both. Wall ventilators should have baffles to prevent light entering.

Making the darkroom light-proof

All darkrooms must be completely blacked out. The test is not whether it looks dark when the light is switched out; it must still be dark when the eyes have adapted ten minutes later.

In temporary darkrooms windows may be blacked out with blinds or black plastic on frames made of wood strips. Use a mat to stop light leaking under the doors. And do not forget keyholes and other crevices. Strips of self-adhesive dark foam rubber made for draft-proofing are useful for stopping light leaks around doors. Double curtains can be hung in rooms used as occasional darkrooms. Black, opaque curtains next to the windows can be hidden by decorative curtains. Be generous with lengths and widths of cloth to allow for overlapping and tucking-in. Test with all the outside lights switched on, or, if the darkroom will be used in daylight, when the sun is shining.

Adding fixtures and fittings

If light is properly excluded, a darkroom doesn't have to have dark walls or ceiling. A white ceiling and light walls help the general illumination from the safelight, especially when you are printing in black and white. The only exception is the wall directly behind the enlarger. Most enlargers leak some light and this must not fall onto the printing paper. A dark area guards against this danger. In a permanent darkroom the wall can be painted with black emulsion paint; in a temporary one matt black paper, such as black background paper, may be pinned up.

A substantial bench or table is required to support the enlarger. Do not use a flimsy construction which wobbles. Height is important – the enlarger head must not touch the ceiling when it is at the top of the column, and too low a surface makes working uncomfortable. An average height is 33 inches (84 cm), but this is only a guide. Separate wet (processing) and dry areas in the darkroom. Keep dishes as far away from the enlarger as possible. If there is no sink in which to place dishes use a bench or table. An old washstand is ideal; otherwise make the top waterproof with paint, preferably bituminous, or a non-staining plastic. The materials sold for kitchen surfaces are suitable.

Assume that, no matter how careful you intend to be, chemicals will be spilled. Take precautions accordingly. If rugs and carpets cannot be removed, cover them with plastic or at least newspaper. In a bathroom trays can be supported on a wooden framework over the bathtub. Have a few inches of water in the tub while printing. This automatically dilutes drips and prevents stains.

A sign hanging outside the door while the darkroom is in use should prevent people entering, but, if you can, lock the door to make certain. To protect the wall from chemical-laden fingers put transparent protective plastic around the light switch, or use a ceiling cord switch.

Designing a darkroom

If a room can be specially designed as a darkroom much can be done to provide excellent working conditions. Floors should be waterproof and easily cleaned. Light-colored vinyl tiles or floor-covering are ideal.

The edges of shelves, cupboard doors, handles and so on can be finished in white to help locate them in dim lighting. Luminous strips or small patches of luminous paint can be used, but not in the area where films are loaded into tanks.

Plenty of wall sockets are an advantage because increasing numbers of gadgets use electricity, and trailing wires are a nuisance. Fix a large darkroom clock to the wall, showing elapsed time in minutes and seconds. A bulletin board can display manufacturers' instruction leaflets, as well as notes on work to be carried out and supplies to be ordered.

Some tasks are best done outside the darkroom. Print mounting and retouching, filing and storage come into this category. Many photographers prefer to dry films and paper outside, perhaps in a drying cabinet. Drying black and white prints in a darkroom is no problem, and can in fact be convenient – prints may be changed without going outside. But drying color prints can produce fumes from the stabilizer which are unpleasant in a confined space.

Choosing and using the sink

It is best to use a rectangular sink, and to rest the trays of chemicals on wooden slats to keep them clear of the bottom. The sink can be ceramic, or enameled metal, in which case it must not be chipped, or of wood, well covered with chemical-resistant paint. Vinyl sheeting is often used in darkrooms but great care must be taken with the joints. Stainless steel is expensive and can be corroded by prolonged contact with some silver-bleach solutions.

When making prints most photographers like to work from left to right, starting with the developer and ending with the wash. Before prints are dried, excess liquid can be drained off by leaving them on a glass or plastic sheet which slopes into the sink. A roll of paper towel is useful for drying hands. Trays can be stored on wooden slats below the sink, and large chemical containers can be kept on the floor.

Installing equipment

Safelights must not shine directly on the enlarger baseboard. Apart from the danger of fogging paper, the light will distort readings on the enlarging meter and color analyzer. Wiring can be arranged so that the safelight goes off when the enlarger is switched on.

It is possible to use two or more safelights. A large one provides general background illumination while a smaller one gives brighter lighting in a confined area. Amber safelight screens are usual for black and white papers; most films and some special papers are used only in a green light which is so dim that most photographers find it easier to work in complete darkness. Safelights must contain low powered bulbs and must not be used too close to light sensitive materials.

An adjustable masking frame is usually kept on the enlarger baseboard with the timer, enlarger meter or color analyzer (if used), at the side. Dodging or shading

Normally, the slowest film is used when big enlargements (such as 10× negative size) are needed, while fast film is used on occasions when the light levels are particularly low.

Kodak has developed a new emulsion with a true film speed of 1000 ASA (31 DIN). This has been achieved by using flat silver halide crystals known as "T-grains". These films, called Kodacolor VR, are the highest speed color negative types presently available. The speed increase has not been coupled with an increase in graininess or a loss of contrast as would be expected with other types of film.

Black and white film
Most black and white films are panchromatic. Special high-contrast films are sensitive to blue, green, and yellow light only. The latest development in black and white film is the introduction of color-type chromogenic technology to produce a monochrome dye instead of silver image. The advantages are a combination of high speed with fine grain and the ability to rate the same film anywhere between 50 and 1600 ASA (18-33 DIN). Despite the fact that different frames even on the same film have been given varying degrees of exposure in the camera, film development itself is simple and straightforward.

Color film
The main classification of color films is into positive (or reversal) film and negative film. The latter is normally used for making prints, while the former produces projection transparencies, but it is possible to produce prints or slides from either type of original.

Color negative film
Nowadays most color negative films are masked. This gives the processed films an overall orange tint which makes the colors purer on the print. Color negative films generally have speeds between 64 and 1000 ASA (19 and 31 DIN).

Reversal film
Reversal films may be divided into two main groups: those with color couplers present in the emulsion, and those where couplers are added during processing. This is why some films cannot be processed at home. Reversal films are made to a variety of speeds, from ASA 25 to 500 (15 to 28 DIN) or even faster. And there is a general (but not invariable) rule that the faster films are grainier and of lower contrast than the slower ones. The visual effect of lower contrast is often hidden by increased color saturation, whereby brighter colors give an effect of brilliance. An advantage of this modern type of film is increased latitude with exposure.

Films for use in daylight and artificial light
Color films are balanced for the color temperature (see p. 231) of the exposing light source. There are two types: daylight, balanced as its name suggests for daylight conditions (5400K) and for flash; and types A or B, balanced for artificial light (around 3400 and 3200K respectively). This latter level of illumination is that provided by most photographic studio lamps.

Special films
The range of special films is very wide. Most need to be ordered. Some are available only as 35 mm reels, often in approximately 100 ft (30.4 m) lengths instead of in cassettes. Others are only made as sheet film.

Special black and white films
Infra-red film
These monochrome films are sensitive to the whole visible spectrum and also to some infra-red radiation

tools can be hung on the wall or put into a nearby drawer. A roller or guillotine type trimmer is useful for trimming paper and prints. Photographic paper should be stored in boxes near the enlarger.

Types of photographic film
Film is a transparent base coated with an emulsion of silver halide crystals suspended in gelatin. Most bases are made of cellulose tri-acetate, but thinner polyester bases are also used.

The speed and grain relationship in film

Speed of film	Slow	Medium	Fast	Extra fast
ASA number	25–64	64–200	200–400	400–1600
DIN number	15–19	19–24	24–27	27–32
Grain	very fine	fine	medium	coarse
Definition	very sharp	sharp	medium	poor to medium

A simple way to classify films is by their sensitivity to light — what photographers call their "speed." The larger the crystals in the emulsion the faster and therefore the more sensitive to light is the film, but large crystals cause the granular pattern, or "grain," to become more pronounced in big enlargements. Fast film is also made with an extra-thick emulsion which allows the film to collect more light, but because light scatters inside the emulsion this tends to blur fine detail.

The darkroom and its equipment
1 Light switch
2 Ventilator
3 Washing tank
4 Paper towel
5 Trays
6 Racks
7 Pail
8 Wastebin
9 Safelight
10 Ceiling light
11 Cupboard
12 Enlarger
13 Flat bed drier
14 Wall safelight
15 Stool
16 Guillotine
17 Masking frame
18 Timer
19 Filing cabinet
20 Drawers

Darkroom Materials

(see diagram below). They are generally used with a filter which prevents blue and green light from reaching the emulsion. An infra-red filter, which is usually opaque, is necessary for scientific work, but for pictorial photography a red filter is usually sufficient. Typical "effects" show snow-white trees against a jet-black sky with all haze removed from the distance. Leaves reproduce white because they reflect infra-red radiation. Only if the sky is clear blue does it record as black. Grain of infra-red films tends to be comparatively

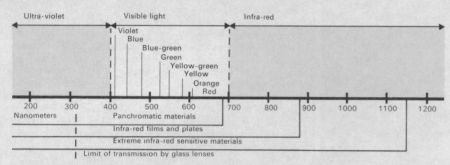

coarse. Read the instruction leaflets carefully and note any remarks about focus shift.

Microfilm
A slow, high contrast film for recording books, plans and other subjects which have no half-tones. Many types are sensitive only to blue light, though panchromatic versions are also obtainable. Grain is extremely fine and definition high, but speed is considerably less than that of the slowest normal film.

Lith film
Intended primarily for the lithographic printing trade, this film produces extremely high contrast especially when processed in a special developer containing formaldehyde, which gives very clean, sharp edged images. It is useful in the darkroom when making derivative prints.

Print film
A name applied to film used for making transparencies from negatives. Monochrome types are usually blue-sensitive and can be handled in ordinary yellow safelighting. The film contains a bromide paper-type emulsion on a transparent base. This film is not to be confused with the material used for making large color transparencies from negatives.

Reversal black and white film
Most slow speed fine grain film can be specially processed to produce positive monochrome transparencies from one camera exposure. Black and white transparencies can also be made from reversal black and white film which is sent back to the manufacturer for processing. A strip of positive transparencies are returned together with the cardboard mounts.

Stripping film
This film is manufactured with emulsion coated on an extra layer of gelatin. Warm water causes this gelatin to soften so that the lith image on top of it can be floated off like a transfer and placed on a variety of other surfaces.

Autoscreen
Autoscreen produces a screened image — an image made up of dots — of the type normally used for photo-mechanical reproduction in newspapers etc. Lith film

Recording infra-red waves
Normal film is sensitive to the familiar colors of the spectrum — the range of wavelengths from 4000 to 7200K (400 to 720 nanometers). Above this range wavelengths are known as infra-red and special films are made to react to them.

Screening photographs
"Autoscreen" film is available to produce screened photographs. Part of the photograph of the man, top, has been magnified to show the dot composition of the autoscreen in the picture above.

is used with a fine screen built in. Processing produce an image composed of very small half-tone dots. Th size of the dots on the final print is determined by th degree of enlargement.

Special films for color work
Color infra-red film
Originally evolved during wartime for detecting camou flage this is employed today for aerial survey worl scientific applications and special pictorial effect The modified color sensitizing of the film produces yellow positive image in the green-sensitive layer the processed transparency, a magenta image in th red-sensitive layer and a cyan image in the laye sensitive to infra-red radiation. A yellow filter is used t absorb blue light reaching the film. Results are n completely predictable.

Internegative film
This is a special color film designed for making colo negatives from transparencies for the eventual produc tion of color prints. The film is not easy to process an is being replaced by methods of producing print directly from transparencies. It is generally used in th darkroom rather than in the camera.

Reciprocity law failure
The reciprocity law states that exposure is the produc of time and intensity: $E = T \times I$. Time and intensit possess a reciprocal relationship in that when tim (shutter speed) is halved and intensity (aperture control is doubled, total exposure remains constant.

Unfortunately, with extremely fast shutter speed (1/1000 second or less) and high intensity illumination or with slow speeds (1 second or more) and low levels o illumination, this law breaks down. This inconsistenc is known as reciprocity law failure.

Failure actually occurs at the edges of a much nar rower band of time than that between 1 second and 1/1000 second, but due to the exposure latitude found ir black and white films, it bears little practical significanc within these limits. But in the case of speeds slowe than 1 second an increase in exposure time or an increas in the size of aperture is required. The amount o correction needed in both cases varies between film types and it is best to refer to manufacturer's data sheets for information. The following table offers a rough guide for correction of exposures in excess of 1 second with black and white film.

Exposure time in seconds	1	10	100	100
Film type	f stop increase required			
Slow			1	2
Medium	$\frac{1}{2}$	1	2	3
Fast		$\frac{1}{2}$	$1\frac{1}{2}$	$2\frac{1}{2}$

At speeds beyond 1/1000 second extra development is required. How much can only be estimated by trial and error. A suggested starting point is a 25% increase of the recommended standard developing time.

Reciprocity law failure in color film
Color films have three emulsion layers, all of which have reciprocity characteristics. These are balanced to match reasonably well within a certain range of speeds Beyond the range recommended by the manufacturer reciprocity law failure will occur, differing by degree in each layer. This creates a color cast in the final result

is better therefore to adjust lighting levels, or increase the size of the aperture, to suit exposure times recommended for the particular material in use.

Manufacturers produce color films which are especially suitable for long exposure times. They also provide information sheets which show the filter compensation required if exposure times go beyond certain limits.

Photographic printing papers

Photographic printing papers can be classified according to base thickness and tint, surface texture and sheen, type of emulsion (which governs speed), color of image and contrast.

Paper bases

Paper is used as the base for almost all printing materials. A special process, involving spinning at high speed, is needed to produce a paper which does not fall apart when wet. The pulp is then pressed between rollers and a smooth surface produced. A top coating of baryta makes the paper base highly reflective and helps to make bright highlights in the final print. The standard paper base is white but other base tints are available, such as cream and ivory.

Resin-coated bases

Waterproof base is becoming increasingly popular. This is known as RC, resin-coated, or PE, after polyethylene, the plastic used. Both sides of the paper are coated with resin and then one side is coated with emulsion. The advantage is that no chemicals are absorbed by the base, thus reducing the carry-over from one bath to the next and greatly shortening washing time. Dimensional stability is greatly improved. Ordinary base stretches during processing and drying, and with highly accurate work it produces problems. Aluminum-based paper, incorporating metal to aid stability, has been largely superseded by RC types for detailed work.

Paper weight

Paper bases are made in various weights or thicknesses. The two most popular are single and double weight. The former is easier to glaze while the latter has more substance, making it more crease-resistant when large sizes are processed. Lightweight paper bases are also available. Different manufacturers use slightly different weights, but in general RC bases can be thinner than the uncoated types as rigidity is retained when the paper is wet.

Surface textures

The most popular surface is glossy; this provides the deepest black and records the finest detail, especially when glazed. Various agents, such as starch, can be introduced into the printing emulsion to provide a matt surface. Different degrees of sheen can be produced in this way, a common description for a surface halfway between glossy and matt being "luster." The more matt a paper becomes, the less deep is its maximum black in reproduction.

Emulsion types

It is common practice to divide printing emulsions into groups according to the particular silver halide used. Slow emulsions containing silver *chloride* are described as contact papers. Faster types, giving a pure black image, contain silver *bromide*; slightly slower papers giving warm-tone images use a *chlorobromide* emulsion.

Exposure and paper grade
The diagram shows how exposure time must be increased with soft paper grades for a good range of grays to appear in a print. It is more difficult to achieve dense black in a print on soft paper than in a print on hard paper.

Fine grain × 30

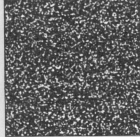
Normal grain × 30

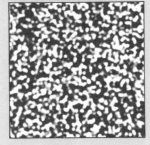
Coarse grain × 30

Film or paper grain
The larger the silver halides in a photographic emulsion the faster it reacts to light. Because of this an image recorded on fast emulsion looks grainier than one recorded on slow emulsion.

A simple grouping is into contact and enlarging papers, the latter being about 20 times as fast as the former. Image tones can vary from blue-black through neutral to warm or brownish black. Processing can influence the tone but normally the image color depends on the emulsion. Remember the base tint also has an influence.

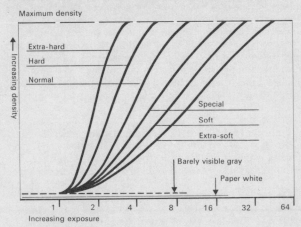

Paper grades

Photographic papers react differently to changes in density on negatives, depending on the grade of paper used. A hard or contrasty paper provides strong tonal variations while a soft or low contrast paper provides very little when exposed to the same negative. Most manufacturers make a range of grades running from extra-soft through soft, normal and hard to extra-hard. Another grade termed "special" is sometimes available between soft and normal. But there is little or no agreement between makers as to what constitutes a soft, hard or normal paper. There is a tendency to use numbers instead of the descriptions listed above.

With some makes speed varies according to the grade; with others the sensitivity, as measured for a particular tone, is kept reasonably constant so that various grades may be tried without exposure variation. The hardest grade papers are frequently slower than the other grades.

Color sensitivity

Ordinary enlarging papers are sensitive to blue and ultra-violet radiation, but some types respond to part of the green spectrum. Most safelights are therefore a deep yellow or amber to ensure safety with all types. Lith printing papers are usually orthochromatic in sensitivity and require a red safelight. Panchromatic paper is sometimes used for printing from color negatives, and demands either a very deep green safelight, or no light at all.

Polycontrast papers

Multi-grade or polycontrast papers are intended to allow all printing to be done with one packet of paper. A mixed emulsion is used, either a hard contrast one sensitive to yellow light mixed with a soft one sensitive to blue, or the converse. By choosing an appropriately colored filter the precise contrast required can be achieved. Various tricks can be used; for example the main exposure might be made on a hard gradation and the highlights burnt-in on soft.

Tone reproduction

Overall contrast effect does not completely describe the tone rendering given by a paper. One particular make or type may give a good separation of shadow

237

Darkroom Materials

tones, another be best for highlights, and a third be especially suitable for pictures depending on the subtle mid-tones. Only experience will teach which is the best type of paper for a particular effect.

Special papers
Any emulsion which can be coated on film may also be put on paper. It is possible to obtain papers with bright colored bases. And some are available with fluorescent bases. One manufacturer produces a linen based emulsion. And a base of translucent plastic with emulsions on both sides can be obtained. Both images contribute if light is transmitted from behind the print, but only one side is seen if light is directed from in front.

Lith paper
Lith paper has a very high contrast emulsion and produces deep blacks and white highlights. It must be used with lith developer made by the same manufacturer. Other special emulsions coated on paper are available.

Papers for color prints
Here there is much less choice than with monochrome papers. There is really only one contrast grade, and white base, usually RC, is used throughout the range. Textures are mostly glossy and silk, though a few others are available. Manufacturers tend to produce a paper suited to their color negative film, with color response balanced accordingly. Papers are also made for direct reversal processing, so that prints may be made directly from transparencies.

Dye destruction prints
These color printing materials work when some of the dye they contain is destroyed by light while the rest remains to color the image. The material is available on a white plastic base for prints, and a transparent plastic for illumination by back projection. The process gives pictures with rich colors and great stability, which makes them ideal for long-term displays.

Using photographic chemicals
The theory of development
Light passing through a lens onto a sensitive emulsion causes definite but invisible chemical and physical changes, producing a latent image. Chemicals known as developers can render this latent image visible, by reducing those grains of silver salts affected by light to black metallic silver.

The function of a developer is to reduce silver bromide to metallic silver and to absorb bromine from exposed parts of the emulsion. The developer therefore must possess an element which combines with bromine in the exposed silver salts, and should not act appreciably on the unexposed silver salts.

Many substances will do this, and the most commonly used are metol, phenidone, hydroquinone and amidol. They are called reducing agents because they have the property of reducing silver salts to a metallic state. They work by combining with oxygen in water, but by so doing they free hydrogen which combines with bromine in the exposed silver salts.

The combination of hydrogen and bromine sets up hydrobromic acid which if left unattended in the developer slows the reducing action quite considerably. Therefore an alkali is added which neutralizes the hydrobromic acid and hastens the action of reducing agents. Such alkalis are known as accelerators – sodium carbonate, sodium and potassium hydroxide and sodium borate, or borax.

Because reducing agents oxidize rapidly in air, a chemical with a strong affinity for oxygen, such as sodium sulfite, is added to absorb oxygen and prevent deterioration of the solution. A solution containing these three constituents, (a reducing agent, an alkali and an oxygen absorber), is impractical, because they also tend to develop unexposed silver salts, causing chemical fog. So a restrainer, such as potassium bromide, is added to regulate development and minimize the risk of chemical fog.

Chemicals for black and white processing
Black and white developers
Developers usually contain a developing agent, an alkali, a preservative and a restrainer. These are dissolved in water before use. Often more than one developing agent will be included. Phenidone and hydroquinone for example, work particularly well together.

Most developing agents work best in alkaline solutions. The stronger the alkali the more energetic the action. The type and concentration of alkali can therefore be chosen to suit the particular purpose of the developer. Sodium carbonate is popular because it is effective and cheap, but sodium or potassium hydroxide is often used for high contrast developers. Alkalis with a softer action, like borax, are used in fine-grain developers for films.

The preservative needed to protect the developing agent from oxidation also acts as a mild silver solvent and helps to produce finer grain.

Potassium bromide is a common restrainer, but in print developers benzotriazol is popular because it influences the print tone towards blue-black. Photographers usually have one developer for prints and another for negatives. A universal developer can be used for both, but chemicals designed for specific purposes tend to produce the best results.

Negative developers
Some negative developers are described as "speed-increasing." The standard is D76, or its equivalent, and a speed-increasing developer usually provides about 60% higher speed. For example, an ASA100 film could be rated as ASA160. In some developers effective emulsion speed is sacrificed for extra-fine grain, or enhanced image sharpness, obtained at the expense of fine grain. But for general work a standard fine grain developer serves well and can be used with any make or type of film.

Formulae for black and white developers
(all weights quoted in grams)

	D76	ID68	FX3	D76b	D23	FX5b	D76d
Metol	2.0	—	—	2.75	7.5	4.5	2.0
Phenidone	—	0.13	0.75	—	—	—	—
Hydroquinone	5.0	5.0	6.0	2.75	—	—	5.0
Sodium sulfite anhydrous	100	85.0	75.0	100	100	125	100
Sodium carbonate crystals	—	—	—	—	—	—	—
Borax	2.0	7.0	2.5	2.5	—	—	8.0
Boric acid	—	2.0	—	—	—	—	8.0
Sodium bisulfite	—	—	—	—	—	1.0	—
Sodium metaborate	—	—	—	—	—	2.25	—
Potassium bromide	—	1.0	1.0	—	—	0.5	—

Water to 1 liter in each case

D76   is virtually identical with ID11, M & B 320 and others; it is usually accepted as a standard.

D68   is a phenidone version with good keeping qualities, giving from 30% to 60% speed increase.

FX3   can be considered a phenidone version of the ASA metol-borax formula which gives slightly better sharpness with a lower contrast effect.

D76b   is a version giving slightly softer contrast which is popular for motion picture work.

D23   is simple and gives almost as fine grain as D76 with slightly lower contrast. The water used for this developer should be distilled.

FX5b   gives the finest grain of these developers but at the expense of 30% loss in emulsion speed.

D76d   is a "buffered" version of D76 giving greater contrast control and more consistency in re-use, together with a slight speed loss. It needs about 35% longer for development.

Acutance developers
Acutance developers give great sharpness but are not fine grain. They are most suitable for slow films with inherently high contrast. Effective emulsion speed is 60 to 100% higher than standard. A typical formula is as follows:

FX1 developer

Metol	0.5 gr.
Sodium sulfite, anhydrous	5 gr.
Sodium carbonate, anhydrous	2.5 gr.
Potassium iodide 0.001 solution	5 ml.

Water to 1 liter. Use once and discard.

Universal and print developers
Most print developers have similar basic constituents although these are used in different quantities. There are special types intended to produce softer contrast, or to provide warmer, browner tones with special papers, but as a general rule any good print developer will work well with any make or grade of printing paper. These formulae are not fine grain but can, depending on the strength of the alkali, provide high contrast and short development times. Ready-made developers bearing the same numbers may not be identical to the published formulae.

Formulae for universal and print developers
(all weights quoted in grams)

	D61a	D163	DK50	D19b	D158	ID2	ID62	ID20
Metol	3.1	2.2	2.5	2.2	3.2	2	—	3
Hydroquinone	5.9	17	2.5	8.8	13.2	8	12	12
Phenidone	—	—	—	—	—	—	0.5	—
Sodium sulfite anhydrous	90	75	30	72	50	75	50	50
Sodium bisulfite anhydrous	2.1	—	—	—	—	—	—	—
Sodium carbonate anhydrous	11.5	6.5	—	48	69	37	60	60
Sodium metaborate	—	—	10	—	—	—	—	—
Potassium bromide	1.7	2.8	0.5	4	0.9	2	2	4
Benzotriazol	—	—	—	—	—	—	0.2	—

Water to 1 liter in each case

D61a   is a general purpose negative developer. Dilute 1:3 for tank development.

D163   may be used for films, diluted 1:3, but is mainly for enlarging papers diluted from 1:1 to 1:3.

DK50   is a film developer to be used undiluted. It is recommended for use with the very fastest films.

D19b   is a high contrast developer especially for X-ray and aerial films. It is used undiluted and keeps well.

D158   is especially suitable for the slow papers used for contact printing. Dilute 1:1.

ID2   is a standard MQ developer for films and a useful non-caustic formula for high contrast materials. In tanks dilute 1:5, in dishes 1:2, or even use undiluted.

ID62   is a general purpose PQ formula for films and papers. For enlarging papers dilute 1:3.

ID20   is a PQ developer for all papers. Normal dilution is 1:3.

Most manufacturers have their own published formulae. Here a representative selection has been shown and many resemblances are obvious. Any monochrome film can be developed in any of these developers, though some give better results than others. There are also many proprietary developers whose formulae are not published. Provided manufacturers' instructions are adhered to, all work well.

Stop bath
This is not essential, especially when acid fixers are used, but it is very useful because it stops development thus keeping development time accurate. Furthermore it protects the fixer from excess alkaline contamination. A regular formula contains about 2% acetic acid. Sometimes an indicator dye is added which changes color when the acid has been neutralized by alkaline developer carried over on the prints of films.

Black and white fixers
The most important constituent of a fixer is a solvent to dissolve those silver halides which are not reduced to metallic silver. Hypo, sodium thiosulfate, was the traditional chemical for this purpose, but it is now largely replaced by ammonium thiosulfate which works more swiftly and is the key ingredient of "rapid fixers." Care must be taken when using rapid fixers with prints because ammonium thiosulfate is a strong solution which will attack the visible image of metallic silver, causing deterioration in the blacks of prints.

The solution should be acidic so that the alkali is swiftly neutralized. Sulfurous acid is normally used since anything stronger leads to precipitation of colloidal sulfur from the fixing agent. This sulfurous acid may be produced by the interaction of acetic acid with sodium sulfite, or by the inclusion of sodium metabisulfite. The sulfite acts as a buffering agent against both acids and alkalis.

The majority of fixers also contain an agent to harden gelatin. This is advisable with films and is generally a slight advantage with papers, except when glossy paper is to be glazed on glass or a chrome-plated sheet. A typical hardening agent is potassium alum.

For general purposes the same formula — sometimes differently diluted — may be used with papers and films, but the used solutions are often kept separately. Formulae vary since concentrations of fixing agent are not critical. The following table shows how different solutions can be mixed.

239

Darkroom Materials

Formulae for fixers
(all weights quoted in grams unless otherwise stated)

	F1	F2	F3	F4
Sodium thiosulfate crystals	250	250	240	—
Potassium metabisulfite	20	—	—	—
Ammonium thiosulfate crystals	—	—	—	200
Sodium sulfite anhydrous	—	25	15	—
Acetic acid, glacial	—	25	13	15
Boric acid crystals	—	—	7.5	15 ml.
Potassium alum	—	—	15	2.5

Water to 1 liter in each case

F1   is a simple acid fixer, easily neutralized by carried over developer.

F2   is "buffered," being more resistant to changes in acidity.

F3   is an acid hardening fixer.

F4   is a rapid acid hardening fixer.

Concentrations of fixing agent are not critical so formulae can change.

Monobaths

The basic idea of a monobath is to combine the developer and fixer for films so that only a single bath is required. The main advantage is simplicity and, since the degree of development is predetermined, there is no chance of incorrect timing. The disadvantages are that grain is coarsened, development cannot be altered to suit specific subjects or personal taste, and the emulsion is not hardened, so extra care is needed in washing and drying. A separate hardener can be used, but this rather spoils the concept of one-solution processing.

Stabilization

This process is generally used with special papers which have the developing or reducing agent incorporated into the emulsion. The developer can be a simple alkali, able to activate the reducing agents present. The prints are stabilized with substances such as ammonium thiocyanate or thioglycolic acid, instead of being fixed. They do not require washing, so prints can be produced in 30 seconds or so although they are not fully permanent.

Chemicals for color processing

The processing of color materials follows the same basic pattern as for monochrome, but with the added complication that a dye image must be produced and the associated silver one removed. Times, temperatures, and the exact formulation of processing solutions are more critical than for monochrome.

Negative color developers

The developing agent used is generally a paraphenyl-enediamine derivative. It reduces the light-affected halide to silver and makes the development by-products react with color couplers to form associated dye images (yellow, magenta, and cyan), in the three different layers. Most negative films are now masked, which means an orange or pinkish dye is also formed, usually in the magenta and cyan dye layers. This improves the purity of recorded colors.

Reversal or transparency film developers

The first development produces a silver image, as with monochrome. The residual silver halide is fogged with chemicals or by exposure to light, and the second or color development produces a reversed or positive silver image together with an associated dye image. The silver image is bleached and then fixed to remove the unwanted halides. The last process is usually stabilization.

Intermediate baths, hardeners and stabilizers

Color film emulsion tends to be softer than monochrome, though much is being done by manufacturers to harden it. Sometimes an initial or intermediate bath is used to prevent excessive swelling of the emulsion, especially when processing is carried out at high temperatures. Hardening is often achieved by highly toxic formalin and allied compounds, as well as by the usual hardening agent, alum. Formalin also stabilizes the colors, helps to reduce fading, and is often used as a final bath.

Bleaches

The unwanted silver image must be removed to leave a pure dye image. Potassium ferricyanide is the traditional bleach in which bromide ions are present to ensure the formation of silver bromide which can subsequently be fixed out. A modern equivalent, which causes less pollution but is more expensive, is a sequestrene agent.

Color fixers

These are used in the same way as monochrome fixers, but greater attention must be paid to the precise degree of acidity.

Bleach-fix baths

To reduce the number of solutions and save time the bleach and fix baths necessary in color processing are often combined. Extra constituents are generally required to avoid precipitations forming, so combined baths tend to be more expensive than separate ones, even if more convenient.

Mixing and using photographic chemicals

Photographic solutions may be made from separate chemicals weighed out individually from ready-made powders, or from concentrated liquids.

Essential equipment

Hot and cold running water is virtually essential. A measuring cylinder is vital; inexpensive plastic ones are adequate and less easily broken than glass. A good size is about 600 ml. although for larger quantities a 1200 ml. is useful.

For concentrated liquids a small measure, such as 25 ml. is necessary. If measurements are in fluid ounces make sure there is no confusion between the Imperial (28.4 ml.) and American (29.6 ml.) ounces. Never mix chemicals in measures made from aluminum, copper, tin or galvanized metal. Glass and ceramic measures are safe; stainless steel may be used for everything except silver bleach.

A good thermometer is necessary, but do not stir solutions with it because it will eventually break. Stir with a glass or plastic rod. A funnel is useful but not essential; a plastic one lasts longer than any other kind.

Making up chemicals with separate constitutents

When making a developer from separate chemicals, dissolve the ingredients in the order stated. For example, metol will not dissolve in sulfite solution so the metol must be dissolved before the sulfite is added. Start with about 3/4 of the total volume required, say 750 ml. if making 1 liter of solution. Most chemicals dissolve more easily in warm water than cold; it is usually safe o use water as hot as the hand will stand. The exceptions to this rule are sodium and potassium hydroxide, which produce so much heat when dissolved that it is afer to start with cold water.

If developer is to be made from prepared packets of chemicals, be sure to read the instructions. Usually there are two separate packages because the alkali and developing agents do not keep well if stored in contact with one another. The smaller packet should usually be dissolved completely before adding any of the larger. Cold water is added last to bring the volume up to the correct total.

Solutions should be bottled and clearly labeled. Dark bottles are best, although they are less important if the chemicals are stored away from bright light. It is best to keep bottles well-filled with developer since any air inside causes oxidation. The bottles should be made of glass or strong plastic and have well-sealing stoppers. Plastic screw tops are usually safe but metal caps or ordinary corks are not really suitable.

If you plan to use these bottles for warming the chemicals by standing them in water, put the labels high up and use waterproof ink. Information written on labels should include the name of the solution and the date of preparation. If the solution is bottled for re-use make a note on the label of the number of times it has been used, and allow for the fact that the solution becomes exhausted. 600 ml. of D76 will develop four or five films but usually each film developed after the second needs 10% extra time. Since individual developers vary, always read the instructions carefully and save leaflets for future reference.

Making up chemicals from liquid concentrates
Procedures are different when making developers from liquid concentrates and in many cases the working solution is used only once and then discarded.

First measure the necessary water into a measuring cylinder making sure the water is at the correct operating temperature. Then add the small amount of concentrated developer. This method is very quick and avoids the uncertainties of exhausted solutions, but it is more expensive than using powders.

Rapid fixers are usually supplied as concentrated liquids, and the working solutions are used repeatedly, like ordinary fixers. There is little difference between the cost of making fixer with powder and with rapid fixer concentrate.

General notes
The greatest precision is necessary when preparing chemicals for color processing. The proportions, the timing and the temperatures must all be exact. Great care is also needed with monochrome developers. The subsequent processes like fixation allow some room for error, but no room for carelessness.

Only make one solution at a time, and always rinse vessels and sinks well. Clear developers soon oxidize and produce unpleasant brown stains. Most photographic chemicals are relatively harmless and exceptions must be clearly marked, by law. Nevertheless, it is always advisable to be careful.

Intensifiers
Intensifiers are used to increase density on negatives, but should not be needed if development and exposure are correct. Do not try chemical treatment if a similar result can be obtained by using a harder grade of printing paper, and always make the best possible print before attempting to intensify a negative.

Chromium intensifier

Solution A.	Potassium bichromate	50 gr.
	Water to 1 liter	
Solution B.	Hydrochloric acid	100 ml.
	Water to 1 liter	

Use one part A and dilute it with six parts water. Add an amount of B from 1/4 to twice the amount of A (before dilution). For example, take 100 ml. of A, dilute it to 700 ml. with water and add from 25 to 200 ml. of B. The lower the concentration of acid the higher the intensification, but the action is slower. When the negative is completely bleached the image is a yellow buff color with no black remaining. Check this by looking through the back of the negative. Wash until the yellow stain is removed, then expose the negative to diffused daylight — not bright sunlight — or strong artificial light before putting in a developer to darken the image. Use a low-sulfite developer; a print developer is suitable, a fine grain developer is not. Wash and dry the intensified negative in the usual way.

There are other intensification methods available, whose formulae may be found in manufacturers' literature. Some can be bought ready for use.

Reducers
Reducers remove silver from negatives or prints. A cutting reducer, which increases contrast, is especially useful for copying line diagrams or other material without half-tones. A local reducer to lighten specific areas is also useful for prints. There is little point in using reducers to bring down the contrast of over-developed negatives — it is easier to use a softer grade of printing paper.

Farmer's reducer

Solution A.	Sodium thiosulfate	100 gr.
	Water to 1 liter	
Solution B.	Potassium ferricyanide	20 gr.
	Water to 1 liter.	

Use 100 ml. of A, 20 ml. of B, and 200 ml. of water. This working solution will not keep. Avoid contamination by iron which produces Prussian blue stains. Brushes with metal ferrules can cause trouble. After reduction rinse and fix.

Iodine thiourea reducer
This reducer is particularly useful for local reduction of prints.

| Solution A. | 10 ml. of water, 6 gr. potassium iodide, 10 gr. iodine, make to 100 ml. with methyl alcohol or isopropanol. |
| Solution B. | 10 gr. thiourea, 100 ml. water. |

Use two parts of B with one of A. Fix without further rinsing.

Toners
Prints intended for toning should be evenly developed. The safest plan is to develop fully. Extreme colors can be obtained by using metallic ferricyanides, but purer tones are produced with color papers. Some suggestions for making toners appear on pp. 202–203.

Color formulae
The processing of color film is far more complex than that of black and white. The easiest and safest approach to home processing is to use the film maker's kits or those produced by specialist firms. These are popular because some color chemicals are difficult to obtain in reasonably small quantities and others are unpleasantly toxic or dangerous to handle in an unmixed state.

Checking for Faults

Recognizing and correcting faults

Try to avoid faults rather than attempt to cure them afterwards. Retake a spoiled picture rather than resort to correction in the darkroom. If the photograph cannot be taken again, or is irreplaceable, make the best possible print or copy before attempting any chemical treatment. As a general rule, do not worry unduly about a single, isolated fault. However, do start checking to find the cause if the same error keeps occurring. While materials and processing are occasionally to blame, most faults are in fact caused by the photographer. Never load film, or leave the camera, in bright sunshine. Always ensure that 35 mm film is properly engaged in the take-up spool and that the perforations fit over the sprocket wheel. A completely blank length of unexposed film can result if the tongue is not engaged in the take-up spool, or if the perforations are torn. Always check that the crank rewind turns when the wind-on lever is activated. If it fails to turn, the film is not winding on and will not be exposed. Make sure that roll-film is running squarely when loaded. Look at the edge signing — the letters and numbers in the film margin — to see if the film has been processed properly. If the letters are distinct, blame exposure rather than processing.

Check the expiry date on the box when film is bought, and avoid using out-dated film. As film ages it loses some sensitivity and tends to fog. With color films the balance becomes incorrect, so process as soon after exposure as possible. Store films, exposed or unexposed in a cool dry place.

Old cameras, especially those with bellows, may have tiny holes which sunlight can enter to cause fog patches. To check this, put a small lamp or a torch bulb inside the camera. Connect the bulb with thin wires to a battery outside the camera; very thin wire will not prevent the camera from being closed. In a dark room the light will show through any worn places.

General fog may be caused by X-ray examination at airports. Carry films in hand baggage; don't rely on protective bags.

Condensation will form on the lens when a cold camera is brought into a warm room, so give it time to clear before use.

When taking pictures, watch the subject all the time, up to the final click. A common error is cutting off subjects' hands, or otherwise upsetting a good frame. The cause may be a faulty viewfinder, but usually the photographer is moving the camera before taking the picture. With cheap cameras, it may be advisable to remove glasses when looking through the finder.

Under-exposed negatives — color or black and white — are identified by being too light and thin while over-exposed negatives are too dark and dense. Under-exposed transparencies, or slides, are dark; over-exposed ones are light. Dark streaks on negatives, light streaks on transparencies can be caused by light leakage, usually from the sides. If similar patterns occur in each negative it is most likely that the fogging occurs when the film is in the exposure position. Alternately, it may have happened when the film was rolled up, or because of a faulty 35 mm cassette. Ensure that the camera back is always properly closed. Wrap exposed films; often the original packing can be used.

Negative and transparency faults

Appearance	Fault	Comments
Heavy negative or light positive image.	Over-exposure.	Check film speed setting, cell in meter, shutter speeds, automat diaphragm in SLR lenses.
Light negative or heavy, dull positive image.	Under-exposure.	Check film speed setting. In very dull weather give extra exposure.
Branching, twig-like marks, dark on negatives.	Static.	Produced in hot, dry, conditions. Rewind 35 mm film slowly.
Tiny sharp-edged areas, clear on negatives, dark on transparencies.	Dust on film during exposure.	Remove dust from camera. Always clean camera, especially 35 mm, inside and out before use
Areas shaped like lens iris, dark on negatives, light on transparencies.	Light reflections within lens.	Try to avoid direct light hitting the lens.
Lines along length of film.	Scratches.	Check camera for rollers not freely rotating. Could be grit in 35 mm cassette.

Print faults

Appearance	Fault	Comments
Fuzzy definition, some distances may be sharp.	Out of focus.	If this always happens have camera checked. Otherwise fault in setting camera.
All-over blurring, possibly with streaking of light parts.	Camera shake.	Squeeze release gently. Use faster shutter speed when possible. Hold camera correctly.
Blurred image in parts.	Subject movement.	Use faster shutter speed or avoid quick-moving subjects.
Overall mottle.	Backing paper off-set.	Occurs only with roll-film. Due to over-long storage or dampness
Overlapping images.	Incorrect winding.	Check camera wind-on mechanism.

Color faults

Color film is prone to all the faults of black and white film as well as several peculiar to itself. The previous tables apply to color with additional variations. For example, light leakage marks tend to be yellow on transparency film.

Color negative films are not covered here since overall bias should be corrected during printing. Excessive contrast in negatives can be caused by faulty developing.

Appearance	Comments
Image much too orange/yellow.	Daylight film used in artificial lighting or yellow filter accidentally left on lens.
Image much too blue.	Artificial light (type-A or B) film used in daylight.
Greenish image, with poor maximum density even in margins.	Old film, outdated or stored badly. Could also be poor processing.
Pink lights in eyes with flash.	Reflection from retinae. Move flashgun further from optical axis. With 110 camera use flash extender.
Bluish bias and poor contrast with flash.	Smoky atmosphere. Take party pictures before too much cigarette smoke clouds the air.
Bluish landscapes, especially in distance.	Haze recording as blue. Use UV or haze filter.
Reddish rendering, usually noticed with portraits.	Picture taken at sunset or dawn.

Processing faults

These faults are grouped together because they tend to occur with home processing. Some obvious faults are left out. We all know that finger-marks are caused by fingers contaminated with chemicals.

Appearance	Fault	Comments
Dimple, or arc-shaped mark, sometimes accompanied by dent in film.	Kink caused when loading film in tank.	Occurs mostly with roll-film. No cure. Try to avoid.
Uneven diffused bands of light density along film.	Wipe static.	Caused by running fingers along film before loading.
Clear, or lighter, area along length of negatives.	Insufficient developer.	Ensure film is completely covered in tank.
Round areas, lighter on negatives, darker on transparencies.	Air-bells.	Tap tank on hard surface during first moments of processing.
Flat negatives, low density but ample shadow detail.	Under-development.	Print on hard paper. Intensify only if unavoidable.
Contrasty negatives, fog level may be high, no over-exposure.	Over-development	Print on soft paper. Reduce only if unavoidable.
Milky negatives.	Incomplete fixation.	Refix, preferably in fresh solution before exposing to bright light.
Short hair lines, parallel to edges of film.	Cinch marks	Do not tighten rolled up film before processing.
Small, sharp areas with streamers.	Chemical marks.	Ensure all powder is dissolved before using solution.
Large spot of lighter density with greater density at edges.	Drying mark.	Use wetting agent in final rinse. Wipe down wet film.
Net-like cracks in gelatin.	Reticulation.	Avoid moving film from hot to cold solutions.
Overall purple color with roll-films.	Regenerated backing dye.	Rinse in sulfite solution or developer, wash and dry. Does not occur with all makes.

Paper faults

Appearance	Fault	Comments
Gray veiling on margins.	Fog.	Unsafe safelight or old paper.
Overall yellow color.	Staining.	Over-long development. Old developer. Possibly fixer no longer acidic.
Gray prints with no full black.	Lack of contrast.	If paper grade suits negative, insufficient development. Try giving $1\frac{1}{2}$ to 2 mins. Developer may be exhausted.
Poor image color.	Contamination.	If full time given in correct developer, suspect contamination of developer by fixer.
Black lines.	Abrasion marks.	May be caused by physical pressure before development. Sometimes caused by trimming before exposure. Can also result from prodding prints with sharp edged tongs during development.
Uneven density.	Development marks.	Usually caused by uneven development when prints have over-long exposure and are taken quickly from the developer in an attempt to compensate.

Points to remember
Hold the camera correctly and trigger the release gently to avoid shake.
Make sure that your fingers do not cover the lens or light meter window.
Change film indoors or in the shade.
When using a 35 mm camera check that the take-up spool is transporting the film by making certain that the rewind knob rotates when advancing the film.
In cold dry weather, wind the film on gently. It may be brittle.
Prevent direct sunlight from striking the lens.
When coming out of the cold into a warm room check to see that the lens is not misted.
Store camera and film in a cool place.
Do not trust old processing solutions. If in any doubt make fresh solutions.
Handle negatives only by the edges and protect in envelopes.
Never cut 110 film into individual negatives.
Store negatives and transparencies in a dry place.

Projectors & Viewing Systems

Transparencies and slides are intended to be viewed with light behind them – that is, by transmitted light. A transparency can give a far richer image than any print because light is going through the film, and doesn't depend on reflection from a white backing. The disadvantage is that special equipment is necessary for viewing.

Viewers

Some viewers are compact enough to be carried, but their magnification and use are limited. Their simple lens system may distort the picture by bending the straight lines at the edges of the frame. These viewers can be used anywhere but usually by only one person at a time.

Projectors

Projectors provide large, bright images with little distortion, but a dark room is usually required.

Back projection

Most projectors throw the image onto the front of the screen, on the same side as the projector. They will also throw the picture onto the back of a suitable screen, the side away from the viewer. (Some projectors are designed only for back projection). This allows pictures to be projected indoors without darkening the room. All the equipment can be carried in a cabinet about the size of an average suitcase. The disadvantage is that the small size of the special translucent screen limits the number of viewers as well as the degree of detail.

Projection lamps

Projectors are usually classified by the type and power of their lamps. The cheapest models have a 100W or 150W mains-voltage lamp, the highest wattage that can be used without a cooling fan. More expensive are the 300W and 500W models which do have fans. Next come the designs using low-voltage bulbs, the

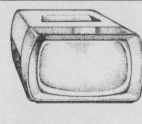

Viewers
The simplest viewers are held up to the light. A diffuser makes illumination even and the transparency is magnified by a lens. More elaborate models have a torch bulb run off batteries to provide the light; a few can be plugged into an electrical outlet. Lenses are usually of transparent plastic for lightness and cheapness. Expensive models use glass, and sometimes two or three element lenses to gain greater magnification without distortion.

most common of which is the tungsten-halogen bulb (originally called QI, for quartz-iodine). These have a longer life, and light output remains constant because the bulb does not blacken inside. But low-voltage lamps need a step-down transformer which makes the projector more expensive. Popular sizes of low-voltage lamps are the 100W, 12V and 150W, 24V. The range is large and constantly expanding. The filament of a low-voltage bulb is more robust than that of a mains-voltage one, and because of its smaller size the light is utilized more efficiently. Much depends on individual design but a 100 or 150W low-volt lamp normally gives as bright an image as a normal voltage 300W. Some projectors have a dimming switch, so that some

Horizontal rotary magazine
Lens
Slide change button
Focusing knob
Remote control
Leveling control
Mains lead

compensation can be made for those slides which are a little thin, due to over exposure.

35 mm projectors

These projectors take 2 × 2 ins (5.1 × 5.1 cm) slide mounts which are used with 35 mm and 126 films. Some models will also take "Superslides" which are 4.0 × 4.0 cm.

The most simple projector is a manual push-pull type, where slides are loaded one at a time. Some projectors with magazines holding from 30 to 40 slides can also be manually operated, but many models have motors controlled by a button on the projector, or a remote-control system where the button is on a lead, enabling it to be operated from an armchair. Some machines allow for slide changing in both directions, so that a slide can easily be shown again.

Focusing can also be done by remote control, using a motor which moves the lens backwards and forwards to compensate for "popping" – a change in slide curvature as the film becomes hot. Automatic focusing is even more sophisticated, a beam of light reflects from the slide surface to a photocell. If the slide moves, or a new one does not come to rest in the same position, the beam misses the cell to activate a motor. It stops only when the beam again reaches the cell, focus having been restored.

Automatic timers change slides at pre-set intervals. If they are used with circular trays the show simply repeats itself until the projector is switched off.

Setting up a 35 mm projector
A projection table is useful to hold the projector steady at the correct height. The lower shelf can be used for boxes of slides or magazines. The projection table folds flat for storage. The projector shown has a horizontal rotary magazine and remote control.

Loading transparencies into a projector

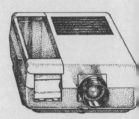

Many projectors are built to be used with magazines in which the transparencies are loaded. This model has a straight magazine which holds about 40 transparencies.

Sometimes rotary magazines can be interchanged on projectors supplied with straight magazines. These hold over 80 transparencies.

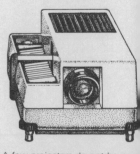

A few projectors do not have magazine loading. Transparencies are fitted into a compartment in the projector.

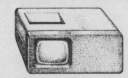

Many 110 projectors employ a carrier-belt system which acts in much the same way as a magazine.

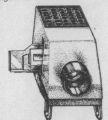

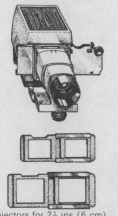

Other 110 projectors have a push-pull carrier which requires no preparation before loading.

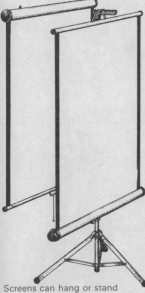

Projectors for 2¼ ins (6 cm) square transparencies are often supplied with adapters for 35 mm slides.

Projection lenses are made in many focal lengths. The most popular for 35 mm projectors are 8.5 cm and 9 cm, since these are suitable for filling a 40 ins (101.6 cm) screen in an average sized room. Longer lenses are useful for larger rooms and lecture theaters. Shorter lenses are used only when big pictures are needed in a confined space. The more expensive projectors are fitted with zoom lenses.

110 projectors

110 slides can be shown in a 35 mm projector but the picture is very small if projected from the usual distance. Should the projector be moved further away, or a lens of shorter focal length used, the image fills the screen but loses a lot of brightness and some sharpness.

A projector made for 110 slides is much more efficient. Many models have modern lamps with integral reflectors and small filaments which push maximum light through the small transparency. Many 110 projectors use a loading system resembling a moving belt which carries the slides around like a circular magazine. The choice of 110 projectors is smaller than with 35 mm models, but the range is continually growing.

Projectors for 2¼ ins (6 cm) square transparencies

These projectors take the larger size transparencies and produce large, bright images, but the choice is limited. Many of them have simple push-pull carriers and are fitted with adapters to take 35 mm transparencies too. The lens is usually chosen to suit the larger size. A 14 cm lens gives the same size image with a 6 × 6 cm slide as the standard 9 cm with a 35 mm slide. If the same lens is used for both formats the 35 mm slide will not fill the screen unless the projector is moved further away. The image will then be less bright than that achieved with an exclusively 35 mm projector.

Screens

Slides can be projected on any flat, white surface, including walls, but a roll-up screen is normally used. Screens can be rolled by hand but most are spring-loaded, rather like roller blinds. Sizes and shapes vary. Square is best for everything except motion pictures, because some slides will be projected vertically and others horizontally. The image need not fill the whole of the screen.

Most surfaces are either beaded, silver or white. The difference is in the way light is reflected. Beaded screens are coated with minute glass beads which bounce the light back in a narrow angle so that high brilliance is obtained. However the audience must sit squarely in front of the screen, and not to one side. For home projection a matt white surface which reflects light over a wide angle may be the best choice. A silver screen has an intermediate effect between beaded and matt types but highlights often appear metallic. Silver screens are used mainly for stereo projection because the surface retains the polarity of the projected picture.

Screens can be hung on the wall but it is often more convenient to have them free-standing. A collapsible structure is good for storage. A popular system is a short, folding tripod, with a central telescopic rod supporting the screen. Always make sure that the screen is parallel to the lens and not tilted up or down or sideways, otherwise it will be impossible to get the whole image in focus.

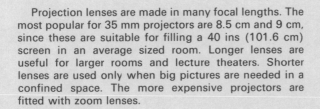

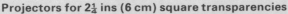

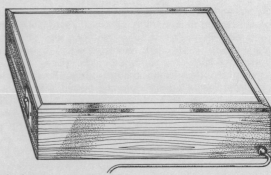

Light boxes

Large transparencies which are too big for projectors are best viewed on light boxes. The top surface is of flashed opal glass or translucent plastic, so that diffused light comes from below. Fluorescent tubes, usually of daylight type, are employed as light sources because they do not easily overheat. These boxes are also useful for examining large negatives or comparing several small transparencies.

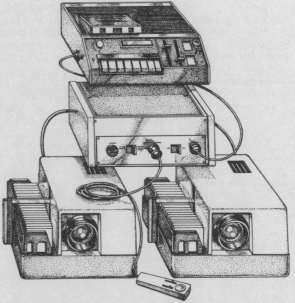

Slide-synchronization systems

Sound can be used to accompany a slide show, either to provide a commentary or to supply background music. A tape recording can be linked to a projector, and special synchronization sockets are provided on many projectors. The simplest method has metal foil on the tape, which sends a signal to activate the slide-change mechanism at the appropriate part of the recording; more sophisticated systems use a recorded pulse for the same purpose.

It is common practice to use two projectors — as shown in the illustration above — so that images can be made to dissolve gradually from one view to another without the dislocation of an abrupt change. There are many systems, mechanical and electrical, for effecting smooth transition, sometimes with parts of two pictures visible at the same time.

Screens can hang or stand according to the space available, and the size of picture required.

Storing & Mounting

Slides and negatives should be stored so that they remain in good condition and can be located when required. Methods can vary from an old shoe box marked with a title to a sophisticated cross reference system. Whatever is adopted, store slides in a dry atmosphere free from noxious gases. There are no problems in the normal centrally-heated house but in damp places sealed containers are desirable. Use silica gel to maintain dryness and regenerate the gel at intervals according to the maker's instructions. In the tropics moisture-proof containers and a chemical such as formaldehyde help to guard against fungus. For long term storage transfer slides from card into plastic mounts. There is no need for mounting between glass; this often causes more problems than it solves.

Storing transparencies in projector magazines
Transparencies can be stored in projector magazines, straight or circular; they are thus always ready for viewing. However, the cost is considerable and storing a large number of magazines is awkward.

Transparency boxes
These are available in many styles and sizes, but they are all the same in principle. Transparencies fit into numbered slots and an index card, usually in the lid, carries a brief description of each slide. Popular sizes are 100 or 120 transparencies to the box. If a lot of data is recorded a card index system can be used, while the transparencies are numbered and stored separately.

Viewpacks
Slides can be stored in viewpacks, which are plastic sheets with envelopes, usually transparent on one side and translucent on the other. The advantage is that a number of slides can be seen at once. Viewpacks can be fitted with a metal strip which allows them to hang inside the deep drawer of a filing cabinet.

Labeling transparencies
Some information can be recorded on the mount, especially the date. Manufacturers only stamp these on card, not plastic. Small self-adhesive labels are ideal for plastic mounts and self-adhesive numbers can also be purchased. Colored inks or labels can be used to distinguish years or categories.

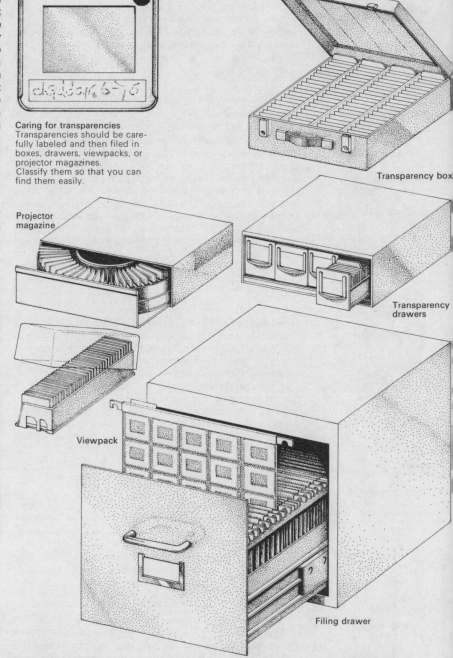

Labeling a transparency

Caring for transparencies
Transparencies should be carefully labeled and then filed in boxes, drawers, viewpacks, or projector magazines.
Classify them so that you can find them easily.

Transparency box

Projector magazine

Transparency drawers

Viewpack

Filing drawer

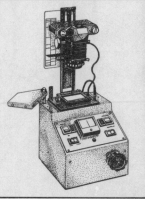

Transparency copying
Transparencies can be copied, but not cheaply. Simply photographing the projected image does not yield good quality. And even if one of the lens extension devices which are made for SLR cameras is used results are not completely dependable. A special transparency copier provides the best results. These generally use built-in electronic flash with an ordinary SLR camera on an arm, like the head on an enlarger. The slide is placed underneath on an illuminated screen. Exposure can be measured and set on the copier, and some correction of badly exposed or color biased originals is possible.

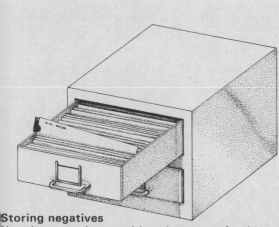

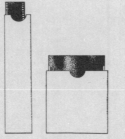

Protective sleeves

Viewpack

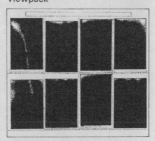

Protecting negatives
Once a negative is scratched or dirty, the quality of prints made from it will suffer. Protect strips or separate negatives from such damage in special sleeves, and keep them in a box, drawer or transparent viewpack.

Storing negatives

Negatives must be stored in strips except for the very largest sizes. Transparent or translucent bags provide excellent protection and these can be stored in albums or in filing cabinets. A common method is to make a contact sheet from the whole film (see pp. 188–189), and to file this next to the negatives. This provides instant visual information and is especially useful when there are several similar pictures. The more subtle expressions in portraits, for example, cannot be judged from negatives. Special albums file contact sheets and negatives together, with plenty of space for the recording of data. Or an album can be made up using negative bags in a cheap binder. Most bags can be written on, either with a ball-point pen or a chinagraph pencil. Never write on a bag when the negative is inside. Contact strips can be stuck on one side of the bag — double sided adhesive tape is ideal — leaving the other side free for data. The negative bag is the best place to record technical information. The date, film and developer used, and possibly the grade of paper, should be all that is needed. Exposure details are rarely important.

If possible store negatives outside the darkroom in a dry place, away from moisture and fumes.

Displaying prints

Photographic prints can be stored flat in boxes or drawers, but they are best displayed on the pages of an album where they can be easily seen. Try to arrange pages creatively, contrast small pictures with large ones and avoid rows of photographs all the same size.

Mounting prints
Prints can be mounted wet with appropriate glue, dry with dry-mounting tissue or with rubber cement. The latter should be used with care because it can cause stains on prints.

Wet-mounting
Wet-mounting prints, in its simplest terms, involves sticking the prints on a mounting board with glue. Before applying the glue, soak the print, then remove excess water from its surface with a squeegee. Brush the glue onto the mounting board, stick on the print, and then, on the reverse side of the board, repeat this procedure with a reject print to prevent the board from warping. The prints dry with a smooth finish.

Dry-mounting
To dry-mount prints use tissue coated on each side with a shellac-like material which melts with heat. One side sticks to the mount and the other to the print. A domestic iron can be used although proper tacking irons and presses are available. Make sure that both print and mount are bone dry before starting. Liquid dry mountant is available; this is brushed on the back of the print, dried then heated.

Soak the two prints in water.

Clean the mounting board and the print.

Squeegee excess water from their surfaces.

Attach tissue to print back with tacking iron.

Apply glue to one side of mounting board.

Trim tissue to fit print.

Align print and press it onto the board.

Secure corners of tissue to mounting board.

Repeat these stages on the reverse side. Trim.

Use hot press to fix print to board.

Glossary

Aberration The inability of a lens to produce a completely sharp image. Rays of light from subject points are not rendered as exact image points.

Absorption When light falls on a surface, part if not all is absorbed by that surface, and is usually converted to heat.

Accelerator General term applied to the alkali found in a developing solution. In greater strength and volume the alkali increases the speed of development.

Acetic acid Chemical used in acid stop baths to stop development and neutralize developer prior to fixation. A 2% solution is usually recommended for negative and print stop baths. Also used to acidify fixing baths (together with sodium sulfite).

Achromat Lens capable of bringing two primary colors of the spectrum to a common point of focus.

Actinic The ability of light to cause chemical and physical change in a material.

Actinometer Early exposure meter. Used a comparison between the effect of ambient light on a sensitized emulsion against a standard tint.

Additive color synthesis Method of producing full color images by mixing the primary colors, blue, green and red.

Agitation The means used during the processing cycle to keep fresh solution in contact with the emulsion surface.

Air-bells or bubbles Bubbles of air formed on the emulsion surface during processing. Avoided by using the manufacturer's recommended agitation times.

Air-brushing Method of retouching photographic prints. Uses high pressure air to spray dye over selected areas.

Alkali See "Accelerator."

Alkalinity Denotes the degree of alkali in solution. Measured by the pH value. All values above pH 7 are alkaline.

Alum (chrome or potassium) Chemical used as a hardener in the photographic process. Can be used as a single solution or in conjunction with acid fixing baths.

Ammonium chloride Chemical used in toners and bleaches.

Ammonium persulfate Chemical used in "proportional" reducers.

Ammonium sulfide Chemical used as a toner (sepia), and in some intensifiers.

Ammonium thiosulfate Main constituent of rapid fixing baths. Converts unused halides to a soluble complex.

Anamorphic lens Lens capable of compressing a wide image in one dimension, so squeezing it onto a standard frame. A special projection system can reform the image on a wide screen.

Anastigmat Lens containing a number of elements which help to reduce astigmatism.

Angle of incidence Light striking a surface forms an angle with an imaginary line at right angles to that surface. The imaginary line is known as the normal. The angle formed between the incoming light ray and the normal is called the angle of incidence. Light is reflected from a surface at an angle with the normal equal to its angle of incidence.

Angle of reflection Light reflected from a surface forms an angle with an imaginary line at right angles to that surface called the normal. The angle formed between the reflected ray and the normal is called the angle of reflection. The angle of reflection is always equal to the angle of incidence.

Angle of view The largest angle obtainable between two rays passing through a lens which will form an image of acceptable quality within the film format.

Angstrom Unit used to measure the wavelengths of the electro-magnetic spectrum.

Anhydrous Free from water.

Anti-halation backing Dye used on the back of (or within) film to absorb light which passes through the emulsion layer(s). This helps reduce spread of light reflected back through the emulsion from the rear of the film or camera back.

Aperture Circular hole in the front of the camera which regulates the amount of light that can pass from the lens to the film.

Aplanat Lens corrected for spherical aberration.

Apochromat Lens corrected for three primary colors: blue, green and red.

ASA American Standards Association. Denotes a speed system with which manufacturers may "rate" their films in terms of its sensitivity to light, e.g. 200 ASA. The higher the number the faster the speed of the film. ASA ratings have a strict arithmetical progression, 400 ASA being twice as fast as 200 ASA in terms of film sensitivity. ASA speeds are printed on all film boxes and packets.

Aspherical Three-dimensional curved surface, whose radius of curvature varies regularly over part of its diameter.

Astigmatism The inability of a lens to focus mutually perpendicular points – such as a cross – onto the same plane.

Autochrome process Early system of color photography using the additive color synthesis principle.

Backing Colored coating on the back of film emulsions which reduces halation. The colored coating is removed from the film during the processing cycle.

Back projection System for producing location scenes in a studio. Location scenes shot previously can be projected onto the back of a translucent screen to form a background for subjects placed in front.

Barium sulfate Compound used as a foundation coating on fiber based photographic printing paper to give clean white highlights.

Barn doors Accessory for spots and floodlamps to control direction and width of light beam.

Barrel distortion Lens aberration where straight lines in the subject, particularly on the edge of the field, are formed as curved lines (in the shape of a barrel) in the image.

Bas-relief Photographic effect using a negative and positive sandwiched together slightly out of register. Simplifies the image tones and emphasizes line.

Bellows Light-tight folding sleeve between the lens and image screen. Three types are used. The first, used with large format cameras, is a concertina type which provides an adjustable range of lens-image distances. The second is a folding cloth sleeve used with small format cameras for close-up work and the third, the bag bellows, is used on large format cameras with wide-angle lenses when the concertina type will not compress to the required lens-image distance.

Between-the-lens shutter Shutter placed within the lens components usually close to the iris diaphragm.

Bi-concave lens Simple lens whose surfaces curve inward toward the optical center. Causes rays of light to diverge from a point of focus.

Bi-convex lens Simple lens whose surfaces curve outward, away from the optical center. Causes rays of light to converge at a point of focus.

Bleaching Chemical process which converts the black metallic silver image into a colorless silver complex. Usually the first stage in toning and intensification processes, and an important stage in most color chemical developing systems.

Blisters Blemishes in the form of bubbles mostly found on printing paper. Caused by gases being formed between emulsion and paper surface either by extreme changes of temperature or excess alkalinity during processing.

Bloomed lenses See "Coated lenses."

Blur Unsharp image areas caused by subject/camera movement.

Borax Mild working alkali, used in many fine grain developing solutions.

Brightness range Subjective term relating to the range of luminance found between the brightest and darkest areas of the subject or image.

Bromide paper Light sensitive photographic paper used for printing. It has a silver bromide emulsion.

B setting Mark on shutter setting ring indicating that the shutter will stay open while the shutter release remains depressed.

BSI Abbreviation for British Standards Institute.

Buffer Chemical system used to maintain alkalinity of a developing solution against liberated hydrobromic acid.

Burning-in Method of local control in printing. The addition of more exposure to selected areas of the print.

Cable release Simple cable system used for releasing the camera shutter. Prevents hand contact with camera body and camera shake during long exposures.

Cadmium sulfide cells (CdS) Cell used in exposure meters. When an electric current is passed through it, the cell offers a resistance directly proportional to the amount of light it is receiving.

Callier effect Prints produced from negatives with a condenser enlarger acquire greater contrast than with a diffuser enlarger. The difference between the two types of source is half a grade in terms of printing paper contrast. This effect, named after W. H. O. Callier, is caused by the scattering of direct light from a condenser system by dense (highlight) areas of the negative but not by clear (shadow) areas. On a diffuser enlarger the light is scattered prior to passing through the negative and the effect on contrast is much less.

Camera movements Mechanical systems mostly found on larger format cameras for manipulating the relative positions of front and back panels. The movements are known as follows: rise/fall; swing; tilt; shift (cross front/cross back).

Canada balsam Cementing substance with a refractive index similar to glass. Used for cementing lens elements together in compound systems.

Carbon arc Light source obtained by passing an electric current through two sticks of carbon.

Cartridge Quick loading film container, often plastic, preloaded by the manufacturer.

Cassette Light tight metal film container holding small format film sizes. Supplied for loading into camera.

Caustic potash Very strong alkali accelerator used in high contrast developing solutions.

Centigrade Scale of temperature where 0 equals water's freezing point and 100 its boiling point.

Characteristic curve Graph representing the performance characteristics of film under known developing conditions.

Chemical fog Overall density produced by an excessive degree of development, due to unexposed silver halides being attacked by the developing solution.

Chloride paper Printing paper using silver chloride in the emulsion. It is very slow and mainly used for contact printing.

Chlorobromide Light-sensitive emulsion using silver bromide and silver chloride. Produces warm tone images on printing papers.

Chromatic aberration The inability of a lens to bring different colors which are on the same plane in the subject, to a common plane of focus.

Circle of confusion An image disk formed from clusters of light rays reflected from one point in the subject. The smaller the disks forming an image the sharper it will appear.

Coated lenses Lenses with coated air/glass surfaces. The magnesium or sodium fluoride coating reduces flare.

Cold cathode illumination Fluorescent light source used in some large format enlargers for projection printing. Low working temperature even when run for long periods. Inclined to soften contrast and edge definition marginally.

Color sensitivity Relative response to the colors of the spectrum.

Color synthesis Methods by which a final color photograph is formed. Color synthesis is either additive or subtractive.

Color temperature Scale, usually measured in Kelvins, for expressing the color quality (content) of a light source.

Coma Lens aberration which causes circular patches and comet-like spots on off-axis image areas.

Complementary colors Two colors are said to be complementary if they make white light when added together in suitable proportions. In photography, the concern is with *light* rather than the traditional painters' pigments and complementary colors to the primaries of the spectrum are as follows:

Primary	Complementary
blue	yellow
green	magenta
red	cyan

Compound lens Lens system containing two or more elements.

Condenser Simple lens system for concentrating light rays from a source into a beam, as in an enlarger or spotlight.

Contact papers Papers of very slow speed used solely for contact prints.

Contact printer Equipment for making contact prints.

Continuous tone Term applied to monochrome photographs that possess a gradation of gray tones — from white through to black — representing varying luminances in the subject.

Contrast Visual judgment on differences in densities and their degree of separation in a negative or print.

Converging lens Lens which causes rays of light from a subject to converge to a point, i.e. a simple convex camera lens.

Convertible lens Compound lens whose elements are so arranged that part of the lens can be un-screwed to provide a new lens of longer focal length.

Convex lens Lens which causes rays of light from a subject to converge.

Copper toning Chemical process used for toning bromide prints. Produces warm purplish-red tones in exposed areas.

Copyright Copyright establishes ownership of a particular photograph or piece of work. Copyright laws vary from country to country.

Correction filters Filters which correct the color sensitivity of the emulsion to match that of the eye.

Covering power Area of the image plane where the lens produces an image of acceptable quality.

Curvature of field Lens aberration causing a curved plane of focus.

Cut film Negative material obtainable on flat single sheets of film. Usually 4 × 5 ins (10.2 × 12.7 cm) or larger. Used with cut film holders in large format cameras.

Cyan The complementary color to red. It is composed of a mixture of blue and green light.

Dark cloth Dark material placed over the head and shoulders to facilitate viewing on the ground glass screen of a view camera in bright light conditions.

Dark slide Term sometimes applied to the container used for cut film in large format cameras. Name for cut film holder.

Daylight color film Color film used with a daylight light source and balanced to 5400K. Type B color film can be converted to the daylight film balance by using the manufacturer's recommended conversion filter. This usually causes the speed of the film to be halved.

Density The amount of silver deposit produced in an emulsion by exposure and development.

Depth of field The distance between the nearest point and the furthest point in the subject which can be brought to acceptably sharp focus on a common focal plane.

Depth of focus The distance the film plane can be moved while the image points remain acceptably sharp without refocusing the lens.

Developer Chemical bath which amplifies and converts the latent image to black metallic silver, producing a visible image.

Development The system of processing the exposed image to black metallic silver. The essential items to check for accurate development are the type of developer, the condition of the solution, the time and temperature of development and the degree of agitation required.

Diaphragm Term commonly used to describe the adjustable aperture in a lens which uses a set of sliding blades to control the size of the hole. Can also be applied to a type of shutter — the diaphragm or leaf shutter.

Diapositive Positive image produced on a transparent base e.g. a transparency.

Dichroic fog Color veiling usually occurring on negative material in the form of purplish-red and green stains. It is caused by the formation of silver in the presence of an acid. It commonly occurs if the fixing qualities of an acid fixing bath are sufficiently diminished to allow development to continue in the fixing bath.

Diffraction The way in which light waves are caused to change their direction or become scattered, when they pass through a small hole or are close to an opaque surface.

Diffusers Any substance that can cause light to diffuse and scatter as with tracing paper. The effect in all cases is to soften the character of the light.

DIN Deutsche Industrie Norm. The German system of rating film sensitivity to light. Represented by a number printed on the film carton or box, e.g. Din 20°. The DIN numbering system is a logarithmic progression and a +3° change in rating indicates a doubling of film speed, e.g. 23° is twice as fast as 20°, 17° would be half the speed of 20°.

Dispersion The ability of glass to bend light rays of different wave-lengths, and hence different colors, to varying degrees.

Diverging lens Lens which causes rays from a subject to bend away from the optical axis; a concave lens.

Dodging Local control in photo-graphic printing achieved by reducing the exposure to specific areas of the printing paper.

Drying marks Marks left on the emulsion or film backing after drying. On the back of film they are caused by scum and can be removed. On the emulsion they are caused by uneven drying and they may show up on the final print. There is no satisfactory way of removing them from the emulsion.

Dye sensitizing All silver halides used in black and white emulsions have a natural sensitivity to blue. Early emulsions possessed only this sensitivity and no others. In 1880 Dr H. Vogel found a method of sensitizing halides to other colors of the spectrum leading to the panchromatic films used today.

Dye transfer prints Method of making color prints from color transparencies and other color prints. Separation negatives are used and color dye matrixes printed in register.

Electronic flash Light source produced by creating a spark between electrodes contained within a gas-filled tube. A single tube will produce many thousands of flashes.

Emulsion The light sensitive material that is coated on a suitable base, to produce the various types of film and printing paper used in photography. Consists of silver halides suspended in gelatin.

Enlargement Print larger than the negative size. Often referred to as as a projection print.

Exposure Exposure, in the photographic sense, is the product of light intensity and the time the light is allowed to act. Intensity is controlled with aperture, time with shutter speed adjustment.

Exposure meter Device for measuring the amount of light originating from or being reflected from a subject. It is usually equipped to convert this measurement to useable information — shutter speeds and aperture size.

Extension tubes Metal tubes used with small format cameras as a means of extending the film-lens distance. Can provide magnifications in excess of × 1.

Fahrenheit Scale of temperature named after its originator G. Fahrenheit. Water's freezing point is 32°F (0°C), its boiling point 212°F (100°C).

Farmer's reducer Potassium ferricyanide/sodium thiosulfate solution used to bleach negatives and prints.

Ferric chloride Chemical used in certain bleaching solutions. Mainly applied to negative materials.

Film Light sensitized emulsion on a transparent base.

Filters Colored glass or gelatin disks which alter the quality of the light passing through them, usually in terms of color content.

Fish-eye lens Extreme wide-angle lens in excess of 100° angle of view and sometimes exceeding 150°. Depth of field in all cases is practically infinite, thus no focusing device is required.

Fixation Chemical procedure in the processing cycle of negatives and prints. Converts unused halides to a soluble silver complex.

Fixed focal length Camera system whose lens cannot be "inter-changed" for another lens of different focal length.

Fixed focus Lens-camera system that has no method of adjusting the focus of the lens. The lens is fix-focused on a predetermined distance most suitable to accommodate the type of subject it is likely to photograph. Many cheap cameras use this system.

Flare Non-image forming light that is scattered through the lens or reflected off the interior of the camera. If allowed to affect the film it causes a lowering of image contrast. Reflection in a lens is present at all air-glass surfaces, therefore the more elements a compound lens contains the greater will be the effect of flare. The light loss and resulting reduction of image quality is offset in modern lenses by a coating technique often referred to as "blooming."

Flash Artificial light source produced briefly in an enclosed envelope, or glass bulb. Provides high intensity luminance. Two types: expendable, where the bulb can only be used once; electronic, where the flash head may be used repeatedly with the assistance of a power pack.

Floodlight Term usually applied to an artificial light source consisting of a dish-shaped reflector and a 125–500 watt tungsten filament pearl bulb.

Focal length The distance between the lens (strictly its rear nodal point) and the focal plane, when the camera is focused for subjects at infinity.

Focal plane An image line at right angles to the optical axis passing through the focal point. This forms the plane of sharp focus when the camera is set on infinity.

Focal plane shutter Shutter system using blinds which lie in close proximity to the focal plane. Exposure is achieved by the progressive uncovering of the sensitized material to light as the blinds move across the film surface.

Focal point Point on the focal plane where the optical axis intersects it at right angles.

Focusing Method of moving the lens in relation to the camera back to form a sharp image on the film.

Focusing screen Ground glass sheet, often with a fresnel magnifier at its center, fixed to a camera as an aid to viewing and focusing the image in a suitable plane.

Fog, fogging Area, or veil, of density on a photographic negative or print, produced by intentional/accidental light effect, or by chemicals.

Format Size of negative, printing paper or camera viewing area.

Fresnel magnifier Condenser lens found at the center of some ground glass viewing screens which magnifies part of the image and aids focusing.

Gelatin Medium used in sensitized emulsion for the suspension of the light-sensitive silver halides.

Glaze Glossy surface produced on some printing papers. Provides greater maximum black, therefore the widest range of tones.

Gold chloride Chemical used in gold toners. Soluble in water.

Gradation The tonal contrast range of an image, e.g. soft, normal, contrasty.

Grade Numerical and termino-logical description of paper contrast characteristics: no. 0–1 soft; no. 2 normal; no. 3 hard; no. 4–5 very hard.

Graininess Photographic image in which silver grains have clumped together during develop-ment to form a visible structure. Most apparent in gray tone areas.

Grains Exposed and developed silver halides form grains of black metallic silver.

Granularity Objective physical measurement of the amount and extent of grain clumping on a particular emulsion.

Ground glass screen Translucent glass panel used for viewing and focusing in most reflex and large format technical cameras.

Halation Secondary, diffused image usually formed from bright areas of the subject. Caused by light passing directly through the film and being reflected from the camera back or film base slightly out of register with the original subject area.

Half-frame Term used to describe a negative format of 18 × 24 mm, which is half the size of the standard 35 mm frame.

Half-tone System of producing an illusion of continuous tone with a black dot formation representing the image. Main application is in photomechanical printing of newspapers, books, magazines etc.

Halogen Group of elements, particularly bromine, chlorine and iodine, that with silver, form the basis of most photographic light sensitive emulsions.

Hardener Chemical, often potassium or chrome alum, that is used to strengthen the physical characteristics of gelatin, particularly against the effect of high temperature processing.

High key Type of print exhibiting many highlight tones, with a few mid-tones or shadows.

Highlights Bright areas in the subject, represented by dark, heavy deposits on the negative which in turn form light tones on the final positive print.

Hydrobromic acid Acid liberated during the developing process by reduction of the bromine. It slows down the process of development and can be offset by an accelerator, e.g. sodium carbonate, which is used in most developing solutions.

Hydrochloric acid Chemical used in a number of bleaching solutions. Highly corrosive.

Hydrogen peroxide Chemical used in hypo clearing agents.

Hydroquinone Reducing agent. Strong developing action when used with vigorous alkali. Basis of MQ and PQ developing solutions.

Hyperfocal distance When a camera is set on infinity, depth of field extends from infinity to a point closer to the camera. The distance from the camera to this point is called the hyperfocal distance. Because depth of field extends in front of and behind a point focused on, the camera can be refocused for this hyperfocal distance whereupon depth of field will extend from half the hyperfocal distance to infinity.

Hypersensitizing System of increasing the light sensitivity of an emulsion prior to exposure.

Hypo Abbreviation for hypo-sulfite of soda, itself a term incorrectly applied to sodium thiosulfate. "Hypo" has become common usage for a fixing solution.

Hypo clearing agent or eliminator Chemical which removes hypo (sodium thiosulfate) from a photographic emulsion: e.g. hydrogen peroxide.

Image plane Plane, normally at right angles to the lens axis, at which a sharp image of the sub-ject is formed. The nearer the subject, the further from the lens the image plane will be.

Incident light Light falling on a surface or subject.

Incident light reading The measurement by some form of meter of the incident light falling on a subject. The light meter is pointed away from the subject *toward* the light source.

Infra-red The part of the electro-magnetic spectrum below red which is invisible to the human eye. Specially sensitized films record infra-red radiations. They produce images not usually obtainable on normal photo-graphic emulsions.

Integral tripack Three emulsions usually of different characters, coated onto one base. Used mainly for color negatives, transparencies and color print materials.

Intensification Method by which the photographic image may be strengthened in terms of density. Most applicable to negative material. Works better on negatives that have been under-developed rather than under-exposed. A variety of chemical formulae are available.

Intermittency effect A number of combined brief exposures does not produce the same density as a single exposure of equivalent duration. This phenomenon is known as the intermittency effect.

Inverse square law States that illumination on a surface is inversely proportional to the square of the distance of the light source (twice the distance, $\frac{1}{4}$ the light). For the law to apply with absolute precision the light source must be a point.

Inverted telephoto Lens construction providing a short focal length with a long back focus, or lens-image distance. Many small format wide-angle lenses are of this construction.

Iris diaphragm Lens aperture continuously adjustable in diameter by means of interspersed metal leaves.

IR or R setting Found on many camera lenses, usually marked in red. Indicates the change of focus position required for infra-red photography.

Irradiation The scattering of light within an emulsion layer. Lowers definition. The thicker the emulsion (e.g. fast speed films) the greater the irradiation.

I setting Speed setting found on some cheap box cameras. I (for instantaneous) usually offers a speed around 1/60 second.

Joule Unit of measurement applied to the output of an electronic flash. Equivalent to a watt-second or to 40 lumen-seconds. In practice used as a comparative measurement between one flash system and another. The higher the number of joules the greater the light output.

Kelvins (K) Units of measure-ment on the absolute temperature scale used to measure the color temperature of light sources.

Kilowatt Measurement of electrical power and so, indirectly, light output. One thousand watts.

Lamps General term describing the variety of artificial light sources available.

Latensification System of increasing the relative speed of the emulsion by slight fogging after exposure but before development. Two systems available: chemical and light effect.

Latent image The invisible image produced by exposure and subsequently made visible by development.

Latitude (of exposure) The degree by which exposure level can be varied and still produce an acceptable result. Faster speed films usually have greater latitude than slow speed ones.

Lens Single element or multiple collection of glass surfaces, capable of bending light. Basically, there are two types: positive (convex) which cause rays of light to converge to a point; negative (concave) which cause rays of light to diverge from a point.

Lens hood Tunnel system made of metal, wood or any opaque substance, that prevents un-wanted light falling onto the lens surface.

Lens system Describes the types of lenses available for use with a particular camera. Alternatively describes the construction of a particular lens type.

Light Form of energy that makes up part of the electro-magnetic spectrum. Wavelengths between 4000 and 7200A (400 and 720 nanometers).

Local control The system of burning-in or dodging-out during printing.

Long-focus lens Lens with a focal length *exceeding* the length of the diagonal of the film format with which it is used.

Low key Print exhibiting a large amount of shadow with only one or two highlights in the picture area. Produced by control of lighting and exposure at the camera stage.

Lumen Unit of light intensity falling on a surface.

Luminance Measurable amount of light emitted or reflected by a surface.

Macrophotography Extreme close-up photography using a camera rather than a microscope. Generally refers to images which are larger in size than the original subject area but not greater than ×10 magnification.

Magenta Complementary color to green. Composed of a mixture of blue and red light.

Metol Reducing agent, soft working. With mild alkali forms the basis of many fine grain developing solutions.

Microphotograph Photograph produced to a very small size. Often used to record documents and books. Image is viewed using a microfilm reader.

Mirror lens Lens system that employs one or a number of mirrors within its construction. Mirror lenses usually have a mixture of reflecting and refracting optics. In this case a more accurate term applied to them is catadioptric. Such lenses can achieve very long focal lengths with short barrel exten-sion, by allowing the light rays to be reflected up and down the lens tube before they strike the photographic emulsion.

Monobath One solution con-taining developer and fixer combined, providing a quick and convenient system of processing. Limits control over end result due to inflexible degree of development.

Montage Composite image formed from a number of photographs, either overlaid or set side-by-side.

MQ/PQ developing solutions Developing solutions containing the reducing agents metol and hydroquinone (MQ) or phenidone and hydroquinone (PQ).

Negative The image produced on a film by the product of exposure and development.

Negative lens Simple lens that causes rays to diverge from a point. Concave in outline.

Newton's rings When two transparent surfaces such as glass are laid together and an area becomes slightly out of contact, rings of colored light are produced. These are known as Newton's rings.

Nitric acid Used in emulsion manufacture and in toners as a asis of bleach. Highly corrosive.

Nodal point There are two nodal points in every compound lens system. The first or front nodal point is the point in the lens where incoming rays appear to aim. The second or rear nodal point is the point in the lens where light rays appear to come from after passing through the lens. These are used for optical calculations e.g. measurement of focal length.

Opacity The light stopping power of a medium.

Open flash System of flash illumination using the following sequence: the shutter is opened, the flash is fired, then the shutter is closed.

Optical axis Imaginary line passing through the center of a lens system.

Orthochromatic Photographic emulsion sensitive to blue and green regions of the spectrum, but insensitive to red.

Panchromatic Photographic emulsion sensitive to all the colors of the visible spectrum but not in a uniform way.

Parallax The difference between the image seen by a camera's viewing system and that taken by its lens. There is a slight variance in image content particularly when subjects are at close distances, 6 ft (1.8 m) or nearer. Only through-the-lens viewing systems completely avoid parallax.

Paraphenylenediamine Reducing agent used in some fine grain and color developers.

Perspective The relationship in terms of size and shape of three-dimensional objects represented in two-dimensional terms. In photography, perspective is controlled by viewpoint. *Linear perspective* is the effect of depth produced by diminishing size and where lines or planes converge to a "vanishing point." *Aerial perspective* is the effect of depth produced by haze in the air on distant views. Most noticeable on photographs produced by long-focus or telephoto lenses.

Phenidone Reducing agent. Often used in general purpose and fine grain developing solutions as a less toxic replacement for metol.

Photo-electric cell Light sensitive cell that either generates electricity when light falls upon it (selenium), or offers a resistance to electricity when light falls upon it (cadmium). Both types of cell are used in electronic exposure meters.

Photoflood Bright photographic lamp employing a tungsten filament source. Used in floodlights.

Photogram Pattern or design produced by placing opaque or transparent objects on top of a sensitive emulsion and exposing it to light and subsequent development. A variety of images can be produced direct on printing paper without the use of a camera.

Photomicrography Photography of objects magnified by a micro-scope attached to the camera. Image 10× life size or more.

pH values Numerical system of expressing the alkalinity or acidity of a solution. 7 represents neutral. Solutions above this figure are increasingly alkaline, solutions below it are increasingly acidic.

Plane Imaginary surface, considered in terms of a straight line, within which points or lines of a subject lie.

Plate Early photographic glass plates which were coated with emulsion.

Polarization Light travels in wave formation along a straight path. It vibrates in a wave form in all directions. By using a polarizing filter, light can be made to vibrate in a single plane thus reducing its power. Polarizing filters are used over camera lenses and on light sources to reduce or remove bright reflections from certain types of surface.

Positive Opposite of the negative. Often the second stage of the photographic process where tones are reproduced similar, in terms of relative intensity, to those of the subject.

Positive lens A simple lens that causes light to converge to a point. Convex in outline.

Posterization Graphic technique employing a number of separation negatives, producing prints with separate, flat areas of tone.

Potassium bichromate Chemical used in chrome intensifier.

Potassium bromide Chemical used as a restrainer in developing solutions.

Potassium carbonate Alkali used to increase the activity of reducing agents in a developing solution.

Potassium citrate Chemical used in a number of toners.

Potassium ferricyanide Chemical used in silver solvent reducers (Farmer's reducer).

Potassium hydroxide Caustic potash. High activity alkali used in high contrast developing solutions.

Potassium permanganate Chemical with a wide range of uses in bleaches and reducers.

Preservative Chemical (usually sodium sulfite) used in a developing solution to offset oxidation.

Primaries The three primary colors of the spectrum in terms of light transmission are blue, green and red. (In painters' pigments the primary mixing is different being blue, yellow and red.)

Prism Transparent medium capable of bending light to varying degrees, depending on wavelength.

Process lens High quality lens used for copying line and colored originals.

Projector Apparatus for displaying enlarged still or moving images on a screen.

Proportional reducer Silver reducer which reduces black metallic silver in direct proportion to the contrast of the negative. Maintains overall contrast.

Quartz-iodine lamp Outdated term for the tungsten-halogen lamp.

Rangefinder Optical mechanical system which measures the distance from camera to subject. Coupled rangefinder is a similar system linked to the camera lens, so rangefinder and camera focusing work together.

Reciprocity law States that exposure = intensity × time (Bunsen and Roscoe).

Reciprocity law failure Photographic emulsions are manufactured to give reasonable reciprocity characteristics over a narrow band of exposure time. Outside this band the reciprocity law fails and extra exposure is required in addition to the assessed amount, either in terms of intensity or time.

Reducer Solution capable of diminishing density on a photographic emulsion, e.g. Farmer's reducer. A bleach.

Reducing agent Chemicals in a developing solution which convert exposed silver halides to black metallic silver.

Reflection When rays of light strike a surface and bounce back they are said to reflect from that surface.

Reflector Any substance from which light can be reflected. Often describes a white or gray card used to reflect light from a source into the shadow areas of a subject.

Reflex camera Type of camera which uses a mirror to reflect incoming image rays onto a ground glass screen so that the image may be viewed and focused. Two types: single-lens reflex, using a retractable mirror behind the taking lens; twin-lens reflex using a fixed mirror behind the viewing lens only.

Refractive index Numerical value used to describe the light-bending power of a medium, such as glass.

Rehalogenization Conversion of black metallic silver back to a halide, as in the bleaching process.

Relative aperture Measured size of the diaphragm divided into the focal length of lens. Described by f numbers.

Replenishment Chemicals added to processing solutions to maintain that solution's characteristics. Developers, for example, require replenishment with more reducing agents as the old ones are used up.

Resolving power The ability of the eye, lens or film to distinguish fine detail.

Restrainer Chemical constituents of a developing solution whose purpose is to lessen the reducing agent's effect on unexposed silver halides. They also reduce chemical fog.

Reticulation Regular, crazed pattern on the emulsion caused by sudden and severe changes in the temperature, and/or acidity, of a processing solution.

Reversal material Photographic materials that can be processed to a positive after one camera exposure, i.e., to give a direct black and white transparency or a color transparency.

Rinse Brief wash in water used between processing steps, e.g. developer, rinse, fixer.

Safelights Many photographic materials, except panchromatic film, are insensitive to certain colors. This insensitivity can be used to provide a safelight in which the material may be handled without light fogging. Orthochromatic film, for example, is insensitive to red, and may be handled in a red safelight. Panchromatic film may be handled under a very dark green safelight, because of the emulsion's relatively low insensitivity to green illumination.

Selenium cell Light sensitive cell used in some exposure meters. Generates electricity in direct proportion to the amount of light falling on it. Somewhat insensitive at low light levels.

Sensitivity The photosensitive response of an emulsion.

Sensitometry Scientific study of the response of photographic materials to exposure and development.

Separation negatives Set — usually three — of black and white negatives taken through filters which analyze the content of a color original in terms of red, green and blue content.

Shutter Mechanical means of controlling the time during which light is allowed into the camera. Two types most common on modern cameras are the focal plane shutter and the between-the-lens leaf shutter.

Silver halide Light sensitive crystal found in photographic emulsions, i.e. bromide, iodide and chloride.

Silver recovery Methods of recovering silver from exhausted fixing bath. Three methods: sludging, galvanic, electrolysis.

Sodium bichromate Chemical used in intensifiers and bleaching solutions.

Sodium bisulfite Chemical used as a buffer in fixing solutions and as a preservative in developing solutions.

Sodium carbonate Frequently used as the alkali in general purpose developers.

Sodium hexamethaphosphate Water softener.

Sodium hydroxide Caustic soda. Hardworking alkali used extensively in high contrast developing solutions.

Sodium sulfide Chemical used in toners. Pungent smell.

Sodium sulfite Common preservative used in most developing solutions. In certain developing solutions can also act as an accelerator, restrainer and silver solvent.

Sodium thiosulfate Chemical which forms the basis of many fixing solutions. Converts unused silver halides to a soluble compound. Commonly called "hypo."

Solarization Pure solarization is the reversal of the image by gross over-exposure.

Spectrum That part of the electro-magnetic spectrum showing the visible colors of red, orange, yellow, green, blue, indigo and violet.

Speed Sensitivity to light of photographic emulsions. Films are given ASA and/or DIN numbers denoting speed characteristics.

Spherical aberration Lens fault

occurring in off-axial rays, where the lens is unable to render subject-points sharply in the image.

Spotlight Artificial light source using a small tungsten filament lamp, a reflector and a lens. Produces a harsh light beam of controllable width.

Stabilization Substitute for fixing. Conversion of unused halides to near stable compounds which are insensitive to light. These compounds remain in the emulsion. Washing is not required.

Stop Aperture of camera or enlarger lens.

Stop bath Chemical bath whose purpose is to stop development and neutralize unwanted developer contained within the emulsion layer.

Stopping down Reducing the size of the aperture.

Subtractive synthesis Synthesis used in modern color materials, where the complementary dyes of yellow, magenta and cyan are formed to create a full color image.

Sulfuric acid Chemical used in some reducers. Highly corrosive.

Supplementary lenses Additional lens elements used in conjunction with a camera lens which provide a new lens combination of different focal length.

Telephoto lens Compact lens construction which provides short back focus with long focal length.

Test strip Exposure procedure used in photographic printing. A number of varying exposures are given to a strip of emulsion to help judge the correct exposure required for the final print.

Tone separation Reduction of the continuous tone image to a limited range of tonal areas. Produced by the technique of posterization.

Transparency Positive image on a transparent base. Commonly called a "slide."

T setting Camera shutter setting. Indicates "time" exposure. The shutter opens when the release is pressed and closes when it is pressed again.

TTL Abbreviation for through-the-lens metering.

Tungsten filament Light source consisting of a tungsten filament contained within a glass envelope. The tungsten produces an intense light when electrical current is passed through it. Tungsten filament lamps are the basic artificial light source used in photography.

Tungsten-halogen lamp Improved design over the tungsten filament lamp in terms of size, consistency of light output and color temperature.

Type-A color film Color film used in conjunction with an artificial light source and balanced to a color temperature of 3400K.

Type-B color film Color film used in conjunction with an artificial light source and balanced to a color temperature of 3200K.

Ultra-violet The part of the electro-magnetic spectrum beyond violet (3900A). Invisible to humans. Most photographic emulsions are sensitive to some of these radiations which are particularly prevalent on misty days and on distant views. The extraneous light causes loss of definition and can be filtered out with a UV filter, which is colorless and has no effect on camera exposure.

Variable focus lens Lens whose focal length can be altered without interchanging or adding supplementaries. Also known as a zoom lens.

View camera Large format stand camera where image composing and focusing are achieved by viewing the subject on a ground glass screen.

Viewfinder Apparatus for composing and sometimes focusing the subject. Can be either a direct vision viewfinder, an optical viewfinder, a ground glass screen or a reflex viewfinder.

Viewpoint Position of the camera in relation to the subject. When viewpoint is altered, perspective is changed.

Vignetting Printing technique where the edges of the print are faded out at the corners.

Washing The part of the processing cycle that removes the soluble silver complexes and residual chemicals from the emulsion.

Wavelength Describes the distance from wave crest to wave crest between two corresponding waves of light in the electro-magnetic spectrum. Wavelengths are measured in nanometers (nm) or Angstrom units (A).

Wide-angle lens Lens whose focal length is *less* than the diagonal of the film format with which it is used.

X-ray Electro-magnetic radiations which, when passed through a solid and allowed to affect a photographic emulsion, can provide a visual representation of the internal structure of that solid.

Zoom lens Variable focus lens.

Glossary of film types

The tables below and right are a *guide* to the films likely to be available in Gt. Britain, Europe and the USA. The lists are by no means complete since many other brands are also available but often only in selected areas. Manufacturers frequently alter their ranges of film so it is wise to check for additions and withdrawals.

BLACK AND WHITE FILM TYPES

Name	Distributor	ASA/DIN speed	Available formats
Agfapan 25 Professional	Agfa	25/15	120, 35 mm
Agfapan 100	Agfa	100/21	120, 35 mm
Agfapan 400 Professional	Agfa	400/27	120, 35 mm
FP4	Ilford	125/22	120, 127, 35 mm, sheet
HP5	Ilford	400/27	120, 35 mm, sheet
XP1 400*	Ilford	variable	120, 35 mm
Agfa Vario-XL*	Agfa	variable	120, 35 mm
Pan F	Ilford	50/18	120, 35 mm
Panatomic-X	Kodak	32/16	120, 35 mm
Plus-X	Kodak	125/22	120, 35 mm, sheet
Recording film 2475	Kodak	1000/31	35 mm
Royal-X Pan	Kodak	1250/32	120, sheet
Tri-X Pan	Kodak	400/27	120, 35 mm, sheet
Verichrome Pan	Kodak	125/22	110, 120, 126, 127
Kodak Technical Pan 2415**	Kodak	variable	35 mm, sheet

*Variable speed chromogenic film   **Variable speed and variable contrast film

COLOR FILM TYPES

Name	Type	Distributor	ASA/DIN speed	Available formats
Agfachrome 50L Professional	Trans	Agfa	50/18	120, 35 mm, sheet
Agfachrome R100S Professional	Trans	Agfa	100/21	120, sheet
Agfacolor 100	Neg	Agfa	100/21	110, 120, 126, 127, 35 mm
Agfachrome 200	Trans	Agfa	200/24	35 mm
Agfacolor 400	Neg	Agfa	400/27	35 mm
Ilfocolor 400	Neg	Ilford	400/27	35 mm
Fujichrome 400	Trans	Fuji, Japan	400/27	35 mm
3M Color Slide 100	Trans	3M	100/21	35 mm
Polachrome Autoprocess	Trans	Polaroid, USA	40/17	120, 35 mm
Ektachrome 400	Trans	Kodak	400/27	120, 35 mm
Ektachrome 160 Professional	Trans	Kodak	160/23	120, 35 mm
Ektachrome 64 Professional	Trans	Kodak	64/19	120, 35 mm, sheet
Ilfochrome 100	Trans	Ilford	100/21	35 mm
Vericolor III Professional Type S	Neg	Kodak	160/23	120, 35 mm, sheet
Vericolor II Professional Type L	Neg	Kodak	80/20	120, sheet
Fujicolor HR400	Neg	Fuji, Japan	400/27	120, 35 mm
Fujicolor HR100	Neg	Fuji, Japan	100/21	120, 35 mm
Fujichrome 50	Trans	Fuji, Japan	50/18	35 mm
Kodachrome 25	Trans	Kodak	25/15	35 mm
Kodachrome 64	Trans	Kodak	64/19	35 mm
Kodacolor VR 200	Neg	Kodak	200/24	35 mm, disc
Kodacolor VR 1000	Neg	Kodak	1000/31	35 mm
Konica SR 400	Neg	Konishiroku	400/27	120, 35 mm, sheet
3M Color Slide 1000	Trans	3M	1000/31	35 mm

Trans = Transparency   Neg = Negative

Acknowledgments

The Book of Photography owes its publication to teamwork. Nobody could put together a book of this scope single-handed. So there are many people I would like to thank for the help they have given. My especial gratitude is due to Adrian Bailey, who gave me tremendous assistance in the writing and styling of the text. I would also like to extend particular thanks to Roger Bristow and Sheilagh Noble, who designed the book and worked out the many diagrams, and to Jackie Douglas, who edited the text, organized the research and was constantly on hand to remind me what needed to be done next. These four people have been absolutely tireless in their efforts, and I owe them a great deal.

Other people I would especially like to thank are: Michael Langford and Fred Duberry, who checked the text and provided much useful advice; Barbara Bernard, who undertook vital research; Tim Mercer, Catherine Murphy, Tom Picton, John Norris Wood, Steve Moore, Roger Bounds and Amy Carroll, all of whom gave invaluable assistance of one kind or another; John Ward of the Science Museum; the staff of the Print Room at the V & A; the technicians of the photography department at the Royal College of Art; the many models and friends who gave up their time to be photographed; and, not least, Julia Hedgecoe for her continual help, support and sympathy.

JOHN HEDGECOE

DORLING KINDERSLEY LIMITED would like to thank the following for their assistance in producing The Book of Photography:

Consultants and contributors
Harriet Bridgeman
Elizabeth Drury
Charles Elliott
Adrian Holloway
David Kilpatrick
Neville Maude
Bill Spencer

Artists and designers
Arka Graphics
David Ashby
George Daulby
Brian Delf
Fred Ford
Gilchrist Studios
Richard Jacobs
Christopher Meehan
Osborne/Marks
QED
Jim Robins
Rodney Shackell
Venner Artists

Picture sources
All photographs were taken by John Hedgecoe, with the exception of the following:
History chapter
Associated Press 31 center left; Mary Evans Picture Library 29 top right; Gernsheim Museum 18 bottom right, 19 bottom right, 20 bottom left, 21 top left, 24 top right; Kodak Museum 23 top left, 28 bottom right, top left; National Film Library 20 top left; National Museum, Munich 21 bottom left; Popperfoto 31 center right, bottom left, 32 top right, bottom left; Royal Photographic Society 22 bottom center, 25 center right; Science Museum 18 center left, 21 center left, 22 top left, center left, center right, 24 top left, 26 top right, 28 bottom left, 29 bottom left, bottom center, bottom right; Edwin Smith 19 top left, 27 bottom right; Société Francaise de Photographie 21 top center; Sothebys Belgravia 21 top right, 24 bottom center, 25 bottom right, 26 bottom left, 30 bottom left; Victoria & Albert Museum 23 bottom left.
Additional photographs
George Perks 47, 212, 216; Research Engineers Ltd 184 top

Equipment was kindly loaned by:
Leopold Cameras, London;
Pelling & Cross, London;
Polaroid UK Ltd.
Photography department, Royal College of Art.

Typesetting
Tradespools Ltd., Frome, England.
TJB Photosetting, London, England.

Lithographic reproduction
L. Van Leer & Co., BV., Amsterdam, Holland.